THE GIFT WITHIN US

THE GIFT WITHIN US

*Intuition, Spirituality and the Power of
Our Own Inner Voice*

MARY ANN BOHRER

Waterside Productions

Printed in the United States of America

First Printing, 2020

ISBN-13: 978-1-949003-18-5 print edition
ISBN-13: 978-1-949003-19-2 ebook edition

Waterside Productions
2055 Oxford Ave
Cardiff, CA 92007
www.waterside.com

My wish? I'm hoping to change the perception of intuition so that everyone can learn to listen to our own inner voice and get divine guidance in the process. We will all benefit greatly if we understand that we all have access to this amazing intuitive wisdom.

For Eric and Lily

"The workings of intuition transcend those of the intellect, and as is well known, innovation is often a triumph of intuition over logic."

Albert Einstein

TABLE OF CONTENTS

INTRODUCTION

A client of mine asked me to promote a new Millennium Clock, which was located in mid-town Manhattan, when I was working as a PR executive in New York City. This clock, which was being unveiled in 1997, was counting the days, hours and seconds until the Year 2000. Since everyone was worried about what would happen after midnight, January 1st, I decided to hold a press conference, called the Millennium Festival. I invited gifted intuitives – psychics and mediums – to meet with journalists one-on-one and share their predictions about the future, as well as to provide personal predictions for any journalists who might want one.

After doing research, I identified 24 gifted intuitives and scheduled the Millennium Festival for Friday, April 4, 1997 – just over a thousand days before the year 2000. When the day came, I sat the intuitives at individual tables at TGI Friday's at 34th Street and 8th Avenue, one of my clients' restaurants.

Incredibly, more than 75 journalists attended the event, including reporters from *The Wall Street Journal*, the Associated Press, CBS Evening News, Reuters and many other respected media outlets. In addition, entertainment media came, including Inside Edition. The reporters could have a few minutes with each psychic or medium, speed dating style, and then move on to talk with the next intuitive.

The response from these skeptical journalists was very interesting. The media people were impressed with the accuracy of these gifted individuals – and many wrote positive accounts of the event, which appeared in the press and on television, nationally and worldwide. Interestingly, after the Millennium Festival press conference was over, a reporter from the *Wall Street Journal* came up to me and said, "I'll be honest with you, Mary Ann, I came to this event today to make fun of these people and to write a silly story. But after I talked to them, I was in shock. They were so accurate that I couldn't believe it." I distinctly remember how pale this man's complexion was, like the blood had drained from his face. He truly wasn't expecting the intuitives to be as gifted, genuine and real as they were.

Thanks to this press conference, I became friends with many of the gifted intuitives I invited to the event. In the following pages, some of them tell their stories in individual profile chapters which reveal how they discovered their intuitive ability, whether they were accepted or shunned by family and friends, and how they made sense of being born with this marvelous and incredible gift, or how they came to it later, a gift that is still largely misunderstood in society.

In addition, *The Gift Within Us* will hopefully inspire you to look at these amazing people with open minds and hearts, and to be in tune with your own gifts, and to be open to the divine guidance that we all have access to simply by listening to our own inner voice.

ONE

THE NEW SPIRITUALITY
And The Essential Role Of Our Own Inner Voice

A lot of people yearn to satisfy their spiritual needs and connect with the divine, but they've experienced a crisis of confidence in recent years. Many have turned away from traditional religion and the idea that one needs to be in a church or to rely on a clergyman to communicate with God. And recent sexual abuse scandals involving the Catholic Church have done little to bolster their confidence in these powerful but flawed religious institutions.

Most of us are still seeking answers. According to the Pew Research Center, the number of Americans who feel a "deep sense of wonder about the universe" has increased dramatically in the past several years. Many of these spiritual seekers are asking: What is my purpose? How can I be happy? How can I communicate directly with a higher power and the universe? However, these individuals are now choosing to seek these answers for themselves, and not looking for guidance within the walls of a church or a traditional place of worship.

This increase in the "spiritual but not religious" category has grown rapidly. As Pew research conducted from April through June 2017 states, "About a quarter of U.S. adults (27%) now say that they think of themselves as spiritual but not religious, which is up 8 percentage points in five years."

But even as these numbers grow, those who identify as spiritual but not religious are searching for a New Spirituality – one that

1

doesn't define God as a storybook character who's looking down on us from some lofty, unreachable place. We're seeking a more modern, real life, attainable God – a loving being that we can talk to directly and who will provide important answers for us – both about our lives, our purpose, and the universe itself.

This point is illustrated by another survey conducted by the Pew Research Center from April through August 2017. It showed that "People who say they are 'spiritual but not religious' largely reject Biblical God, but believe in a higher power of some kind." While only 12% of respondents in the spiritual but not religious category said that they believe in God as described in the Bible, those who said they do not believe in God were asked if they believe in some kind of higher power or spiritual force in the universe, and 64% responded positively.

Interestingly, in another Pew Research Center study about religion entitled "The Religious Typography," among those that consider themselves to be "Highly Religious" (39%), a significant portion of this group (11%) were categorized as "Diversely Devout" – individuals who were traditionally religious, but who also believe in psychics, reincarnation, and that spiritual energy can be located in physical objects.

As these studies illustrate, the concept of "religion" is changing rapidly – many people are turning away from traditional religion towards "spirituality," and even those who consider themselves to be "highly religious" are becoming more open to intuitive ability, psychometry, and reincarnation. They are seeking new ways to explore their spirituality, and they yearn to receive guidance directly through "a higher power or spiritual force in the universe."

According to Archbishop Harry J. Flynn, former Archbishop of Saint Paul and Minneapolis, people have always had the ability to receive direct spiritual guidance, even if they choose to attend traditional religious services. "This direct connection has always been available to all of us," explained Archbishop Flynn. "Some receive this guidance through prayer, some through meditation, and others by simply listening to their inner voice. We all have access to divine wisdom – it's just a matter of knowing and trusting that we are loved and worthy of receiving that guidance."

Archbishop Flynn continued to illustrate this point by quoting St. John of the Cross, a Spanish priest and poet who became friends with Theresa of Avila and who was eventually canonized as a saint by Pope Benedict XIII in 1726. "As John of the Cross, a great mystic in the Catholic tradition once wrote: 'God has spoken only one word, and he speaks that word eternally and in eternal silence. And it is in the silence of the heart that makes itself heard.' This is why listening to your soul is extremely important. The more one listens, the more one can get in touch with deeper realities and divine insights."

With more people feeling disillusioned and increasingly untethered from their religious institutions, it is easy to understand why so many are now looking for new ways to get in touch with their spirituality. Many may have lost faith in their church, but their faith in a higher power remains strong. So they feel that it's now up to them to move in a new direction, and chart a new path to realizing their spiritual goals.

This belief in a higher power – and our ability to access its wisdom and divine guidance – is directly tied in with intuition and the power of listening to our inner voice. And even if some people attempt to degrade intuitive ability, its role in creating spiritual connectiveness has been known throughout history.

"Down through the centuries, we've had people who were canonized saints who had instances of mysticism and were able to foretell future events and things like that," said Archbishop Flynn. "The spirit of God enlightens certain souls in different ways, and we can't control what God does – God is beyond us. People can have illuminations and foresee things that other people cannot, and sometimes that is a gift from God which we don't understand, sometimes it's the fruit of their prayer, sometimes it's a fruit of silence, when they can really go into the desert of their souls and see things that they would not ordinarily see.

3

"We have so many wonderful people and saints in the Church – canonized saints — who have gone deeply into their own hearts and, as a result of that, had profound experiences of this sort. I would call it a gift – a real gift."

I believe that we have always had the ability to communicate with this spiritual force – we just have to know that we have an *intrinsic* ability to connect. It's the very definition of *The Gift Within Us.* Just by knowing this fact, we've already made great strides to realizing that amazing, empowering connection.

In the following pages, scientists who are studying intuitive ability share some amazing facts, and gifted intuitives tell us their stories and provide advice on how to connect with our higher power and the universe, information that enables us all to gain much desired access to the greatest and, in some ways the simplest, form of communication available to each and every one of us every day.

Two

Access Your Own Inner Voice

I've wondered why I have been inspired – or divinely guided – to write this book. After months of interviewing many highly gifted intuitives and respected researchers who are studying intuitive ability, I think I have the answers. One is to get the word out that people with psychic and intuitive abilities can be a tremendous help to us. The other one is to let everyone know the message: that we are all born with the ability to tap into our "inner voice" – that quiet knowing people describe as a "gut feeling." A "hunch." A "feeling in my bones." That feeling we often get when we are confronted with a difficult or challenging situation. It's a distinct feeling that we know is not coming from our brains, but we feel it anyway, and it informs us of what decision to make or what path to take.

Multiple studies are being done by scientists to measure our brains during these instances to see what is happening. It is possible that the "vibes" we are getting at certain times are due to more than simply measuring how our intuitive right brain is interacting with our conscious left brain. Just as the gifted intuitives in this book often get their profound messages from their guides, angels who are there to protect and guide them, we each have a connection to spirit – wise, loving spirits who are looking out for us and who want to lead us down the right path. Perhaps we don't have the ability to communicate with these guides as clearly as highly gifted individuals do, but this wise "inner voice" is there for us to access, if we choose to.

The challenge is that many people may not know that they can access this inner voice. Some may choose not to try, because they think that the notion of intuition is absurd. Part of the reason they might think this is that society has spent years – actually centuries – denying or belittling intuitive ability. To some, *intuition* a subject to make fun of, and no sensible people would entertain the notion that they can tap into their "inner voice" and receive valuable information.

It is easy to understand why the concept of intuition has become so maligned. People who call themselves "intuitives" have been lumped into one ugly and unattractive stereotype. If you identify yourself as a gifted intuitive, you have to be a charlatan who is out to trick your clients and take their money. This image has degraded the entire concept of intuition and – due to this negative connotation – has essentially robbed some individuals of the ability to access that wonderful voice – the gift of divine wisdom – that we all possess.

One person I interviewed for this book, Gabbie Deeds, told me that the one question many of her clients ask is: "What is my purpose in this life?" Gabbie explains, "If every one of those people would simply open their minds and allow their guides, their inner voice, to lead them in the right direction, they would automatically be on the right path, fulfilling their purpose. The people who turn off that connection are the ones who are wandering around aimlessly, frustrated and confused, and ultimately unhappy."

It is my hope that by demystifying intuitive ability, we can leave misconceptions about this marvelous gift in the past. The message is that if we actually open our minds and listen to our inner voice, we can start traveling down the path that our individual souls are meant to follow. We are not alone in this world. We have loving guides who are there for us, and who can help us become the best people that we can be. If we can realize this – and become humble and just listen – we can fulfill our destiny and achieve great things – for ourselves, and for the world we live in.

So the purpose of this book is twofold: to get the word out that there are gifted people to help us, and that it is good, and even important, to listen to your own inner voice. God, a higher power, the universe, the greater good, our guides – whatever we choose to call it – wants us to succeed, to be happy – to learn what we need to in this life, and to fulfill our purpose. These divine beings, these spirits, are on our side – they're rooting for us!

THREE

TODAY'S BRAVE PARANORMAL EXPLORERS

*"I can't understand why people are frightened by new ideas.
I'm frightened of the old ones."*

John Cage, American musician and philosopher

Today, studying the subject of intuitive ability – "psi" – is still largely shunned by many conventional scientists and the scientific community at large. However, even in this hostile, unwelcoming climate, there are some amazing people who are researching psi. These bold scientists are persevering and moving forward because they believe, based on experimental data, that there is a truth out there, a greater knowing, that has not yet been discovered, and that we – human beings, the planet, the universe – could all benefit from understanding.

These scientific visionaries, Dean Radin, Gary Schwartz and Russell Targ, are quite different from each other, but they share a common goal – to bring us to our next level, the evolution of consciousness.

Each of these scientists has published many papers, studies and books. This is an overview of their research, to provide an idea of the enormous contributions that these scientists have made to better understand the potential of psi and, thanks to their findings, the subsequent and, hopefully, inevitable advancement of human consciousness.

DEAN RADIN

Dean Radin, PhD, is a leading research scientist and parapsychologist who has been studying paranormal phenomena and the nature of consciousness for almost forty years. Even though he is often confronted by skeptics and critics, Radin has steadfastly carried the psi research torch and will continue to do so until he discovers more about the nature of consciousness.

As Radin writes in his autobiography:

"My interest in psi was originally motivated out of a child's intuitive sense that the mind is far more mysterious and powerful than we know. Through education and experience I've also come to appreciate that these experiences are also responsible for most of the greatest inventions, artistic and scientific achievements, creative insights, and religious epiphanies throughout history. I discovered while working on these topics that I enjoy the challenge of exploring the frontiers of science, and that I am comfortable tolerating the ambiguity of not knowing the 'right answer,' which is a constant companion at the frontier."

http://www.deanradin.com/NewWeb/bio.html

Dean Radin is currently the Chief Scientist at the Institute of Noetic Sciences (IONS), an organization that is at the forefront of consciousness research. Prior to joining IONS in 2001, Dean held appointments at AT&T Bell Labs, Princeton University, the University of Edinburgh, and SRI International. He began his career as a concert violinist, but ultimately followed his interest in science, earning a BSEE degree in electrical engineering, *magna cum laude,* with honors in physics, from the University of Massachusetts, Amherst, and then an M.S. in electrical engineering and a Ph.D. in psychology from the University of Illinois, Urbana-Champaign.

Radin is author or co-author of some 250 technical and popular articles, three dozen chapters in books, and three books, including the award-winning *The Conscious Universe*, *Entangled Minds*, and the 2014 Silver Nautilus Book Award winner, *Supernormal*.

According to Radin, most people privately believe that intuitive ability does exist. "From a popular perspective, all of the surveys have said that the majority of the population believes in these phenomena because it happens to them, or it happens to somebody that they know and trust," says Radin. "Within the scientific community, it's the same. Except that, within science, you learn very quickly that you don't talk about this ever, because if you do you'll put your career in jeopardy."

One of the reasons that scientists are reluctant to talk about intuitive ability is that they can't explain where it comes from or how it works. "Even sympathetic scientists are reluctant to talk about this because after we present empirical evidence that, yes, psychic ability is really real, and we can show it under rigorous conditions, the next question is, well, how does it work?" Radin explains. "And science has yet to understand how it works. And I think that the reason why we don't understand it is because we need to have a different paradigm on which science rests."

Currently, science bases its beliefs on the material or physical world. "Every neuroscientist out there, at least most of them, fully believe that subjective awareness and consciousness are an effect of, or an outgrowth of brain activity," says Radin. "So, if you're now talking about people who say that they can talk to dead people who have no brains, and they can get information from the future, it is literally impossible within that paradigm. And that's why, even if a scientist will talk to a psychic on their own time, if somebody raises this topic they'll deny it because it sounds anti-scientific."

However, regardless of the taboo in the scientific community, Radin continues to do research on psi because he believes it is important for humanity. "I think that it's actually important for the survival of the species, to understand a lot more about the nature of consciousness, and who we are and what we're capable of from an intuitive perspective, because if we're walking around half blind to who and what we are, we're going to be walking into walls. And given what we see happening in the world today, we're collectively walking into walls all the time."

When I was doing research for this book, I was amazed at how difficult it was to find scientists, or academicians who study religion, who would agree to discuss the topic of intuition and psychic ability. Some professors of religion and some scientists balked at my requests to talk about these subjects, saying "Oh no, I don't go in for that New Age stuff. That would be a waste of my time." So I was thrilled to learn that Dean Radin had discovered the very same thing over the years.

In his latest book, *Supernormal,* Radin muses about the fact that both scientists and religious scholars turn away from studying psi and the subject of intuitive ability, and are often adamantly opposed to the possibility that these abilities exist at all:

> "It is hardly surprising that these topics are too disturbing to be studied either by religious scholarship or by science. The presence of real siddhis, real psychic effects lurking in the dark boundaries between mind and matter, are so frightening and disorienting that defense mechanisms immediately snap into place to protect our psyches from these disturbing thoughts. We become blind to personal psychic episodes and to the supportive scientific evidence, we conveniently forget mind-shattering synchronicities, and if the intensity of the *mysterium tremendum* becomes too hot, we angrily deny any interest in the topic while backing away and vigorously making the sign of the cross. Within science this sort of behavior is understandable; science doesn't like what it can't explain because it makes scientists feel stupid. But the same resistance is also endemic in comparative religion scholarship, which is supposed to be the discipline that studies the sacred."
>
> Radin, Dean, *Supernormal, Science, Yoga and the Evidence for Extraordinary Psychic Abilities,* New York, Random House, Inc., 2013, p. 309-310.

Even though there are significant challenges ahead, Dean Radin is determined to continue his research. "I think that the way that I persist in the face of a huge amount of resistance in the scientific community, is that I see this more as a long term effort that simply needs to be done. So I'm part of a stream that is happening and, maybe I won't live to see the paradigm change, but somebody needs to be working on it at some point in history, because otherwise, it will never change and humans may well run headlong into extinction. Perhaps we're all on some kind of a long term thrust to raise the collective consciousness, or to gain a better sense of who and what we are and what reality's all about. It's just surprisingly difficult to get most people to think beyond what's directly in front of their face."

GARY SCHWARTZ

Gary Schwartz, PhD, is a professor of psychology, medicine, neurology, psychiatry, and surgery at the University of Arizona and director of its Laboratory for Advances in Consciousness and Health. After receiving his doctorate from Harvard University and teaching there as an assistant professor, he served as a professor of psychology and psychiatry at Yale University, director of the Yale Psychophysiology Center, and co-director of the Yale Behavioral Medicine Clinic.

He is the author of many books, including *The Afterlife Experiments*, *The Energy Healing Experiments*, *The G.O.D. Experiments*, *The Sacred Promise*, and *Super Synchronicity*. Unlike some researchers, Schwartz doesn't identify himself as someone who's studying psi. "First of all, I wouldn't use the word psi because I am really not a psi researcher, even though others would label me as such because I do research on life after death and the survival of consciousness hypothesis," says Schwartz. "I've never approached this area as paranormal. If it is real, it is normal. And I believe that it's real and that it's normal. It may be *supernormal* or *supernatural*, but not in super as 'beyond,' but super as in 'exceptional' or 'strong.' So supernatural to me is not *not* natural, it's just some of the highest forms of natural."

When asked why he chose to study intuitives to better understand consciousness, Schwartz has concluded that he was called to pursue this path. "I think that the universe has been providing me with both the evidence and the inspiration to take on this challenge because I am, as far as I know, the only tenured professor at a major university in the world doing experimental mediumship research. That's how rare it is."

But Schwartz is very clear about his purpose in his role as a researcher in this field. "When people ask me, are you trying to prove survival of consciousness, I say absolutely not. What I am trying to do is give survival of consciousness, if it exists, the opportunity to prove itself. All I am doing, which is my responsibility as a scientist, is to provide the optimal conditions for discovery whether something is true or not with appropriate controls. And for the record, if I could do all of this anonymously I would. Not because of the fear of ridicule, but because it's not about me, it's about the energy, and it's not about you, it's about the universe."

According to Schwartz, the study of mediums and mediumship research is a critical test of a core belief of materialist science. "Materialist science says very clearly that the brain creates consciousness. Matter first, mind second," says Schwartz. "Therefore, when you die, your mind is dead because the brain is dead. Case closed. The new science is saying no. Matter does not create mind. Mind is separate from brain and mind can interact with brain so that the mind uses the brain in order to exist in the physical world. Therefore, when the brain dies, the mind does not die. So how do we determine whether that is true or not? The answer is you have to do research, which is what we're doing." As Schwartz explains, what is emerging is a new paradigm called post-materialist science, and it bridges conventional science, consciousness and spirituality.

However, there are very few scientists and academicians pursuing this area of study. Conversely, there are a great number of scientists who reject parapsychology and any research related to psi, psychic ability and mediumship, and even the study of consciousness itself.

"We have very few scientist leaders," Schwartz points out. "So when are we going to be inspired to step forward and to come together? What I've come to realize is that the future may lie in our breaking the veil. One of the biggest discoveries is the topic of survival of consciousness after death. And the next closest one is the realization that, under the right conditions, technology can be used to detect the presence of spirit."

Although Schwartz believes that we are on the brink of important discoveries in parapsychology, he also sees the challenges that lie ahead. "I would say that there are three major challenges. The first is that we need to open people's minds to looking at the data. When Galileo made significant discoveries about the planets, literally there were both priests and scientists who refused to look through Galileo's telescope to see evidence which challenged their core beliefs. So one of our biggest challenges is to try to awaken people who are threatened by the information about psi, and who don't want to see the information or recognize that it's not only real, but it's extremely important, for both themselves personally and for the world. That's one of the biggest challenges."

Schwartz continues, "I would say that equally big challenges are that it's virtually impossible to get funding to actually support the research, and most journals won't publish experiments about these topics, no matter how carefully conducted they are. There is a taboo and censorship about the material so it's very hard to break into the mainstream academia. There is very little research funding for parapsychology, and so consequently students can't become involved with it and you can't conduct the kinds of studies that would provide the convincing evidence. So those are the three biggest challenges that people who study psychic phenomena are facing today."

But Gary Schwartz remains hopeful, and plans to continue on his quest for the truth about intuitive ability, synchronicity and the survival of consciousness. He believes it is his responsibility to "walk the talk" concerning research that bridges science and spirituality. "What I feel is that this is the path I'm meant to be on, and things are happening at the pace that it's supposed to happen," says Schwartz. "And I am trusting the process and the universe. If it's not meant to be, then my request of the universe is that it tell me so. But if there is a higher purpose, and this work helps us fulfill that higher purpose, then I will continue to be of service to the universe."

RUSSELL TARG

Russell Targ, PhD, is a physicist who was a pioneer in the development of the laser, and who is also a prominent ESP researcher and cofounder of the Stanford Research Institute International's (SRI) investigation of intuitives abilities in the 1970s and 80s. At SRI International, Targ and his colleague, Harold E. Puthoff, were in charge of this breakthrough research program, which studied psychic abilities for U.S. intelligence organizations, including the CIA, Army Intelligence and the Defense Intelligence Agency.

Targ and Puthoff's SRI International research program, which lasted 23 years and received $25 million in funding, yielded a number of significant findings about intuitive ability and "remote viewing," which were published in several prestigious scientific publications, including *Nature, The Proceedings of the Institute of Electronic and Electrical Engineers* (IEEE), and the *Proceedings of the American Association for the Advancement of Science* (AAAS).

An accomplished author, Targ wrote and co-authored several books which take a scientific look at ESP, intuitive ability, remote viewing, and consciousness, among other topics. They include *The Reality of ESP: A Physicist's Proof of Psychic Abilities*; *Limitless Mind: A Guide to Remote Viewing and Transformation of Consciousness*; *Miracles of Mind: Exploring Nonlocal Consciousness and Spiritual Healing* (with Jane Katra); and his first book, *Mind Reach: Scientists Look at Psychic ability* (with Harold E. Puthoff).

In addition to being a scientist, Targ is also a Buddhist, and he writes about ESP and Buddhism in his book, *The Reality of ESP: A Physicist's Proof of Psychic Abilities*:

"ESP allows us to have a direct experience of spacious awareness – transcending space and time. Many people find that
their first introduction to such psychic abilities is exhilarat-
ing, even life changing. They instantly catch on to the idea
that they themselves are obviously much more than just a
physical body, as they learn to see into the distance and the
future. This idea has been articulated in great detail for
the past twenty-five hundred years in Buddhist and Hindu
writings, particularly in the encyclopedic Buddhist meditation, *The Flower Ornament Scripture*, and the inspirational
Hindu volume, known as the *Yoga Sutras of Patanjali*. In
such ancient texts psychic abilities were studied, examined,
and considered an important part of life; they weren't just
deemed weird stuff and shuffled off into a supernatural or
metaphysical corner as much of our society is wont to do."

Targ, Russell, *The Reality of ESP,*
A Physicist's Proof of Psychic Abilities,
Wheaton, Illinois, Quest Books, 2012, p.240.

Targ was aware of his deep interest in studying ESP and intuitive ability from a very young age. But he also knew that in order to
have his research taken seriously, he would have to become a physicist. "I knew that I was going to do this work as a child, from very
early on. And I was aware that many people who research psychic
ability get nowhere, career wise. This is not fair, but it's the way it
seemed to be," says Targ. "I was reading ESP papers in high school,
technical papers, and I realized that all of these people were professionally nowhere, and I didn't want to do that. So I realized that I
would have to do business and research as a physicist first, and then
go into parapsychology."

As a physicist, Targ was better able to address the notion that
people could communicate telepathically with other beings, if
they're not in the same room, or country, or even the same realm
of the universe. "The idea of nonverbal connectivity is much more
accepted in physics. So I would say that physics is helping the

acceptance of parapsychology. In physics, it was understood thirty-five years ago that photons or other particles that are born together, even though they traveled away from each other at the speed of light, are still connected to one another and that's true, but you can't use that to send a message."

Targ talks more about this theory, called nonlocality, which is one of the cornerstones of quantum physics, in his book *The Reality of ESP: A Physicist's Proof of Psychic Abilities:*

> "The view of many quantum physicists is that we live in nonlocal reality, which is to say that *we can be affected by events that are distant from our ordinary awareness.* That's the evidence. No one presently knows how ESP works. But I see a striking similarity between the nonlocal functioning of remote viewing in our SRI laboratory – independent of distance and time – and the descriptions of EPR (Einstein, Podolsky and Rosen) optical experiments in the physics laboratory."
>
> Targ, Russell, *The Reality of ESP,*
> *A Physicist's Proof of Psychic Abilities,*
> Wheaton, Illinois, Quest Books, 2012, p. # 204.

Targ continues, "The idea of nonlocality tells us something about the universe. An example would be identical twins. Identical twins also live similar lives even though they are raised apart. There is one set of identical twins who lived and were raised separately, who both got named Jim because their adopting parents both named them Jim, even though they lived hundreds of miles apart and never met. But the two Jims who were raised separately both became fireman. They both married women named Linda, and then they divorced Linda. After that, they each married women named Betty and there were many, many other things that they did that were the same. They wore the same steel rimmed glasses. They smoked the same cigarettes. They were both were fireman."

Targ explains, "You can say that they became fireman because they were genetically born as risk takers. That would be my guess – that they had the extra testosterone that made them be risk takers. But there is no Betty gene and no Linda gene. They were not sending each other messages of the form, "Marry Betty, marry Linda.' But because they are entangled, they each feel an inclination to do the same things for reasons we don't understand. The story of the Jim twins is very, very well known. They finally met each other when they were brought together by the Minneapolis Twin Study, a big organization in the Twin Cities studying twins at the University of Minnesota."

In addition to nonlocality, quantum entanglement is another aspect of quantum physics that Targ mentioned when talking about psychic ability. Most people, even scientists, have difficulty understanding the concept of entanglement. Put simply, entanglement means that multiple particles are linked together, and that one particle's quantum state can possibly determine the quantum state of the other particles. Therefore, even if the particles are separated by a great distance, changing one particle can create a similar change in the other particles. The important thing to note is that this apparent "correlation" isn't dependent on the location of the other particles in space.

"Entanglement is a scientifically understood idea, but it is like psychic ability in nature, so consequently it is not part of our lexicon," explains Targ. "What the Buddhist would say is that separation is an illusion. That is, in consciousness, we observe that our physical bodies are in different places, but our consciousness is entangled, filling all of space and time. One of the things we know about nonlocality and remote viewing is that it's no harder for someone in California to describe what is going on in Pittsburgh than it is for them to describe what going on across the street in Palo Alto."

Targ says, "The answer to understanding and explaining psychic ability is not in the fields. It's in the geometry. So you are not going to get an electromagnetic field explanation for psychic ability. It would be a geometrical explanation. We misunderstand the nature of the space and time in which we live. And the reason you know that psychic ability is not electromagnetic is that it's independent of space and time, and nothing electromagnetic is independent of space and time."

When asked what he believes about what happens to our consciousness when we die, and if we reincarnate, Targ answered, "The evidence for survival is much greater than the evidence for reincarnation. I am convinced that after people die, there is some aspect to their consciousness that survives, because the evidence for that is overwhelming. There are hundreds and hundreds of current books with information from deceased people. There is also pretty good evidence for reincarnation, but that evidence is weaker."

Overall, Russell Targ feels that having a greater understanding of intuitive ability is necessary for humankind to evolve to the next level of our evolutionary process. "My message is that psychic abilities are available, and that they're real. That's my story. And the explanation will be in the geometry, not in any fields. Because we have done experiments with people in a submerged submarine, where there are no fields, and their friends are on the land. So the explanation for psychic ability will be geometrical."

FOUR
AHEAD OF THEIR TIME
Scientific Breakthroughs That Were Ridiculed

In the same way that researchers who are studying paranormal or psi phenomena are often ridiculed and dismissed, many great scientists and visionaries from the past were laughed at, ignored and even jailed or committed to mental institutions for their beliefs. Thankfully, over time, society has come to understand these beliefs, which have ultimately proved to be highly valuable and beneficial to mankind. Here are some stories about these amazing, tenacious pioneers who were truly ahead of their time.

Alexander Graham Bell

Alexander Graham Bell was a Scottish-born scientist and inventor who was the first person to be granted a patent for the telephone. After receiving his patent in 1876, Bell contacted officials at one of the nation's largest communications firms, Western Union, and asked them if they would be interesting in purchasing rights for the device for $100,000. The company officials declined, saying that they had made their decision about the telephone because of the "obvious limitations of the device, which is hardly more than a toy."

In addition to Western Union, there were other critics of Bell's telephone, including President Rutherford B. Hayes, who said, "It's an amazing invention, but who would ever want to use one of them?" Undeterred, Bell created the Bell Telephone in 1877 and, about a decade later, some 150,000 people in the United States had telephones in their homes.

Ernst Chladni

In the early 1800s, German physicist Ernst Chladni wrote a book entitled *On the Origins of the Iron Masses,* which supported the theory that meteorites originate from outer space, not volcanoes, as was previously thought. Chladni found that the meteorites were totally different in composition from earth rocks, and he stated that he believed these strange stones were of extraterrestrial origin. By taking such a controversial stand, Chladni was the subject of much ridicule by the scientific community, including Georg Lichtenberg, a scientist and satirist, who said that he "wished that Chladni had not written his book" and that he felt that Chladni "had been hit on the head with one of his stones."

Opinions about Chladni's finding began to change when a fellow scientist, Jean Baptiste Biot, performed his own research after a meteor shower dropped thousands of stones on the town of L'Aigle in northern France. After studying the strange stones, Biot wrote a report that confirmed that the stones came from asteroids or comets that had disintegrated, and the scientific community finally came around to accept Chladni's initial research, dubbing him one of the founders of modern meteorite research.

Galileo Galilei

Born in 1564, Galileo was a brilliant mathematician and scientist who made major discoveries that influenced how we view modern physics and astronomy today. Although geocentrism, the belief that the sun revolves around the earth, had been widely believed for 1,500 years, Galileo embraced the mathematical model for the universe called heliocentrism, put forth by Nicolaus Copernicus a century earlier. Galileo wrote about heliocentrism in *Dialogues Concerning the Two Chief World Systems,* which was published in 1632. This angered the Roman Catholic Church because the teachings of the Church favored geocentrism and Galileo was challenging these teachings and violating Church doctrine.

Galileo was summoned to Rome, subjected to Inquisition hearings, and was convicted of heresy. Galileo recanted, had all his works destroyed and promised not to write again. The Church banned any publications which advocated heliocentrism. In spite of all this, Galileo was kept in the dungeons in Rome. His friends begged for his release, and Galileo was allowed to go home to his villa as long as he never ventured outside the villa walls. Galileo kept his promise, dying there nine years later.

Galileo was eventually vindicated for supporting the heliocentric model of the universe which we take for granted today, thanks in part to significant contributions by Johannes Kepler and Sir Isaac Newton. Like many other scientific theories that were ridiculed, true science eventually won out. In 1758, the Church lifted its ban on most writings which supported heliocentrism and Copernican theory, and the Church stopped opposing heliocentrism in 1835.

Similar to the roadblocks and skepticism that psi researchers are facing today, prominent scientists in the 16th century adamantly refused to look through Galileo's telescope, which he had greatly improved, to see evidence of the fact that, indeed, the earth does revolve around the sun.

Robert H. Goddard

Robert Goddard was a physicist who conceived, built and tested the first liquid-fueled rocket which he launched successfully on March 16, 1926. His discoveries helped pave the way for future rockets and space exploration, and today, he is known as the American Father of Modern Rocketry.

But his quest wasn't always easy. Goddard funded his early research entirely with his own money, beginning first with powder-fueled rockets, but later moving on to liquid-fueled rockets, which were much more effective and efficient. Even though his research was truly revolutionary, he didn't receive much attention from the public or the U.S. Government. Finally, in 1917, Goddard received $5,000 from the Smithsonian Institution which enabled him to continue his research. In 1919, the Smithsonian published Goddard's research paper entitled *A Method for Reaching Extreme Altitudes*, which included the concept that, one day, a rocket could reach the moon.

Unfortunately, once the media learned about Goddard's research, they ridiculed him mercilessly. On Jan. 13, 1920, The *New York Times* printed an editorial on page 12 titled "A Severe Strain on Credulity" that was particularly scathing, writing:

> "Professor Goddard with his 'chair' in Clark College and the countenancing of the Smithsonian Institution does not know the relation of action to reaction, and of the need to have something better than a vacuum against which to react – to say that would be absurd. Of course he only seems to lack the knowledge ladled out daily in high schools."
>
> (https://en.wikisource.org/wiki/
> The_New_York_Times/Robert_Goddard)

Although the press belittled Goddard and his theories, he responded to one reporter's question by saying, "Every vision is a joke until the first man accomplishes it; once realized, it becomes commonplace." After the media firestorm, Goddard stayed away from the media, and in 1930, he moved to New Mexico to continue his research in private, until his death in 1945.

Eventually, Goddard was vindicated. After the launch of Apollo 11 in July of 1969, the *New York Times* printed a correction to its earlier 1920 editorial, saying "it is now definitely established that a rocket can function in a vacuum as well as in an atmosphere. The Times regrets the error." In addition, NASA named its space laboratory in Greenbelt, Maryland, the Goddard Space Flight Center.

Joseph Lister

Joseph Lister was a British surgeon, born in 1827, who is credited with discovering the "germ theory of disease." When Lister was a surgeon at Edinburgh Hospital, nearly half of the patients died from infection, or sepsis, as it was called. While most surgeons accepted this high death rate as inevitable, since it was thought that infections spontaneously began in the wound, Lister refused to believe that these fatal outcomes were the norm, and he began to research ways to prevent these deadly infections.

Lister noticed that when someone broke a bone but the breakage was not exposed to the air, the patient would not get an infection. But if the break was open and exposed to the air, an infection would often set in. Lister began to wash his hands and change soiled surgical clothes, but he was often ridiculed by his colleagues, who considered it a badge of honor to be covered in blood after an operation. Lister continued his research, and he discovered a study by Louis Pasteur about the use of carbolic acid to eliminate germs. Although germs couldn't be seen, and many colleagues rejected his theories, Lister started to experiment with carbolic acid as a way to prevent infection in patients. His efforts were successful, and today he is considered to be the Father of Modern Surgery.

Ignaz Semmelweis

Ignaz Semmelweis was a Hungarian physician who outraged the medical community in the mid-1800s when he suggested that physicians should wash their hands when performing surgery. His theory was widely ridiculed by his colleagues, and he was dismissed from the hospital where he worked in Vienna. Semmelweis became angry, and he wrote numerous letters to obstetricians, insisting that cleanliness and hand washing could reduce the incidence of puerperal fever, also called childbed fever, which was responsible for the deaths of many new mothers at the time. His colleagues, as well as his wife, believed that he was losing his mind, and he was committed to a mental institution, where he died shortly after.

Several years after his death, Semmelweis's germ theory earned widespread acceptance, and today he is often referred to as the Savior of Mothers for his insistence about the importance of the use of antiseptic practices in medical settings. Interestingly, there is a term called the "Semmelweis effect" that describes incidences when new theories or scientific research is ignored or rejected simply because they go against the thinking or the established paradigms of the day.

FIVE

A BRIEF OVERVIEW:
The Treatment Of Gifted Intuitives Throughout History

Since the dawn of time, there have been people who have highly gifted intuitive abilities, often referred to as prophets, seers, shamans, psychics, and mediums. Sometimes, these people were revered and respected; at other times, they were mocked, scorned and even put to death because of their gifts. The way they were regarded often depended upon the era and the culture they were born into.

Early Intuitives - The Shamans and Prophets

According to Jeffrey Kripal, the J. Newton Rayzor Professor of Religion at Rice University, and the author of six books, including *Authors of the Impossible* and *The Super Natural*, individuals who have extraordinary intuitive abilities have been present throughout history.

"No doubt, for much of human prehistory, and for most of the world inside and outside of what we today call the 'world religions,' shamans, medicine men, and religious prodigies of all kinds just trafficked in these abilities," notes Kripal. "That's what made one a shaman, or what made one a religious specialist in one's community or tribe — the ability to leave the body, see the future, receive communications from the gods or God, and heal people. I mean, that was the function of the religious specialist, and the religious specialist alone. It wasn't that everybody had these special gifts, and the shamanic vocation comes with real risks and real social costs. The shaman was *different*, set apart from ordinary society."

William Barnard, a Professor of Religious Studies at Southern Methodist University, agrees. "There were probably shamans in every culture from the Paleolithic era on, which was 2.6 million years ago. I don't think that too many religious scholars would dispute this," Barnard says.

"What we call the shamanic cultures, the hunting gathering cultures, and tribal groups, were often people that didn't have doctors, or other people who did different specialized tasks. And so they had to develop some pretty fine tuned intuitive senses, so that they would know, for example, where the food and game is, and when the enemy is going to attack."

In a course he teaches about primal religions, Barnard refers to a book called *Black Elk Speaks*, which was written by John Neihardt, a poet laureate, based on a series of interviews he did with Black Elk when Black Elk was an old man, looking back on his life. In the book, Black Elk, who was a shaman, explains that the tribe was always looking for the shamans among them, and that they believe that the spirits of the shamans were selected to be the medicine people and the healers for the tribe.

"The shaman could act as the intermediary between the human community and the spirit realm," says Barnard. "They believed that certain young men and women were selected to be shamans for the tribe, to heal them, to know what other people are thinking – to be deeply intuitive, deeply psychic. In his book, Black Elk describes having the intuitive sense of being guided to different plants for healing, or having a clear sense that some enemies were just over the hill."

Barnard believes that the shamanic figure was perhaps among the first religious specialists recorded in history. "Shamans were deeply valued, deeply prized by the tribe, because they served so many roles. If there was a drought, they could call on the gods and spirits to overcome the drought. They found game and warded off enemies. Shamans were like crucially important people, so the community was on the lookout for those who had been selected by the spirits to function in that role."

How Prophets Were Viewed in the Bible

Parts of the Torah (or what the Christian tradition calls the Old Testament), written in Hebrew, might have come into being as early as 1,450 B.C.; the first five books, the Torah proper, were consolidated between 538-332 B.C. People with intuitive abilities were often featured. "If you read something like the Hebrew Bible or what the Christians call the Old Testament, there are all kinds of paranormal powers discussed in it," says Jeffrey Kripal. "Joseph reads dreams, and predicts the future through the dreams. Priests would cast lots to determine what to do in a given situation. People consulted oracles and mediums and all sorts of things. Jesus, too, of course, performs all kinds of magical or miraculous healings. He uses his spittle in one scene, and in another he even curses a fig tree to wither and die when it provided no fruit, when it wasn't even in season, no less. I mean, these things are just *everywhere* in the Bible."

In the Bible, prophets are discussed in both positive and negative terms. In the King James translation of the Bible, Amos 3:7 says:

> "Surely the Lord GOD does nothing, unless He reveals His secret to His servants the prophets." A passage in Numbers 12:6 states: "Hear now My words: If there is a prophet among you, I, the LORD, make Myself known to him in a vision; I speak to him in a dream." And another reference appears in 2 Chronicles 20:20: "...Hear me, O Judah and you inhabitants of Jerusalem: Believe in the LORD your God, and you shall be established; believe His prophets, and you shall prosper."*

---

* www.apostolicrevelation.info/2011/10/who-is-true-prophetic-leader.html

Prophets were often highly valued in the Old Testament because it was understood that they were delivering the word of God, not their own messages. "In the Old Testament, the prophets are often considered to be the vessel or channel that God is speaking through," explains Barnard. "They don't have that knowledge personally. God has just chosen them to communicate to His people, and it's usually a community that's going astray. So the prophets were often warning and chastising the people for doing something bad, and they often said, 'This is what God is telling us. If you don't change, then you're going to get punished in the future.'"

The Old Testament prophets include Ezekiel, Daniel, Jeremiah, Isaiah, Hosea, Jonah, and others. Some of the prophets in the New Testament are Paul the Apostle, John the Baptist, Anna, Barnabas and John the Revelator.

The Bible also warned people not to follow "false prophets." For example, in the King James version of the Bible, a passage in 1 John 4:1 reads: "Beloved, do not believe every spirit, but test the spirits, whether they are of God; because many false prophets have gone out into the world." And Isaiah 8:20, states: "To the law and to the testimony! If they do not speak according to this word, it is because there is no light in them."

Kripal notes that the topic of false prophets is often addressed in the New Testament as well. "The prophets are deeply controversial figures throughout the Bible – at once revered and reviled. In the New Testament, for example, there are accusations or warnings against false prophets. That was a real concern, since it was not at all clear where (or from whom) the prophetic utterances were coming from. So they had to come up with mechanisms or doctrinal points that could be used to distinguish between the 'true' and the 'false.' And that's, frankly, one reason the New Testament was put together. So that there was a rulebook, as it were, a measuring rod or 'canon' that could determine the true from the false prophetic teaching or trance utterance. Those are *these communities'* judgments, however, not the historian's. The historian makes no such judgments between 'true' and 'false' prophecy. He or she simply observes that people often go into trance states and utter words or teachings that claim to be 'from the Gods' or 'from God.' And these trance utterances in turn often end up playing important roles in human history."

Saints, the Catholic Church and the Protestant Reformation

In addition to the prophets, the Catholic Church has often recognized certain individuals as saints. Although saints have been canonized (the formal Church declaration of a saint) since the 10th century, for hundreds of years prior to that, saints were often chosen based on public acclaim.

"Prior to the 16th century, Catholicism in Europe already had a very elaborate cult of the saints," says Kripal. "Different saints were venerated (as opposed to worshipped). Human beings like St. Francis and St. Teresa of Avila had these abilities, and they performed miracles, but they and the Church attributed these powers to God. Very early on, around the 13th century or so, the Church decided that it had to determine when an extraordinary event is a miracle from God and so 'miraculous' and when such an event is from a human being and so simply a 'marvel' or evidence for 'magic.'

"So in order to decide who was a saint and who wasn't a saint, they began to institute an actual legal process. You needed evidence of genuine miracles to become a saint, and there was a court proceeding complete with canon or Church lawyers to prove that these miracles had been performed through someone who should be recognized as a saint, that God had actually worked *through* them."

Conversely, during the Middle Ages (5th to 15th centuries), many people – including non-gifted people who were simply thought to be "different" – were rounded up, tortured, and often put to death by hanging or being burned at the stake. It was not a good time to be identified as an outsider, because it could cost you your life. A classic example for this time is Joan of Arc, born in 1412 and burned at the stake on May 30, 1431. However, most of these people who were identified as "witches" were not gifted intuitives – they just stood out as targets for other reasons.

When the Protestant Reformation occurred in the 16th century, reformers changed the way people viewed saints. "They felt that the cult of the saints was just idolatry, so they decided that none of the saints or their miracles were real, or that they were the work of the devil," Kripal says. "So they eventually articulated this position sometimes called the doctrine of the cessation of miracles, which basically says that the age of miracles ended with the Biblical period, and that no miracles could take place after that. And that was their way of dismissing the Catholic Church, its saints and their miracles."

Why Witch Hunts Were Not About Intuitives

About this same time, between the 15th and 17th centuries, witch hunts were occurring throughout Europe and in some areas of the United States. Although one might assume that the individuals who were identified as witches were people who were psychics and intuitive individuals, that was usually not the case.

According to Brian Pavlac, a Professor of History at King's College in eastern Pennsylvania, and the author of *Witch Hunts in the Western World: Persecution and Punishment from the Inquisition through the Salem Trials*, the people who were accused of being witches were often perceived as being different from others, but they weren't necessarily people who were psychic or intuitive. "I don't think there's any good evidence of that," says Pavlac. "That kind of thinking just didn't exist back then."

Instead, during this period, an obsession about people who "worship the devil" began to grow, and was often fueled and carried out by religious and political figures of the day. "To me, what led to the witch hunts was that the leaders of Christian society, theologians and then politicians, got it into their heads that witches existed, and that these witches were trying to destroy society," continues Pavlac. "No one thought much about witches prior to the 1400s. But in the 15th century, this belief grew that witches exist and that they were casting spells and killing babies.

"So the officials began prosecuting accused witches without really investigating the crimes. They believed that these witches were forming partnerships with the devil, and that the devil was giving them the power to cast magical spells. But there was no good evidence that these things actually existed."

The majority of people who were accused of being witches were women; a small number who were tortured and killed during the witch hunts were children. "Many of the women who were labeled as witches were outsiders, or older women or marginalized women," says Pavlac. "There were some women who were involved in magical healing and things of that sort, but they were a small minority. The methods by which they identified these witches didn't really have much to do with looking for people who are intuitive or gifted. They just identified people for arbitrary reasons or because they were outsiders in society. A lot of witch hunts started with neighbors quarreling with each other, and accusing each other of believing in the devil, and it just snowballs from there. A hysteria, or mob mentality took over."

After more than two hundred years of panic, and the torture and killing of thousands of innocent people, the witch hunts began to abate in the 17th century. "One of the things that ended the witch hunts was that better legal procedures were put in place to protect innocent people," says Pavlac. "They began to require better evidence and better court procedures, which helped to put a stop to the hunts. It's my contention that almost everybody convicted in the witch hunts was not doing witchcraft. They were simply the victims of false accusations."

Even though the witch trials were mostly over, associating supernatural or intuitive ability with the devil has continued to persist. "Here's the problem," Kripal explains. "When you have a monotheism (or belief in a single true God) of any kind, what you've essentially done is locate all religious power, and all religious authority, in a single being – 'in one God.' And so, according to this way of thinking, any human being who displays any kind of power or ability that is godlike, such as intuitive or psychic ability, is a big problem. As long as this power is attributed to the human being (and not to God), one of two things must be going on: (1) the person is either faking that he or she has this intuitive ability, or (2) it is from the devil. A demon is behind it. And therein lies the danger of this kind of exclusive monotheistic thinking, of this whole way of asserting 'true' and 'false' prophecy or distinguishing between a 'miracle' or 'a work of magic.' It too easily leads to the demonization of human beings who are different and to the persecution of people who have special gifts."

The Controversial Legacy of Nostradamus

One of the most famous seers in history, Nostradamus, was born in 1503 as Michel de Nostredame in the south of France. When he was fourteen, Nostradamus enrolled at the University of Avignon to study medicine. Due to an outbreak of the bubonic plague, he was forced to drop out of the university after only one year. Five years later, he resumed his medical studies at the University of Montpelier. According to some accounts, he received his medical license in 1525 and, in the tradition of other medieval academicians, Latinized his name from Nostredame to Nostradamus.

For the next several years, Nostradamus turned his attention to treating victims of the plague in Italy and France, and he became well-known for his progressive treatment methods and cure rates for this widespread scourge. After traveling to other countries, including Greece and Turkey, Nostradamus became increasingly interested in the occult. He began to explore meditation and to have visions and, in 1550, Nostradamus wrote his first almanac, which included predictions for the coming year.

The almanac was a success, and Nostradamus decided to continue to write one or more almanacs annually. Eventually, in 1555, he published a book called *Les Propheties* which contains a collection of his prophesies and has rarely been out of print since his death in 1566. Many of his prophesies were written in the form of *quatrains,* which are four line poems or stanzas. He rejected the title of prophet over and over, but his most famous prediction – the strange death of Henri II of France in 1559 – cemented that title.

Although many of Nostradamus' prophesies were about natural disasters, such as floods, earthquakes and droughts, he has also been credited by enthusiasts as predicting such significant events as the rise and fall of Hitler, the French Revolution and the 9/11 terrorist attacks. However, a number of scholars and critics believe that Nostradamus' predictions were too vague and non-specific to be considered evidential, or an indication of his genuine prophetic abilities. So, while Nostradamus continues to be held in high esteem by many, a shroud of controversy continues to swirl around a number of his predictions.

How the Perception of Intuitives Has Changed During the Past 200 Years

The notion that psychic ability is "the work of the devil" has been one reason why people who have these intuitive gifts are often reduced to negative stereotypes. During the past two centuries, a number of influential individuals have attempted to enlighten the public about the true nature of intuitive ability.

William James (1842-1910) was a physician and Harvard professor of physiology and psychology. He was a founder of the American Society for Psychical Research (ASPR), which was created in 1884 and still exists today. Often referred to as the "Father of American Psychology," James was an intellectual and an influential philosopher who interacted with other great minds of his era, including Bertrand Russell, Mark Twain and Sigmund Freud. One of the mandates of the ASPR is to investigate "supernormal psychology" or parapsychology, and the group has studied telepathy, clairvoyance and mediumship, among other topics.

Another influential figure regarding intuitive ability was Edgar Cayce, a gifted intuitive who was nicknamed "The Sleeping Prophet," because he often did psychic readings and answered questions while in a trance state. In addition to generating hundreds of predictions about upcoming events, Cayce founded the Association for Psychical Research and Enlightenment (A.R.E.) in 1931; it is a nonprofit organization that does research on intuition, reincarnation and holistic healing, among many other topics. Based in Virginia Beach, Virginia, the A.R.E. explores many of the spiritual initiatives that helped to establish Cayce as one of the catalysts of the New Age Movement.

In his trance states, Cayce would receive prophesies about the future that he would record and share with others. One of these predictions was that the world would eventually evolve into an era of enlightenment, where humans would become more united with one another. Cayce believed that people would develop supernatural abilities and possess a new, uplifted consciousness that would result in a heightened level of spirituality and peace in the world. In 1944, he was asked which religious theories could lead to "spiritual light and understanding." His answer: "You shall love the Lord your God with all your heart, and your neighbor as yourself."*

Another person from the past century who was influential in raising awareness about intuitive ability was Ruth Montgomery. Prior to embracing her own ability in her later years, Montgomery was a journalist and a syndicated columnist who wrote for United Press International, the *New York Daily News*, Hearst and other top media outlets. After she began working as a psychic, Montgomery wrote a number of books about spiritual and New Age topics, including reincarnation, past life regressions and the afterlife.

Montgomery was a founder of the Association for Past Life Research and Therapy, and she continued to pursue her mission to educate the public about the psychic realm and the paranormal. In 1965, she wrote a bestselling book called *The Gift of Prophesy* about the life and predictions of the psychic Jeanne Dixon. Although some of Montgomery's own predictions didn't come to pass, which she attributes to free will, she did predict that the earth's axis

---

* www.near-death.com/paranormal/edgar-cayce/future.html

would shift, that global weather changes would threaten the future of planet Earth, and that humanity would enter a new and more enlightened era after the year 2000.

Today, many people believe in paranormal and intuitive experiences. According to a Gallup poll conducted in 2005, some 3 in 4 Americans believe in at least one paranormal activity, with the most popular belief being extrasensory perception (ESP). However, it is still largely considered a taboo to profess an interest or belief in psychic ability, particularly in the scientific and academic communities, but also among the general public. Even gifted psychics and mediums themselves are often afraid to "come out" about their intuitive abilities, and many remain closeted, because they fear that they will be judged and negatively perceived by others if they knew they were gifted.

Let's hope that these attitudes begin to change, so that we can learn to appreciate these gifted individuals, and to value the power of our own inner voice. When we become more enlightened about this topic, and we learn to look for guidance from those spirits, guides and angels that have much more wisdom than we do, we will all benefit.

Six

Six Simple Steps
To Access Your Own Inner Voice

Throughout this book, I've mentioned that everyone has access to their inner voice, and to the divine guidance and wisdom that comes to us through that inner voice. But how do we actually get in touch with our inner voice? Are there some guidelines or tips that will help us recognize and learn from this divine resource? The answer is yes – that every single one of us – regardless of if we are religious or not, can tap into this great support system. Our inner voice and this divine wisdom transcend religion. It's there for all of us to access, and to use for guidance and direction.

Here are some simple guidelines that will enable you to recognize your inner voice and to connect with it in a meaningful, profound way:

1) Quiet your mind

If you want to access your inner voice, it's important to clear out your mind and become as peaceful and relaxed as possible. Unclutter your thoughts, and open up your mind to receiving the messages and impressions that the powers that be want to share with us. Be open and receptive, and the messages will come. There are many ways to achieve this goal – find the best method that works for you.

2) Be humble, and take your ego down a few pegs

In our world today, in the era of reality TV, we're often encouraged to be a star, to be the center of attention. Yes, you are important and smart, and maybe even brilliant, but you don't need to take credit for every single thought that comes into your mind. Some of those thoughts or inspirations may actually be coming from divine guidance, from wise spirits or protective entities that are looking out for your best interest. So in order to be able to hear your inner voice clearly, it's imperative that you keep your ego in check.

3) Trust your gut

Everybody has had gut feelings – perceptions or strong thoughts that come to us out of the blue, and that make a deep impression on us, regardless of what our rational mind is thinking. Pay attention to these gut feelings. Chances are that these thoughts and ideas are coming from our wise inner voice that's trying to alert us to something important. It's a good idea to heed these impressions and take them seriously.

4) Ask for help

Do you think that God, the universe and the powers that be are too busy to care about our personal problems and to answer our questions or assist us in finding the right path going forward? You would be wrong. Remember these famous words, "Ask and you shall receive." In the New Testament, during the Sermon on the Mount, Jesus says: "Ask, and it shall be given you; seek, and ye shall find; knock, and it shall be opened unto you: For everyone who asketh receiveth; and he who seeketh findeth; and to him that knocketh it shall be opened." [Matthew 7:7-8]

These loving entities want us to do well and to succeed, and they often respond directly to us when we ask for their help and guidance. I have had several experiences when, faced with a difficult dilemma or decision – I asked for help with the problem, and an answer or solution instantly appeared. Either I was inspired to follow a new course of action that I hadn't considered before, or I suddenly had a new idea that just "came into my mind." Certainly, there are times when this doesn't happen, perhaps because I'm still meant to struggle with the issue for various reasons, but many times, help does come. So don't be afraid to ask for help, and listen to your inner voice for the answer.

5) Be open and believe that we are not alone in this world

Sometimes being able to access our inner voice is as simple as just realizing that we are loved and not alone. If we're open to the concept that we all have access to divine guidance and wisdom, we've already taken a giant step toward being in touch with our higher self, the greater good, God, or whatever you choose to call it. In your heart of hearts, you may already realize this truth – you just have to have the confidence and courage to truly believe what you probably already know.

6) Become adept at "hearing" your inner voice

After you take the previous five steps to learn how to access your inner voice, you will begin to become more adept at actually recognizing and "hearing" your inner voice. At first, you may have difficulty distinguishing between your own thoughts and those inspirations that are divinely guided, but in time you will feel a distinct difference between the two ways of receiving and processing information.

One of the best ways to recognize this difference is to ask yourself if the "idea" or thought that you're having seems to come out of nowhere, and represents a completely new or inspired way of looking at something. If the thought is coming from your brain, it will feel completely rational, because it was created in your head. But divinely guided inspirations that we access through our inner voice have a fresh, clear and somewhat unusual quality, as if someone planted the thought in our heads from another place.

Listen to these divinely guided thoughts. They are the basis of understanding the gift within us. We all have caring collaborators who want to use their divine wisdom to help us on our path in life. By listening to our inner voice, we can help our guides – the collaborators – and us, achieve our shared goal.

"We are not human beings having a spiritual experience.
We are spiritual beings having a human experience."

Pierre de Chardin French philosopher

SEVEN

33 INTUITIVES
Share Their Stories

Here are the profile chapters of thirty-three highly gifted intuitives. Because 33 is considered to be a "master number" in numerology, I decided to focus on thirty-three individuals. The number represents a deeply spiritual teaching energy, with the desire to improve and advance humanity, and do all of the good that we're capable of achieving in this world.

These thirty-three intuitives have very different stories to tell, and they come from all walks of life and different geographical locations. One thing that they do share, however, is the desire to help others by communicating messages from spirit, God, our higher selves and the universe that will enable us to walk on the path that we were meant to take in order to fulfill our personal destinies. Here, in alphabetical order, are their unique, personal stories: how they came to realize that they were gifted, and how they learned to embrace their gift and to be of service to others.

THE INTUITIVES

PAUL ADZIC

Paul Adzic is from Australia, and he worked as a model for several years in Australia, Milan and the United States. He also worked in the film industry - as a production coordinator and an assistant director - on major films, including **The Matrix** *and* **Superman Returns.**

A gifted intuitive, Paul can give a person a crystal clear perspective on both the current situation and the ultimate purpose of one's life. Readings with Paul are refreshing, like a breath of fresh air, because he cuts through the clutter and provides people with a no-nonsense look at life and any issues they're facing. In addition to doing readings, Paul is continuing his film career, currently working on projects such as documentaries and films that are spiritually based.

At the beginning of my reading with Paul, he said that he saw that I was one of three children in my family - that I had two siblings - which was correct. But Paul went on to say that he saw a fourth child, another sibling who had died at a young age. I got goose bumps. There was a fourth child - a brother named Michael who was born a few years before me, but who died of pneumonia when he was 1½. Michael's death was understandably very hard on my mother, and we rarely spoke of it in our family. Most of my friends never even knew that I had an older brother who had died as a baby. But Paul knew, and he said that Michael was always around me, watching over me with love.

Paul knew he was intuitive from a very young age. "My earliest memory would be when I was around five or six years old. I would be talking to people in my room, and my mother or sister would walk into the room and say, 'Who are you talking to? Your toys? Because there's no one in the room with you.' And I'd say 'I'm talking to my friends.' Obviously I was connecting to spirits and they were sending information to me, so I was just interacting with them. At the time, of course, I didn't fully comprehend what was going on either."

Paul's mother was also psychic, although she never chose to formally use her ability. Paul remembers an incident when his mother had a very strong intuitive impression that saved his family's lives. "My family was all in our car, driving somewhere to go on vacation," Paul remembers. "Suddenly, my mother started telling my father to 'Stop! Stop! We need to stop this car and take a break from driving!' But my father didn't want to stop the car, so my mother got really angry and said, 'You have to stop!' and so my father finally pulled into a rest stop, and they had some coffee and relaxed for about a half hour before we got back on the road."

Shortly after Paul's father started driving again, they came upon a huge accident – a twenty to thirty car pile-up – that claimed a lot of lives. "If we had continued driving, and my mother hadn't insisted that we stop, our family would have been part of that accident. She definitely saved our lives that day, but the incident freaked my mother out so much that she shut down and tried to ignore her psychic abilities from that day on."

Although Paul enjoyed talking with his "friends" as a young boy, he was also a bit frightened of his gifts. "At the time when you first notice that you have this ability, it's very scary – because you're very small and have never experienced anything like this before," Paul admits. "And you think, 'What's going on? Am I going crazy – what's happening here?' Frankly, it can be a bit of a shock to a young child."

Paul said that his mother took his intuitive ability in stride, partly because she believed that Paul would "grow out of it." But Paul's ability only continued to grow, and he could create quite a stir when he was out shopping with his mother and sister.

"When I was about six or seven, we would be in a store at the local shopping center, and I would go up to people – complete strangers – and tell them things." His "friends" would send him messages and information about a particular person in the store, and they would ask Paul to deliver that message.

"I remember going up to this woman and saying, 'You need to leave your husband – he's very mean to you,' because my spirit friends would say, 'Go and speak to this woman, go and help her out.' And I would just walk over to her and give her the message they sent to me."

Paul's mother didn't react well to him giving these random, often intensely personal messages to strangers; she decided to keep Paul in the basket of the shopping cart so that he wouldn't wander up to people.

"After I said these things to people, they would come up to my mother and say, 'How does your child know this about me?' and she didn't know what to say to them," Paul recalls. "But after awhile, I didn't do this anymore, because my mother told me, 'You can't do that – people don't understand.' So I stopped delivering the messages to strangers."

As Paul grew older, he learned to accept the fact that he was different from other children, and to deal with that fact. "I always knew I was not a normal kid. You see it, you feel it – other kids would be playing in a certain way, and I was very strange in the way that I would play, the way I would interact with them. As a result, I liked to be around the adults much more than being with the children."

Paul went to college in Australia and studied many different things when he was trying to decide upon a career. At first, he chose architecture as his major, but changed to computer science about halfway through college. "And after jumping around for much of my college years, I decided to go to film school, and that's how I finally finished my degree."

After graduating, Paul traveled around for a few years, working as a model in Milan and Australia. Eventually, he started taking jobs in film production, and finally landed a position on his first major film – *The Matrix*.

"I was in the art department, and was one of those people who create the sets and different sorts of machines that were in the film," Paul explains. "I wasn't actually designing the props – my job was to buy the material to make these amazing things. After

The Matrix, I transitioned more into the production end of films, and I eventually became an assistant director (AD) on other films, including *Superman Returns*."

Beginning his career in Europe and Australia, Paul then moved to the United States when he was 33 and started working as a psychic and giving readings, in addition to continuing to work as a model and a film producer.

"Being a psychic gave me the freedom to pursue other passions that I have, which includes documentary filmmaking. Some of the projects I'm developing are either documentaries or films that are very spiritually based, that will teach humanity about the universe, and that will eventually create a better life for all of us. It's a passion of mine – it's something that I love to do."

Paul is in the process of developing a website that will give people a better understanding of why we're currently here on the planet, and how to find the ultimate purpose in life.

"I try to teach people that if you align yourself to all your desires and your beliefs, and you allow the universe to bring it to you – it does come," Paul explains. "I encourage people to just trust the universe and you'll get what you want. It might not be on your terms, and it might not be the way you think it's going to happen, but it doesn't really matter – you'll be in the right place, living the life you're meant to live."

Even though Paul is now an adult, he still gets strong intuitive feelings about strangers when he's out walking around or shopping. "Once, I was in a bookstore looking at books about crystals, and I got a flash of the sun shining brightly and a baby being born – a baby boy, so I started to look around me, and there was a pregnant woman standing next to me. I said to her, 'Hi, my name is Paul. Do you know when you're going to have your baby?' And she said, 'Oh, in the next week or so – we have a little time.' And I told her, 'You're going to have that baby boy tomorrow morning – not in a week.'

She took my phone number, and the next day I got a call from her husband, who said, 'My wife wanted me to call you – today, when the sun started to rise, she gave birth to our son, and she wanted to thank you for telling her that yesterday.' So I thought, 'Wow – this is just like when I was a little child, getting impressions about complete strangers!' It even amazes me to this day."

Regarding death, Paul has some specific thoughts that may help us to expand our perspective on what for many is a difficult subject.

"We humans are always looking at death from the standpoint of thinking that our lives are so important, how could this happen, how could my loved one die?" notes Paul. "But if you look at the bigger picture and stand back, you'll know that we're all eternal beings – we never actually 'die' – the lifetime we were just in was just one experience. Then we go back to the 'nonphysical' plane, and eventually, we'll come back here again in another body."

Ultimately, Paul believes that people need to treat others with love in order to help the world change for the better. "When people are coming from a place of ignorance and fear, they often think that war is the answer. But negative energy only creates more negative energy. By constantly bombing people, it's never going to end – it's a vicious cycle."

Conversely, Paul thinks that love is a powerful, positive energy that can make great changes happen. "Look at Nelson Mandela – it's amazing how much he changed the world with love rather than with war. That's how the universe works. You can only have good changes in this world if you send out good energy. I hope people begin to understand that soon."

According to Paul, it's important for people to open their minds and to see the world – and the universe – differently. "If we just sort of listen, and to acknowledge what is beyond our limited human understanding – we would see life in such a different way. In time, humans – and how we're treating each other and how we're treating the planet – are going to have to change, because the system we've got in place does not work. And the planet is slowly starting to tell us. And the planet can't speak to us, so it's going to teach us in other ways. And that's what has to happen for humanity to change."

PRAJNA AVALON

Prajna Avalon grew up in Brazil among a community of healers, psychics and mediums who were part of a "healing community" where she and her family lived. As a young girl, she gradually developed her healing and psychic abilities with the help and encouragement of her father, who was also a very gifted medium. After Prajna graduated from high school, she worked for a couple of years, saved her money, and moved to the United States when she was twenty. Prajna studied English in Boston, and she was eventually hired as a medical interpreter at a local hospital, where she translated medical terms, and used her healing abilities to do research on the effects of energy healing and surgery.

Prajna loves the healing work she does, and she feels deeply grateful for her intuitive abilities. She believes that our purpose in life is to grow and to heal here on Earth, so that we can ultimately be more enlightened, fulfill our destiny, and raise the vibration of the world to its highest, best level. During my reading with Prajna, I felt the effects of her healing energy because, while she was very accurate, her comments were also very inspirational, supportive and affirming.

Growing up in Brazil, Prajna Avalon always knew that she was gifted with intuitive abilities. "I've known it all my life. I was really lucky, because I was born and grew up in a community of healers and mediums and so all of that was very normal to me," she says. "There wasn't a memory where I said, 'Oh my God, I know I'm psychic, or I know I'm a medium.' I never had a spiritual awakening moment that changed my life. Everything was very normal and very familiar from the beginning."

In fact, Prajna has detailed memories of her existence in spirit before she was born. "I had memories of planning this lifetime, and what my work was going to be here," says Prajna. "I even had memories of the specific beings that are part of my soul group. These memories have been strong guiding forces for me in this life."

Prajna received support and encouragement about her abilities from her father, who was also a psychic medium. "He always encouraged me with all of my abilities. I think he saw it in me since I was very young."

As she was growing up, Prajna noticed that the other psychics seemed to be surprised at the high level of her intuitive gifts, compared with their own abilities. "The healers, mediums and psychics within the healing community, including my own teachers, were surprised at the level of my psychic and mediumship abilities. And as I got a little bit older, I noticed that I had surpassed even my father's abilities."

Intuitive experiences were routine in Prajna's life. When she was about eight, she had an experience that even amazed her father. "One day, my father was working in the garage and I was drawing with chalk on the sidewalk. He told me that my 83-year-old grandmother was very sick and that no one, none of the doctors, were able to determine the cause of her illness. And he told me that they were going to take her to the hospital to try to figure out why she was sick," remembers Prajna.

"Suddenly, out of nowhere, I said 'She has labyrinthitis.' And my father just looked at me with a surprised look, as he often would, since things like that often came out of my mouth, and he said, 'What does she have?' And I said, 'Labyrinthitis.' And he said, 'How do you know that?' And I just kind of shrugged my shoulders, and I went back to drawing on the sidewalk.

"A few weeks later, he came to me and gave me a hug, and he said, 'Well, we waited for two weeks, but the doctors still didn't know why your grandmother was sick, so we asked them if she could have labryinthitis, and they looked into it, and that's what your grandmother has, that's what's making her sick.' None of us had ever heard of labryinthitis – I now know that it's an inflammation of the inner ear, which causes extreme dizziness," says Prajna.

"But when my dad told me about my grandmother being sick, I just heard that word and it just came out of my mouth. That's usually how things work for me. The thought will come, or the vision will come, and I instantly know the answer. This has happened to me many, many times, and it's been proven to be right, so I don't question it anymore. But this was my first memory of using my medical intuition."

Although Prajna grew up in a community of intuitives and healers, she attended a traditional grade school. "I've always loved school and loved learning," says Prajna. "But I was very bored in school, because I found it too easy, and I wasn't challenged. I missed being around others who had a deeper connection with the spirit world, and who understood the teachings that I felt within myself. But nobody outside of the healing community knew that I had these abilities, and I kept them to myself."

As a result, Prajna often felt isolated and alone, and that she was different and didn't fit in. But she was very independent and actually enjoyed spending time alone. "I had fun exploring my psychic abilities in day to day life, and would often experiment with them to see how far my abilities could go," she explains.

Sometimes, Prajna used her intuitive abilities to help her in the classroom. "I was really shy as a kid, so when I was in class and I had a question about something, but I didn't want to raise my hand and be the center of attention, I would look at another student and think into their head, 'Could you please ask this question,' and two seconds later, the person would raise their hand, and ask the question I wanted answered. That always worked for me, and it was nice to play with energy and consciousness in different ways."

Prajna also used her abilities when playing childhood games. "I grew up playing outside, and we used to play hide and seek a lot," recalls Prajna. "I used to play a lot with my father. He was very fast and agile, so I could never find him. One day I realized that, because I could connect with other people's minds, I was able to find their hiding places more easily. So the next time my dad and

I played hide and seek, I connected to his mind and I could see where he was hiding right away. Every time! He couldn't believe it!

"But the funniest part is that after I told him what I was doing, he tried to do the same thing with me," Prajna continues. "Except that I knew he was doing that, so I would still connect with his mind first. I would think of places I didn't intend to go and send him all over looking for me in different spots. It drove him crazy!"

When Prajna was about ten years old, her father abruptly left home. "That was a huge loss for me, because my father was my main source of support and development. In a way, he was the only person who truly understood who I was. I felt very alone."

In her early teens, Prajna's intuitive gift began to grow rapidly. "My abilities started increasing a lot – to the point where it became overwhelming to me. I was having very strong premonitions all of the time. I would see spirits a lot, I would do astral travels, my things would disappear from one place and show up in another. My mom asked the psychics and mediums from the healing center to help me, but they weren't sure what to do. So I actually asked my guides to please shut down my abilities for awhile. And they did. My psychic abilities didn't shut down completely, but they decreased significantly, which was a huge relief, and my life became more manageable."

During Prajna's teenage years, some of her friends found out about her intuitive and healing abilities, and they would ask her for help. "When I was fourteen or fifteen, my friends would ask me to put my hands on them when they were sick. If they had a headache, I would put my hands on their forehead, and their headache would go away. Even my friends' parents would ask me to come to their homes and do readings for them. It was a lot of responsibility for a young person to handle, doing readings about major life decisions for an adult."

Prajna graduated from high school when she was eighteen, and because her family was very poor, she didn't have the financial resources to go to college. So she took a job as a salesperson at a telemarketing company and began to save money to move to the

United States. "When I was about thirteen years old, I started feeling that I was meant to move to the U.S.," Prajna says. "I had no idea why I was coming, or how long I was going to stay, and I didn't even speak English. But the guidance, the intuition, was so strong that I knew I had to move to America."

When Prajna was twenty, she moved to Boston and dedicated herself to studying English for a year. "I really studied a lot, so after one year, my English was very good," says Prajna. "I was always interested in using my medical intuition, and I was able to get a job as a medical interpreter at a local hospital, where I worked for almost ten years. My main job was to interpret medical language to patients who were Portuguese or Spanish, but I eventually did healing work."

In addition to working at the hospital, Prajna took courses at the Barbara Brennan School of Healing. "I completed the four year professional program and the two year advanced studies program and teacher training," she explains. "It was an extraordinary program, and it allowed me to start working as a healer in the United States."

Prajna always knew that she was meant to be a healer. "It felt very natural to me. My guides always told me three things: that I would be a teacher, that I was a healer, and that I would write a book. So those three things I knew. They told me not to ever lose sight of that. So I knew that I had a purpose, and that I was going to fulfill that purpose."

As part of her graduating project for the Barbara Brennan School, Prajna developed a research project at the hospital where she worked which looked at the effects of energy healing in patients who were undergoing surgery. "My research project was approved by the hospital almost immediately, and I began doing healing work with patients pre-op, inside the operating room and post surgery. I worked with a control group and a healing group, to compare specific results.

The results of the research project were overwhelmingly positive, impressing both Prajna and the medical team at the hospital.

"The results showed a significant benefit to the patients who received energy healing," says Prajna. "In fact, over 70% of patients who received healing treatment didn't need any pain medication after surgery. And the healing group also reported a significant increase in their sense of well-being and calmness around the entire surgical experience."

One case in particular stands out for Prajna. "They were going to do a lumpectomy on a woman who had breast cancer, and they asked me to do my healing work with her before the surgery. So she came to me and I worked with her for a half hour, preparing her energy field, working with the tumor, just working energetically to prepare her for surgery, so that she would have a very easy recovery and healing afterwards."

After Prajna finished her healing session, the patient was sent for an ultrasound to identify the exact location of the lump prior to surgery. But, after three hours, the patient still hadn't returned to the operating room. "The nurses called the radiology department to find out the reason for the delay. And the ultrasound technician reported that they had done numerous ultrasounds on the women, but that they could not find the lump. They had looked at her previous x-rays and confirmed the lump, but now, somehow, it was no longer there. So they cancelled the surgery and sent her home, because the lump disappeared. We all looked at each other in astonishment and celebration."

From then on, after seeing repeated positive results with patients in the healing group, the hospital staff would often ask Prajna for help. "If they had a patient whose blood pressure was too high, or if the patient was very nervous before surgery, the nurses would page me and ask, 'Could you come over and do some of your healing hands?' And even if it wasn't my shift, I would come and do the healing work, because the staff saw how much it worked."

After Prajna completed her research project and graduated from the healing school, her life and work as a psychic healer began to accelerate. "Opportunities began to arise from many sources. I developed a thriving private practice, taught at the Barbara

Brennan School, did interviews on Hay House Radio, started running my own healing groups, and I collaborated with other healers at different events. I was even invited to be a part of a worldwide peace vigil at the border of Syria. It was as if the universe was saying, 'Okay, you've graduated from your regular life, you're ready to be a healer, you need to surrender and let go, it's time.'"

Over the years, Prajna has been able to help many people from all over the world, most of whom come to her for healing work, which she feels grateful to do. "So many times, after I finish a day of work, I am in such deep gratitude, and feel so honored to be able to be trusted with transmitting these healing energies, and to help people heal. In fact, very often, I'm brought to my knees in gratitude, with tears in my eyes, feeling so humbled, and so grateful for still being trusted with this sacred, sacred work."

Prajna believes that one of the main reasons we experience life on Earth, with all of its ups and downs, is to heal and grow our souls. "The message that I feel is very important is that we are all here to heal – that's why we're on this planet," explains Prajna. "Regardless of our life's circumstances, regardless of what we're going through, or how easy or hard our life is, the purpose of why we're here is to heal. To be better. To be happier. To be healthier – within our soul and within ourselves."

Prajna thinks that everyone has a purpose in life. "I believe that we all come to life with very specific purposes, and gifts – some people are gifted artists, some people are incredible doctors, and some are caring teachers. And some people are extremely gifted healers, and psychics and mediums. And gifted healers and psychics have a really big responsibility. We have to embrace ourselves, and embrace our abilities through the highest of its capacity, so we can help others raise themselves up to a higher vibration as well. By doing this, we can become a template for others to find the light that is already within themselves."

Prajna continues, "If people can focus on being the best that we can truly be, if we can focus on the deep love within our hearts, or compassion, or happiness – the more we raise our vibrations like that, the more we help the vibrations of the world to rise. And the higher vibration always wins. The negative and lower vibration cannot compete with the higher. Higher frequencies will always be more powerful.

"So let's forget about focusing on healing the negative. We've been doing that for too long. Let's focus on raising our vibrations, and connect straight to the source of happiness and love and trust. And then darkness cannot help but dissipate, because the vibration will be so much higher here on Earth. This is the secret to healing our own personal wounds, and healing our beautiful planet."

NORMAN BLANCHARD

Norman Blanchard is a gifted intuitive who currently resides in Berlin, Germany and who has had an interesting life, working as a dancer, a hair and makeup artist in the film and television industry, and a wig designer for celebrities. He has clients all over the world, and he regularly visits many countries, including Canada and Costa Rica. Although he has many famous clients, and has been sought after by television and radio producers, Norman believes that being a celebrity can be a dangerous thing, and he prefers to stay out of the limelight.

When Norman does a reading, he accesses a person's energy from the highest plane, and often conveys information about a person's life and purpose that is truly inspiring. After the reading, his client has a clear picture of which path to take to make the most of life on Earth.

As a little boy, Norman had a couple of intense intuitive experiences that he remembers to this day. "When I was four years old, living in Wales, I would play in the fields, and down by the water, all by myself, and my mother used to say to me, 'Norman, please don't go near that water. You can't swim, and it's dangerous.' And I'd think, 'How crazy is this woman. I've got all of these people with me, holding my hand and taking care of me.' That's my first recollection of knowing that spirits were with me, watching over me, but other people couldn't see them."

A year later, Norman's family bought a new house, which they converted into a bed and breakfast. "My father had a very bad accident which made it impossible for him to work, and my parents had to create a new business for themselves," explains Norman. "In back of the house, there were four acres of land, and there were about twenty apple trees in this very small orchard. I remember looking at these trees and I told my mother that they were all dead. And my father overheard what I said, and he told my mother, 'You know, there's something wrong with this child. I think we should have him seen by someone.' The trees looked just fine on the outside. They didn't have many leaves, but they looked okay.

"About nine months later, a young woman, a nurse, came to stay at our bed and breakfast, and one day she invited me to take a walk with her. So we walked through the orchard, and I said to her, 'The apple trees in our orchard are dead.' And she said to me, 'Oh, really? Let me sit for a moment.' And she just became very quiet. I knew she was connecting to spirit. Then she opened her eyes and said, 'You're right, young man. There is no life in those trees.' So we went home and told my mother, and we went out to take a look. When my mother leaned on a tree, it fell over. She did this to eight more trees, and they all fell over. Apparently, the sap in the trees had been keeping them going, but they were really dead. After that, my parents realized that I was gifted, and they listened to me more."

Norman went to elementary school, but he had trouble connecting with the other children in the classroom. "I never had a school friend. I had my own friends, my spirit friends. I didn't play with my classmates, the real people. I was just there in physical form. I used to sit with my spirit friends and read and play games. Luckily, my classmates left me alone. I was very fortunate because usually, if you're an isolated child, you get bullied. But I never had any of that. Even the teachers never seemed to see me. They just let me be," Norman remembers.

As he grew up and entered high school, Norman continued to rely on his spirit friends for his social life. "When I was older, I'd hear people talking about going to high school class reunions and other school gatherings, and I realized that I never had any of that social connection when I was in high school," says Norman. "I never had a sleep over or did the things other kids did. I can't remember ever having a school friend in real, human form. Mine were all in spirit form. So I wasn't your average high school kid."

After graduating from high school, Norman went to college, but he left college very quickly. "I didn't want to be at school. I hated anything to do with education," says Norman. "But my father insisted that I get an education. He wanted me to be a court reporter. So he found someone who could teach me shorthand and typing but, after awhile, I thought, 'This is not for me, it's boring, I can't do this,' and I left. On my way home from my teacher's house, I saw a shop called Gladys Smith School of Dancing, and I decided to go in out of curiosity.

"Inside the shop, there was Gladys, an old show girl from way back, with big boobs, big red lips, bright green eye shadow and hair bleached to within an inch of its life. And she said to me, 'Hi dearie, what do you want?' And I told her that I wanted to know about her school, and she told me that she taught dancing. She said that she had a quick step class and a jazz ballet class starting soon, so I signed up for jazz ballet. So I took these dance classes without telling my father."

Norman learned how to dance, and eventually got dancing jobs, including a job in Cairo. After awhile, he decided that he wanted to do something else. "When I got off of the plane after the Cairo job, I clearly heard a voice telling me to 'go to Market Street, walk down Market Street' and I came home, dropped off my luggage, and went to Market Street. When I arrived, I immediately saw a sign for Arthur's Hairdressing School, and I went in, signed up for a hairdressing course, and became a hairdresser."

After he learned how to cut hair, Norman became quite good at his new profession, and he worked at top hair salons, where he developed a following. "I had clients who would return over and over again. But it wasn't just for my hairstyling skills. I would tell them things that were coming up for them, things that were going to happen in their lives," recalls Norman. "So my psychic ability was coming through. And my clients used to say to me, 'You know, Norman, when I leave this salon, I'm a different person. I have an energy that I didn't have before.' So I realized that I was really reading my clients while I was doing their hair."

After leaving the hair salon, Norman moved to Sydney, Australia, and began doing hair and makeup for film stars and famous people on television and film sets. It was glamorous work, and he continued to work in hair and makeup for two decades. "I also worked for a place called Simon Wigs, where I made wigs for celebrities like Elizabeth Taylor," says Norman. "It was very detailed work, and I used to design all of the front parts, all of the very fine edges. It was my forte, really."

In addition to doing hair and makeup, Norman was also building a steady clientele for his psychic readings, including people who worked on the film sets, as well as a host of celebrities and movie stars. "I did a lot of spirit work with the celebrities while I was doing their makeup. When you're applying someone's makeup, you're in very close proximity to the person, so it was a natural thing for me to give them a reading at the same time."

Eventually, however, Norman grew tired of doing hair and makeup. "After twenty years, as glamorous as the film industry was, I felt that I'd had enough of this work. So my partner and I decided to leave Sydney and move to the country to open our own business. The first day I was there, living in the country, I felt like I was in heaven."

Norman and his partner bought a plot of land in the Australian countryside and built a house on the property. "We built a big house, quite a large home, that we eventually turned into a gay bed and breakfast. And I kept seeing a lot of people on my land, in spirit form, so I knew I was in the right place. One of the spirits was an Aboriginal man, and when I asked him why he was appearing to me, he told me that he belonged to this land, and that he was 60,000 years old. I turned away briefly, and when I turned back around, he was gone."

Even though Norman had moved away from Sydney, people kept coming to him for intuitive readings. "I don't know why, I just had people coming in carloads to my house in the country," says Norman. "They used to come and sit in my garden and wait for a reading. I had become quite well known, and people from all over Europe and Australia were seeking me out. I began to realize how easy it was to get caught up in the adoration of people, and having people look up to you.

"It was like an adrenaline rush in a way," continues Norman. "I could feel it, and I was fighting it constantly, saying, 'Norman, you are Norman Blanchard from Australia. That's all I kept saying to myself to keep myself grounded. For about three months, I really fought becoming famous, because I could see how dangerous it was, and I didn't want that part of it. I didn't want to become a guru, that's not for me. So I turned down television and radio appearances, and tried to stay out of the limelight."

Norman wants people to know that we all have access to a greater spiritual energy, if we would only open up ourselves and embrace it. "I do believe that we are all psychic, we are all connected to spirit, and that we can experience this spiritual energy if we just let go of our preconceived ideas about religion and spirituality," explains Norman. "If we realize that there is something greater than all of us, whether you call it God or spirit or whatever, and connect with it, we can find that peace within ourselves. If you ask spirit for help, the answers will come. The more open to spirit you are, the more at peace you'll be. To me, that's the magic of life."

CHARLEY CASTEX

Charley Castex is an internationally known clairvoyant spiritual counselor who lives in Asheville, North Carolina with his wife, Kathryn and their cat, Cornelius. Gifted since he was a child, Charley has a calm, caring demeanor, and his goal is to "read for the heart and from the heart." Charley has read for more than 45,000 people all over the world, and covers a variety of topics - but he's best known for his clairvoyant life guidance and medical intuition.

During our reading, Charley immediately picked up on a complex personal issue that I'd recently dealt with, and he was accurate about other aspects of my life as well. After talking with Charley, I felt refreshed, and he confirmed that I was taking the right steps to achieve my purpose and goals for the future.

When he was a young boy, Charley slowly became aware that he was gifted and that his gift could protect him from harm. "At first, I became aware that I had an 'early warning system' that could sense danger," Charley explains. "There were times when I was in grade school that I would be bullied, just like other kids who don't fit the norm. I would know ahead of time that these guys were going to try to beat me up, so I would take another way home from school. As a boy of about nine or ten, I intensely identified with Spider Man, so I came to rely on what I called my 'spidey sense' to protect me."

As a child, Charley played little games with himself to test his intuitive ability. "I'd listen to a friend talking, and in my mind I'd try to fill in what they were going to say. I found that I could do that. I also had lots of times when I would feel really stuck in life, just being a kid. I had a tough family upbringing, and sometimes when things were especially hard, I would stop everything and just sort of clear my mind. I would go blank and ask a question that was troubling me and the answer would arrive in some way. Sometimes I would get subtle sensations about what was going to happen – either in a verbal message or in images. That's when my cognitive talent first started becoming clear to me."

Around that time, Charley began to have intense dreams of beings that appeared and gave him spiritual information. "I remember having these powerful dreams as a child where I would be in a beautiful place surrounded by beings of light, more like columns of light than human forms. I would ask these complex questions about the nature of time and human existence, and I would be given the answers. I would also be given different cues about events that were going to happen and things that were changing in my life. Then I would wake up and just go back to my normal experience, but I knew that something really important was happening to me because of these dreams."

One of the things that changed in Charley's life was when his father died of lymphoma when he was ten years old. "That turned out to be a really transformational experience, because I was very attached to my dad. After he passed, I had these incredible experiences just about every night, where I'd have a lucid dream of seeing him in my grade school. He would be sitting in an empty classroom, and I'd walk in and hug him, and I'd ask him all these questions about everything that was happening in my life and about the challenges of growing up. Then I started asking him questions of a more spiritual nature, of an existential, cosmic nature, and he would provide the answers. These dream sessions continued for several years and helped me through the loss of my dad at such a young age. That was an extraordinary blessing."

When Charley was in middle school, he began to use his intuitive gifts to his advantage. "As a teenager, I remember getting into trouble, like any kid – for being the class clown or playing around with my friends," Charley recalls. "And the ones who acted out would have to stay in for detention. But I always got out of detention. I would just focus my mind on my teacher, and I would be able to take my name off of the list of boys who were in trouble. It never failed. The other boys would turn around and say 'Well, what about Charley? He threw the book at Sally – he should be staying in at detention.'

"But I would focus my third (spiritual) eye on the teacher's mind, and I would clear my name from the list. It was kind of bizarre! Of course, I stopped doing that because I had an inherent sense that this qualified as a misuse of the gift. I realized that with great power comes great responsibility. I learned that spiritual sight is sacred and had to be leveraged in a really positive way."

Although he knew he was gifted, Charley didn't tell anyone. "I kept it a secret. I thought it was some strange, aberrant little gift or curse that I had, and I didn't quite know what to do with it. I felt that if I talked too much about it, that either a) it would go away, or b) people wouldn't understand and I would be an outcast. I didn't share my intuitive abilities with anybody until I got older."

After Charley graduated from high school, he did a drumming residency at the Collective Music School in New York and then was accepted at the Musicians Institute of Technology in Hollywood, California, where he studied to become a professional drummer. In addition to his drumming, Charley began to use his intuitive skills professionally at a metaphysical bookstore in Asheville, North Carolina called A Greater View.

"During the first five hundred readings, I was so nervous and scared that I would say the wrong thing, or somehow ill advise somebody, and not be accurate. Really – I was a bundle of nerves. My co-worker at the bookstore said, 'Charley, you're either psychic or you're not, and you either trust it or you don't.' That simple advice really changed my life. I had to diligently work at it, but I started to embrace the scope of my gift. I got a clear message from my guidance that I could either fully embrace my cognitive abilities or, wind up really batty. So I finally began to trust my inner perceptions."

Eventually, Charley decided to leave A Greater View bookstore and venture off on his own to create a career in private practice. "I remember pulling out of my driveway one spring morning and I heard this message internally: 'Well, if you don't make a decision about leaving the bookstore by June, a decision will be made for you.' I decided to start my own practice as a spiritual counselor, and – sure enough – the bookstore went out of business in June.

They had decided to close, even though their first year's commission revenues from my readings provided nearly thirty thousand dollars."

Since he opened his own spiritual counseling practice, Charley has read for thousands of people all over the world. "I went to a psychic once, and she said to me, 'You are going to help so many people with your gift. I just see thousands and thousands of people that you're going read for and help with their lives.' And she was right on.

"But I was very slow on the uptake to figure this gift out. My conscious mind couldn't grasp how I was able to do this. Even though I was very spiritual, I thought 'How can this be?' I would be reading for a client and I'd see a real estate sign in my mind's eye. I'd look up and say, 'Wait a minute, are you about to sell your house?' and my client would say 'yes' with raised eyebrows.

"I'd see a leaf falling off a tree and I would say, 'Okay, you should sell the house in September,' and that's when the house would be sold. I realized that these people were paying their hard-earned money for my readings and that they had solid expectations. I learned from trial by fire that I genuinely possessed a gift and could use it to help people."

Charley believes that every one of us has direct access to heaven and a resounding, deep inner bliss. "I feel that heaven exists within us, that the kingdom of heaven is accessible within each of us," Charley explains. "That's not metaphorical, that's true. That's literal. My sense of it is, when we get in touch with those inner resources, then we can make changes. The idea is, there is abundant bliss inside of us. There is joy placed inside of us. There is peace inside of us. And we must communicate with and claim our internal spiritual powers. As simplistic as it is, as trite as it sounds, that has really profound implications. If you get in touch with that power inside you, you can heal, you can effect change and you can inspire."

Charley continues, "My goal is to get people back to a sense of personal empowerment, via a return to an attitude of play, wonder and deep perceptual sensing. I'm a spiritual cheerleader who's encouraging folks to quiet their minds and internalize their focus, because we are all so used to an externalized focus. We don't really know what it means to interiorize our thoughts and our energy, unless we meditate or do yoga or some kind of internal practice.

"My message is basically about finding your power from within – not from without. If you quiet down and internalize your consciousness, you'll be guided to realize your own true path much more effectively. Which is what we all want – we all want clarity about our life direction."

VIRGINIA ROSE CENTRILLO

Virginia Rose Centrillo (known to her friends as Ginger) is an extremely warm, funny and disarming woman whom people would never guess is a gifted psychic medium and ghost hunter - or "house whisperer" as she likes to call it. Virginia spends much of her time visiting haunted houses and helping spirits who are "stuck" on this side to cross over to the other side. While this may sound scary, Virginia uses love and compassion to reach the spirits and help them move on. She has also helped numerous homeowners reclaim their homes after the houses were haunted for many years.

The reading I experienced with Virginia was amazingly accurate on every level, and included the full names of my loved ones and specific details about circumstances that were only known by my family. At the beginning of our reading, Virginia picked up on an elderly couple who had lived in our house before we bought it more than a decade ago. She correctly identified the name of the woman as Bernice, but kept insisting that the name of her husband was Adolph. I told her that Bernice and her husband Mickey lived here previously, but no Adolph. After the reading was over, I looked up the previous owners on the internet, and was shocked to find out that Mickey's first name was actually Adolph! No one, not even our neighbors, knew that Adolph was his real name because Mickey was Jewish, and he had hidden his given name from everyone.

As a child, Virginia had intuitive experiences and saw deceased relatives, but she thought that it was a natural and normal ability that everybody had. When she was two, Virginia had a very bad earache, and she was standing and crying and holding her ear, when a kind old woman lay her down on her bed and started patting her. Virginia remembers the woman's smile, and how gentle and loving she was. Years later, when Virginia was looking through old photographs, she realized that the woman who had comforted her was

68

her great-grandmother, Julia, who had passed on before Virginia was born.

A couple of years later, when Virginia was four years old, she had a friend she would play with. "He was an older man, maybe in his late seventies. We would play hide and seek for hours. He would hide behind me and pop out. And I'll never forget, my grandmother would say, 'Virginia Rose, who are you talking to?' And I would just point. And my grandmother would say, 'I know you see the man – play nice.' But the man was from the other side – no one else could see him. But I learned later that my grandmother was psychic as well."

As Virginia got older, she could actually see the spirits as if they were real people. "My grandmother would say that I was getting stronger in my visions," Virginia explains. "I could describe the people to her, and my grandmother would say, 'What do you see now, who do you see, what do you hear? You see very good – Grandma doesn't see as good anymore.'"

Virginia's grandmother encouraged her to develop her gift, but told Virginia that if she ever got scared, to call on her guardian angels, to pray, and to tell the spirits that she was a child of God, and that they shouldn't bother her.

Virginia's grandmother also warned her not to tell anyone about the spirits that she saw. But Virginia made the mistake of doing so anyway. "I remember that I was in kindergarten one day, and I saw a teenage boy wearing knickers, brown shoes and a tweed suit, and I remember thinking, 'It's really hot outside, he must be uncomfortable.' He was just standing in the corner – he was staring at me, and I was staring at him. And the teacher told us to get our blocks, and this little girl, Graciella, went over to that corner and I said, 'Don't go over there, the man's there.' And our teacher turned around and looked at me and said, 'What man? There's nobody there – you can't tell that to people.' And she was very intense with me."

Then Virginia saw the man point to himself and then point to the teacher, and she realized that he was a relative of the teacher's. "The teacher seemed really upset," Virginia remembers. "And I thought that maybe it was her father coming back at a young age or something. But the teacher went over to the corner and moved the blocks and said, 'See, there's nobody here.' And the spirit went out the window – I guess it knew it was in trouble."

Virginia continued to see spirits, but became better at keeping her visions to herself. Yet, when she was in middle school, some of her friends would ask her questions. "A certain group of my friends knew I was psychic. We would sit around and they would ask me, 'Does this boy like me, does he not like me,' and I would say yes or no, and I became popular and would get invited to slumber parties."

But eventually these friends would turn on Virginia. At one party, a girl brought out a Ouija Board from her mother's closet – but Virginia refused to use it. "The board had a very negative energy. And I said no and pushed the board away. And from then on my girlfriends got mad at me and made fun of me. They would say 'You have no gift,' and everybody was trying to beat me up. And my teenage years were very uncomfortable after that – from about age twelve on. I didn't have a lot of girlfriends anymore, because everyone knew what I did – that I was psychic and could see things that other people couldn't."

Eventually, Virginia did make a couple of new friends, including a French girl named Jean. "I loved Jean – we hung out a lot. Her parents were into spiritual stuff – they had books on ghosts and Hans Holzer,* and they said that spirit is everywhere, and let's hug this tree; they were wonderful people."

Jean had a brother named Patrick who was involved with a rough crowd of kids. "Patrick was never up to anything good," Virginia remembers. One day, Jean invited Virginia to a party her brother was having at their house. "But I got a bad feeling, and I said, 'Don't go to the party, Jean – I get a bad feeling.' I refused to go. Before Jean left to go to the party, we switched coats – like little girls do – she wanted to wear my coat and I said, 'All right, I'll take your coat.'"

---

* Hans Holzer (1920-2009), author of more than 100 books, wrote about his own paranormal research. Born in Austria, he moved with his family to New York City when he was 18.

Later that night, Virginia fell asleep, only to wake up because she felt Jean's hand on her shoulder. "I woke up and started shouting, 'Jean, Jean, are you here?' And my mother, who shared my bedroom, jumped up and said, 'What's the matter, Virginia? Why are you shouting Jean's name?' So I told her that Jean was in our bedroom, and that she wanted to return my coat. But my mother told me that it was one o'clock in the morning and that no one was in the bedroom."

Virginia insisted that Jean had been in her room, trying to return Virginia's coat, and that Jean also said, "You were right, Virginia, I shouldn't have gone to my brother's party."

Now that Virginia and her mother were awake, they heard a commotion in the street outside of their house in Astoria, so they went outside to see what was happening. "All of the sudden, another friend of mine ran up to me and asked me if I was all right. And I said, 'Yes, why are you asking?' And she said to me, 'Don't you know? Your best friend Jean died tonight at the party.' Jean was dead because someone had put a drug in her drink – probably acid – that made her brain swell and she died. I was in shock.

"The next thing I know, Jean's mother was running across the street, holding my coat in her hands," Virginia continues. "She was hysterical. And she said, 'My daughter died in this coat, I don't know whose coat this is, is this your coat? Do you have my daughter's coat?' I said, 'Yes, I'm wearing it.' And she said, 'May I have my daughter's coat? And I said yes, and I took it off and handed it to Jean's mother."

That's when Virginia finally realized that Jean had visited her in her bedroom shortly after Jean died. She wanted to return Virginia's coat, and to say goodbye to her good friend. "That was really difficult for me. It was one of the most difficult times in my life."

Throughout her teen years, Virginia continued to "see" things and events before they happened. She began learning to meditate when she was about 19 or 20. "I didn't really know what I was doing – I would just sit quietly for five minutes and let things come in to my head. Finally, things started to click," Virginia says. "It's like my brain cells started to pop open like pods."

For the next ten years, Virginia continued to explore her intuitive gifts. She began to read books by paranormal investigators Hans Holzer, Lorraine and Ed Warren and Peter James, and she consulted with other gifted psychics to learn more about how she should use her ability. "They all told me that I was also really gifted, and that I should teach meditation to others." So Virginia took some classes about meditation at the New School in New York City, and started to hone her psychic ability. Eventually, Virginia began to do psychic readings for people, and she developed her strong ability as a medium.

Today, Virginia is nationally known as a "house whisperer," has appeared on Animal Planet's TV show, *The Haunted*, and lectures on metaphysical topics across the country. She is a member of the Pennsylvania Paranormal Association (PPA), which investigates reports of paranormal activities and hauntings in Pennsylvania and around the world.

In addition to her work with the PPA, Virginia has been working closely with *Face OFF Productions*, a boutique production company in New York City, developing new programming for television. Over the past several years, she has been integral in assisting to solve unsolved missing persons and cold cases. Virginia has also taught meditation classes for the past 30 years – helping people get in touch with their intuitive abilities.

Although Virginia was bullied for having these abilities as a child, she learned that it is very important to love people, regardless of their outward behavior. "What my guides have taught me is to never judge anybody, love everybody, treat everybody with great reverence, because God is in them," Virginia says. "No matter how different or twisted another person may behave, God is in them, and God loves them. So we have to learn how to truly love others."

Over the years, Virginia has been very involved with animal activism and is an advocate for animal rights. She has taken a personal interest in the Billy the Bull Anti-Bullying Foundation, (www.BillytheBull.org), an organization which helps to educate children about bullying and abuse. Today, Virginia continues to make every effort to help people, animals and spirits wherever there is a need.

LIBBY CLARK

Libby Clark is a spiritualist medium and trance healer who is based in Nottinghamshire, England. Although she was gifted as a young child, Libby learned to keep her intuitive ability to herself so that she "wouldn't get into trouble." When she was 16 years old, she was introduced to the Spiritualist Church, where she was encouraged to develop her gift and to do readings for church members.

Today, Libby is a tutor and course organizer at the prestigious Arthur Findlay College in Essex, England, where she helps others access their psychic and mediumship abilities. She also travels around the world, attending speaking engagements, doing private readings and teaching workshops and seminars on mediumship and intuitive ability.

During my reading with Libby, my mother came through and weighed in on some issues that I had been discussing with my husband earlier that day. It was as if I had just picked up the telephone and was asking my mom for advice about run of the mill, everyday issues, just like I did when she was alive. It was a profound and comforting feeling to know that my deceased mom knew what was going on in my life, and that she was still there to offer motherly advice if I needed it.

As a young child growing up in England, Libby had the ability to know things about people that others could not see. "I've always seen colors around people," remembers Libby. "I'd always watched what I called their light. So if I went to see a new baby, for example, I'd look to see what their light looked like. Or if somebody wasn't very well, I would see that in their colors. This was just normal for me."

Libby remembers one incident very well. "When I was about eight years old, my mum and I went to visit Mrs. Townroe, the elderly lady who lived next door. My mother used to go and have a cup of tea with her, and I used to go along, because I'd get a pink wafer biscuit and a glass of orange squash, orange juice. And this particular time we'd gone 'round there, my mum and Mrs. Townroe were talking, and I said to Mrs. Townroe, 'What's that funny mark on your leg? Well, it's not on your leg, it's sort of above your leg, and it's a grey and brown color.'

"Well, of course they both looked down at her leg and they didn't see anything, and my mum said, 'What are you going on about? There's nothing there.' And I said, 'You know mum, I can see it in my head.' My mother told me to be quiet and stop saying such things."

But later that day, Libby's premonition proved to be valid. "A couple of hours later, there was an ambulance outside, and Mrs. Townroe was being whisked off to hospital – she had a blood clot in her leg," Libby recalls. "And when she came home from the recuperation hospital six weeks later, my mum and I went 'round to see her. And of course, being a kid, the first thing that I said was, 'That funny color is gone off your leg now – you're all right!' And my mom got mad and told me to stop talking. So I learned to keep quiet, because if I told somebody what I could see, it got me into trouble."

When Libby was about 12, she and her family moved to a new house, where she experienced more unusual, paranormal things. "After we moved, I would be in my bedroom, and an elderly lady, an elderly gentleman and a young boy used to come at night and sit around the fireplace in the corner of my bedroom. I used to tell them my troubles, and they would comfort me, saying things like 'Don't worry, it will be all right.' They were always encouraging me," says Libby. "The only thing was, as far as I knew, there had never been a fireplace in the corner of my bedroom. But I could see these people in my head sitting by this fireplace."

A few years later, Libby's parents decided to renovate some of the rooms in their house. "When I was seventeen, mum and dad had some work done around the house. It was a four hundred-year-old cottage, so it needed repairs," explains Libby. "When they took the plaster off of the wall in my bedroom, I couldn't believe it – the wall was marked with soot where there had once been a fireplace! So what I saw in my head was actually real, there behind the plaster."

Libby had her first introduction to the Spiritualist Church when she was 16. "My dad took me to Beaconsfield Spiritualist Church at Nottingham," says Libby. "He had his own business and was very stressed about things, so he started looking into spiritual healing and after he joined the spiritualist church, he became much calmer. He wasn't shouting as much, and he just seemed to deal with things better, so I said to him 'What are they doing to you at that place? You seem so much different.'

"So my dad said, 'Come with me.' And I said, 'Oh, I don't think so – I don't want to sit there in the dark with strangers.' He said, 'No, the church is fully lit, there are beautiful flowers there, and the people are lovely. It's not scary.' And then he said, 'I'll tell you what – come with me on Sunday, because we all go for a drink at the pub afterwards, and I'll buy you a drink.' So I went to the church, because my dad offered to buy me a drink. And when I went, I was overwhelmed. It was just like going home. It just felt right."

Libby's previous experience with church had been less pleasant. "I got thrown out of the Church of England when I was fourteen because I asked too many questions at confirmation classes. "Right before confirmation, at the dress rehearsal, the vicar asked me if I believed in God. I was fourteen, and I didn't know who I was, never mind who God was. And he said, 'You must answer me honestly.' I said, 'Well, then I have to say I don't know if I believe in God.' And the vicar said, 'You heathen child – get out of this church and don't come back.' So he basically threw me out of the church."

Unlike her experience with the Church of England, Libby loved going to a spiritualist church. "During the next eighteen months after my dad introduced me to the spiritualist church, I went to church every chance I got," says Libby. "It just felt so right. I could see the medium working on the platform, and I could see the people in spirit who were talking to her. And I also got messages from the spirit. So the other people in the church told me, 'You should be a medium, you should be working as a medium on the platform.' And I told them that no, I didn't want to talk to spirits, I can't do this.

"But we used to go for drinks at the pub after the service, and people would give me things to hold, like their watch or their wallet, and they'd say, 'Hold my watch, tell me what you can get for me, Libby.' And I would hold their keys or whatever, and I would see things about them. It was kind of a fun thing, like a game. And they'd say, 'How did you know that? You're right! You need to be doing readings for people.' That's how my psychic and mediumship abilities started to develop."

Libby began to do regular readings or "services" at the Spiritualist Church, where she was encouraged and mentored by other gifted mediums, and she received spiritual instruction from teachers from the Arthur Findlay College who attended her Spiritualist Church at Beaconsfield Street. "It started slowly, and thanks to word of mouth, more churches started to book me for services," says Libby. "Eventually, I was doing services at different churches every month, and then every week – on and on it goes."

After graduating from high school, Libby married the boy she'd been dating since she was fourteen. "I married at nineteen, and we separated when I was twenty – very quickly it all went wrong," Libby says. "He was extremely violent, and put me in the hospital on occasion. He was an only child, and he couldn't cope with the responsibility of being married and not being at home with his mum and dad. Being an only child, he had whatever he wanted, and when he suddenly had to hand over his wages to pay the mortgage, he wasn't so happy about it."

One month after Libby separated from her first husband, she met her second husband, Bob. "Two days after I met Bob, he moved in with me, and thirty-seven years later we're still together," laughs Libby. "Everything fell into place. We got together in January, and our first child, Sarah, was born in the end of November. We talked about having a child – it wasn't a case of 'Oops, we forgot and you got pregnant.' We knew it was right for us, and we wanted to start a family right away. And we had two gorgeous girls within the first three years of our relationship."

Before she had children, Libby worked in various companies, often as a sales representative. "I've always worked in the corporate world," explains Libby. "My first job was for the DuPont Company, and then I worked for other companies, including Rover Cars, IBM and Cannon Street Investments. But I stopped working when I had the girls, because I'd had two children in under two years. So I used to make handmade wedding dresses, evening dresses and lingerie for people. I'd always made my own clothes. I did that from home when the girls were little for extra money. But I also did readings at the Spiritualist Church on the weekends throughout my twenties."

When Libby's daughters were approaching middle school, she went back to work in the corporate world. But her work life didn't flow as easily as it had earlier in her career. "In 1991 and 1992, I was made redundant – lost my job three times in five years from very good corporate jobs," says Libby. "Although the companies were doing well, they were bought out by other companies, and they wanted to replace our management team with their own people. And then I lost my job with IBM. We were starting to struggle financially. I couldn't even get interviews, it was really weird. So Bob said, 'The thing is, Libby, you've already got a job, but you're just not doing it.'"

Although Bob believed that Libby should start doing readings full time and move on from the corporate world, Libby wasn't so sure. "I said to Bob, 'But my readings are not going to feed us. They're not going to pay the mortgage, and the bills, and allow us to treat the girls to the things they want. Bob said, 'Well, look, why don't you give it a go?' And I said, 'Okay, I'll give it three months. If things haven't picked up in three months, I'm quitting, and I'll just get a job somewhere doing anything.' And Bob said, 'No, give it three years.' I said, 'I can't, we'll starve!' And Bob said, 'No, no – then come on, just trust that you can do this.' Three months later, my diary was full for the next eighteen months. And I've been fully booked for readings ever since."

In addition to doing readings and healings, Libby teaches courses in healing and mediumship at the Arthur Findlay College. "I'm a course organizer – I book tutors who I want to work with me. And I can only book tutors who are trained and accepted at Arthur Findlay College," Libby explains, "so I have about five courses a year. A course might be a week long, it might be a weekend – it depends on what the course is about. It's a residential college – we can host about one hundred students at a time."

After almost 40 years of working as a medium and doing readings for a wide variety of clients all over the world, Libby has a unique perspective on what happens to us when we pass on, and what should be of importance to us during our lifetime. "The first thing I want people to know is this – that we do not die. Whatever happens to us in this physical world, when we leave it, that life energy carries on. But while we're here, we are here to learn to experience life and to share what we've learned," says Libby. "And one of the biggest things I've learned that I tell people is, 'Don't sweat the small stuff. Don't let your life become bogged down with small things, like do we have enough toilet rolls, is there enough coffee to last 'til the end of the week? Because at the end of the day, these things aren't really relevant.

"Instead, spend your time with good people – with your family and friends. And enjoy the time that you have, because, although we don't die, you've got to find a good medium to come back. And that's not always easy, you know? So from my point of view, it's about letting go of the small stuff. Not getting wound up in it. I did that in my corporate life, God knows I did it. And it's not worth it. Just find the time to do the things that you enjoy doing, and every day – every day – I try to do something for somebody else. But I also do something for myself."

Libby also wants people to know that many of our deceased loved ones are very happy where they are, and have little desire to come back to the earthly realm. This is often why some of our relatives don't come through in readings. "Many people are happy when they go to the nonphysical. They are, they are!" maintains Libby. "And for many people, that's why they don't want to come back. That's why they don't want to communicate, because they're quite happy where they are. They're surrounded by their family, their friends, their dogs are there, their cats are there – they're quite happy in the spirit world. And when I'm doing a reading, sometimes it's like, 'Yeah, well just tell the kids I'm fine, you know – let the family know I'm all right, I'm fine, I'm okay now. Bye – I'm going to get back to what I was doing!'"

Finally, Libby has learned that we often reunite with our long-term partners, such as husbands and wives, when we transition to the other side. "People do meet up with their partners on the other side. They do. It's like Bob and I – we've been together all of these years. And whichever one of us goes first, trust me, we're going to be waiting for the other one on the other side. You can count on that!"

EDDIE CONNER

Eddie Conner is a Southern boy from North Carolina who grew up in an abusive home, but discovered that he had a strong intuitive ability that could protect him and keep him out of harm's way. After harnessing his ability and developing his intuitive skills in the South, Eddie moved to Los Angeles and has developed a substantial client list, including many celebrities and A-Listers. It is easy to see why he's so popular - his warm charm and Southern sense of humor make him instantly likable.

During my reading with Eddie, he suddenly asked me, "Did you recently have a puppy who's passed on?" And I told him, "Yes, our sweet little dog died a couple of months ago." Eddie said, "Well, your mother is handing you a new, fluffy white puppy right now." Which was incredible, because we were in the process of trying to get a new Bichon Frise puppy to help us get over the loss of our adorable eight-year-old Bichon Frise, Snowball; we loved her very much. And although the waiting list to get a Bichon puppy from a reputable breeder was about a year long, a female Bichon puppy magically became available just one month after my reading with Eddie. We named her Lila Faith.

Eddie Conner is a third generation intuitive who grew up in a troubled, abusive family in a trailer park in North Carolina. Although he had a difficult upbringing, and it's hard to imagine how he survived such a challenging childhood, Eddie is extremely lighthearted and funny.

Eddie's father regularly beat his mother – in fact, when his mother was pregnant with Eddie, she was also pregnant with a second baby – he was one of twins. But after a particularly severe beating, Eddie's mom lost one of the twin babies, which Eddie believes would have been his twin sister.

"One of my earliest memories, when I was about three and a half or four years old, was when my dad came home one day, and busted through the front door, and began beating the crap out of my mom. We were in the kitchen – she was going to make something for supper – and he burst through the door and grabbed my mom," recalls Eddie.

"The next thing I knew, somebody grabbed my shirt sleeve and pulled me underneath the table – one of those old Formica tables with metal legs – they pulled me underneath the table and we cowered down there, between the chairs," continues Eddie. "And it was a little girl. And she and I were down there, under the table, and I could see Dad kicking my mom, and pulling her hair, and there were broken glasses everywhere, and it was just terrifying. After he stormed out of the apartment and left – he took her tip money, took everything that she had worked for that day – I crawled out from under the table and chairs, and the little girl was gone. And I'd never seen her before – she was just gone. But later, I realized that she must have been my twin sister, who came from the other side."

Right after his mother's beating, Eddie had his first psychic vision and his first experience with angels. "When I got up from under the table, the light was all different. You know how when you're swimming in the lake or the ocean and you open your eyes and you see the sunlight coming through the water? That's the way the light looked," remembers Eddie.

"It came out of the ceiling and the wall, and it was all around my mom, just like you see it when you're snorkeling under water. And then this feeling went from this horrible, powerless, vulnerable terrible feeling to … first of all, is she alive? And then to … everything's gonna be okay. And then, in the light, these figures started coming forward, and that's the first time I'd ever seen angels. They were letting me know that she was going to be okay – it was all telepathic – and all of the fear was erased in no time at all. That was my first-ever psychic experience that I remember, consciously."

Eddie continued to have these experiences as he was growing up – and sometimes, these experiences saved his life.

"When I was in the first grade, I was on the school bus one morning and we were driving on a brand new, freshly bulldozed dirt road that the construction workers were still building. And I heard a man's voice, as clear as a bell, say to me, 'Leave school after lunch today.' But there were no men on the bus – our driver was a woman. And I looked around to ask if anyone else heard it, but they didn't hear anything. A few moments later, the male voice repeated itself, only stronger and more direct, 'Leave school after lunch today!'"

So Eddie went to school, and when lunchtime came, he had his lunch and then he started to pretend that he was sick. "They took me to the office and called my mom, who came to school to pick me up. And as soon as Mama walked in, I just started crying, but I didn't tell her that I was faking. So she took me straight to my grandma's house, and she went right back to work."

Eddie's grandmother took care of him that afternoon, and after awhile she came outside where Eddie was snapping peas for dinner, and she asked him a question. "So I'm snapping peas, and Grandma comes out of the house and comes right up to me, and she says – with this dead serious look on her face – 'What bus do you ride? What bus number do you ride?' And I told her, and she put her hands on her hips and looked right down at me and said 'I knew you weren't sick today.' And I said, 'Ma'am?' And she said 'You weren't sick today. Your bus just fell off a cliff, because that new road that they're building gave way.' And she turned on her heel and walked straight back into the house and slammed the door. We never talked about it again. And I never told my mom. I found out later that the kids on that bus were hurt, but that they survived the accident."

Sometimes, Eddie would see terrible things that were going to happen to people he knew. "Once when I was in the eighth grade, I was walking to the school bus stop with my brothers and these neighborhood bullies started to beat us up. So we fought back, and one of the bullies hit me so hard that I saw stars."

Eddie continues, "Out of nowhere, I shouted at the top of my lungs, 'Your bus is gonna turn over and send every one of you to the hospital.' Everything came to a screeching halt, and the bullies stopped beating us up. Then their bus came, and the bullies and my brothers got on their bus and went off to school. I was on a different bus because I was older than them, and my bus came a few minutes later."

Eddie got on his bus and started to read a book. Suddenly, his classmates on the bus started shouting 'Oh my God, look at that!' So Eddie looked out of the window. "I couldn't believe what I saw. There was my brothers' bus – the one with the bullies on it – and it was flipped over on its side. It had been hit by a tractor trailer. And there were ambulances there and they were pulling kids out of the emergency door of the bus, and as we drive by, I saw my brothers and those bullies sitting and standing at the back of the ambulance."

Eddie recalls, "That was around the time that I just prayed and prayed that whatever this thing was that I had, this psychic ability, it would just go away."

It took Eddie years to understand why he was experiencing these disturbing visions, and to realize that he wasn't responsible for the terrible things he saw as a kid. "Everything that I psychically saw was bad, horrible stuff. And I was too young to understand that I wasn't making this bad stuff happen," says Eddie. "Later, I realized that because we lived in a volatile household with lots of abuse, I was highly, acutely sensitive as a psychic to predicting bad stuff happening. But I wanted it to go away, I couldn't take it anymore. And it finally did go away, in my later teen years."

Eddie went on to graduate from high school, and then he moved away from his hometown. He began to work as a dancer, a choreographer and a visual marketing designer, designing department store windows. "After I moved away, got a job and turned twenty, my psychic ability came flooding back like gangbusters, like a dam had opened."

The next time Eddie had an intuitive experience, it was when he became certain that his partner was cheating on him. "I started dating a man who was abusive, just like my mama did. And I remember that I just knew that Lee, my partner, was cheating. I had no physical proof or evidence of it, but I knew it to the very core of my being," says Eddie. "So one day, when Lee picked me up from work, he told me that he'd met a new man, and that they were madly in love. I was right, all along."

Eventually, Eddie met another man named Tim, who became his best friend. "We were inseparable up until he passed away from AIDS in 1993. And he was the only person I ever told about my psychic experiences and my twin sister in spirit and all that stuff. I never told anybody but Tim," notes Eddie. "Tim helped me go back and heal certain things in my life. He was really my best friend. And he encouraged me to cultivate my gift and harness my psychic abilities."

Eddie took Tim's advice and began to read everything he could about intuition and psychic ability. He went to workshops and seminars, and took classes about how to read Tarot cards. "As soon as I started to harness my psychic ability, all of these people came out of the woodwork and wanted psychic readings from me, including my bosses at work," Eddie says. "But I was still in the closet as a psychic at that time. I didn't want to tell people that I was gifted yet."

Regardless of Eddie's desire to stay closeted about being a psychic, word about Eddie's intuitive abilities got out, and he was invited to be a guest on the biggest radio station in North Carolina, G105 FM, along with Sharon Capehart, who, as he was told, was the official psychic on the movie *Ghost*. "Sharon and I did a guided meditation together to pull in the spirit of Nostradamus," Eddie explains. "Everybody was blown away, including Sharon and the DJs at the radio station. So I went from no one knowing that I was psychic, to blowing the doors off and beginning my intuitive career."

One of Eddie's clients, a radio executive named Randy, got a job as the program director at Star 98.7, a prominent radio station in Los Angeles. Randy invited Eddie to fly out to LA to share his intuitive abilities as a guest on one of the station's radio shows. So Eddie booked a flight out to Los Angeles in September 1995, did live psychic readings on the air, and was offered a weekly spot on the station.

In December of that same year, just before Eddie moved to Los Angeles, Star 98.7 restructured their format and Eddie's new show was canceled, even before he ever left North Carolina. But Eddie decided to move to LA anyway, because he felt strongly that he was supposed to start his soul intuitive career in the City of Angels. Soon after Eddie moved to Los Angeles, he began to teach classes on how to communicate with spirit guides and angels at the Learning Annex, which had a built-in audience of thousands of people.

"In addition to teaching at the Learning Annex, I began to appear at every psychic fair in Los Angeles for the next three months," says Eddie. "That's how I was able to pay the bills. But after a few months, I stopped doing the psychic fairs and I started getting calls from clients from all over LA, including an amazing base of celebrity clients."

According to Eddie, "I came out as gay when I was in the eleventh grade. It was devastating, I was terrified, terry-a-fied. So I told my mom, and she was cool about it – she didn't like it, but she was cool about it. About ten years later, I came out to her as psychic. And that was hard. About a year after that, I came out as a medium – I didn't know that was the same as being psychic. So my mama said 'Okay Edward, that's enough. You've come out three times, I think that's enough for one lifetime!'"

Eddie admits, "It was way harder to come out as a psychic. I just felt like I was a freak. I already felt like a freak for being gay, and I'd gotten over that hurdle, because I didn't know anything else than being gay from the time I was born. But being psychic, that was hard because it was a part of me that I had buried deeper inside of me, underneath my being gay. So being psychic was like being a triple freak. It was hard, it was way harder coming out as a psychic than it was coming out as a gay person."

Eddie believes that everyone is intuitive, and that people who open themselves up to that side of themselves will live much more fulfilling lives. "We all have intuitive ability, and it's a gift that will literally change your life in ways that you can't even imagine – if you learn how to harness it," Eddie says. "Also, when you call on your soul and on your higher self and ask that part of you that's nonphysical to guide you, and attune you to your purpose on this planet, that's when more doors and windows open for you on the Earth plane. Your life on this planet will start to get easier, and you'll feel divinely guided by a greater power – it's really your power – but it's a greater power, and it just keeps putting you at the right place at the right time with the right people."

Eddie adds, "But it takes some practice, and getting used to the fact that most of our energy is nonphysical, even though we have this physical body. So if I could share anything with people, it's that we're really ninety-nine percent nonphysical – we're pure positive energy in this little body. Instead of using just the one percent that is your physical self, utilize all of the universal consciousness, and pull it to you and through you so that your life is happier and better. When you get into that relaxed, meditative place, then you're going to receive divine guidance, and your life will get better."

GABBIE DEEDS

Gabbie Deeds lives in the Ozark Mountains near Eureka Springs, Arkansas with her partner, Kelli. She had her first intuitive experience at the tender age of three, after she nearly died and was in a coma for three days. During that time, she crossed over into heaven and met her angel guide, who cared for her in a beautiful meadow until Gabbie was ready to return to her body. And her guide, Ariel, is still with Gabbie to this day.

In addition to being a medium, a teacher and a healer, Gabbie has also worked on national missing person cases and has been a guest on radio shows. She feels that we can all know what our purpose in life is if we just listen and realize that God is in all of us, guiding us to fulfill our mission.

My reading with Gabbie was amazing, because my father-in-law - who had died two years before - immediately came through and was laughing about the fact that "I've finally made it - and I can't believe that there are so many Jews in heaven!" That sounded very much like my father-in-law, who was Jewish, and who was a very funny, irreverent man.

Gabbie Deeds became aware of her intuitive ability at the age of three, when she became very ill and nearly died. "My parents first thought that I had a cold or the flu, but when I developed a high fever and began hallucinating that I was seeing huge butterflies flying over me, they took me to the hospital," Gabbie says. "By the time they got me to the emergency room, my heart had stopped, and apparently, I died."

The next thing Gabbie remembers is that she heard the doctors talking, and "all of the sudden, I felt like I was floating and then, when I opened my eyes, I was standing in this garden. There were flowers, beautiful flowers, colors that I didn't have names for, and there was this tree that had a swing on it. And standing next to me was this lady – whom I now know was Ariel, a guide of mine – and she told me that I was only going to stay in this garden until I could go back to my family, and that she was with me when I was born, and that she would be with me forever – all I needed to do was call her name. And I remember that she was swinging me on the swing, and there was a little pond in front of us, and it was really foggy, and I looked out across the water, and I saw that there were people out there, but I couldn't see them well because of the fog. And I asked the lady who they were, and she told me that they were guides and angels, and that they were there to watch me too. But, even with all this happening, I never felt frightened at all."

Gabbie's guide, Ariel, continued to talk to her, and to sing to her. "And then, right before I was pulled back, Ariel said, 'They're ready for you now, I love you,' and the next thing I know, my dad is saying, 'Are you okay, Sissy? Now, everything's going to be okay,' and I was back in the hospital room. My dad told me that I had been unconscious, put in what they called a coma, and that I had been in the hospital for three days."

After Gabbie's near death experience, she continued to hear Ariel talking to her when she was playing, saying, "Don't climb that tree, go easy, I love you," and other messages. "I remember the next time I actually saw Ariel, it was probably a year after I was sick. My parents were fighting, and there was a big Texas storm happening, and the lightning was so loud that I woke up. And I looked down at the foot of my bed, and Ariel was sitting there. And she looked at me and said, 'Just because your parents are fighting, they still love you, and you can go back to sleep.' I don't remember anything after that, because I apparently went back to sleep."

Eventually, Gabbie told her parents about Ariel. "My mom just sort of wrote it off, as if it was just an imaginary friend. My dad, on the other hand, didn't. He just told me that we all have angels around us all the time, and that it's a gift from God, and that if I can see and hear them, that it would be best if I kept it to myself, or to talk to him about it."

As a child, Gabbie preferred to be on her own. "I had friends, but I didn't really play with them. I was always very content to play with myself or with my guides. I always wanted to be outside – I would go into the woods, or play in the creeks, and my guides were always my friends. And I would talk about them, but the other kids would make fun of me. They used to call me a witch throughout grade school, middle school and even in high school. So I was pretty much a loner."

When Gabbie was sixteen, her mother left the family, and Gabbie was forced to grow up fast. "I love my mother, but she was never much of a hands-on parent – she was in and out of our lives ever since I can remember. She would leave my dad and leave us for a year, six months, and come back and then leave again."

When Gabbie's dad was diagnosed with colon cancer, her mother came back and stayed with him until he died. But the weekend after her dad died, her mother packed up and left again. "I went to school, and when I came home, everything was gone," remembers Gabbie. "Fortunately, I was dating a boy named David, and I called him after this happened, and he and his mom came and took me away from that little bitty town. And I married him, and we were together for 13 years after that."

Gabbie's husband David was in the military, and the couple moved to Germany and raised their family. "We had Robin first before moving to Germany, and after the move, we had two more babies," said Gabbie. "Living in Germany was interesting, and we traveled through the country and saw castles, and even went to the place where the Holocaust took place. That was the most intense thing I've ever experienced in my life." Gabbie had a lot of spiritual experiences, especially regarding the Holocaust, but she kept her intuitive ability to herself. "I didn't let anyone know about my intuitive side, but when we moved back to the U.S. three and a half years later, I started to open up. I started to come out of my shell and not be embarrassed about my ability – but it wasn't until my kids were teenagers that I really started acknowledging spirit."

After returning to America, Gabbie and David separated for a few years, and then were divorced. To pay the bills, she started to work on a psychic hotline, and she learned how to do readings quickly. "I learned fast in that arena. There were some wonderful readers on that hotline, but it's not for spiritual awareness – it's basically for entertainment. I mean, it was great, it paid the bills – but spirit was really pushing me to step out of the box, so I just started readings for friends, and then friends of friends – so I finally decided to put up a website, and I've had clients ever since."

Before Gabbie started doing regular readings for clients all over the country, she was reluctant to use the word 'psychic.' "In the beginning, the word 'psychic' was a dirty word to me, because it had such negative connotations. People think it's all smoke and mirrors. But I think that God gives us this gift for a reason – I think it's divinely inherited. I do my work from a spiritual aspect – not a metaphysical aspect. To me, that's just a groundbreaking way to look at this, because it's not about being a 'medium,' it's about being able to help somebody through their grief, and I think that's a beautiful thing – to be able to help somebody see that this life is very temporary, and that love and life go on. That's what I see in the future. I feel like people who are divinely inspired and divinely gifted are the next generation of – almost ministers, spiritual ministers – because that's what people need."

Gabbie's clients often thank her profusely when she gives them a reading, especially a reading that sheds light on sensitive areas. But Gabbie feels that her clients should really be thanking God. "You know, I'm just the facilitator. I am the in-between. I am the one that actually speaks out for spirit. It always – not embarrasses me, but I feel very humbled when somebody says 'Thank you' to me, because it's really not me, it's what God and spirit wants that specific person to know. I always tickle myself, because I think of myself as – if you think of two people and somebody is on one end of the phone, and the other person is on the other end of the phone – I'm just AT&T. I just deliver the messages, I am not the creator of the messages."

Gabbie believes that organized religion has its place, and that it can be good for the community – but that one doesn't need to belong to a church, temple or mosque in order to be close to God. "People don't need religion – they need God. They're two totally different things," says Gabbie. "When people think of mediums or psychics, they don't necessarily think about God. However, I believe that we're here to help take the fear and the separation out of spirituality so that people can learn to love and coexist in a world that was meant to be one – not a collection of different churches with different beliefs. God is not in four walls. God is in each individual, and I think that's what people are looking for, at least in my experience.

"And I shock people when I talk about God. People just are shocked. They say 'You believe in God?' And I say, of course I do, because if I didn't, I wouldn't be doing what I'm doing, I promise you. But, you know, our intuitive ability is really divinely inspired, and I just think people need to know that."

MARY DEVENEAU

Mary Deveneau, an upbeat, joyful person, is a psychic medium who lives in the Sacramento, California area and often travels to give lectures and workshops across the country. She is also incredibly accurate, both as a psychic and a medium who can connect clients with loved ones who have passed on.

When I first interviewed Mary, I said next to nothing about myself and just turned on the tape recorder to begin our first reading. Right away, Mary picked up my parents, who are deceased. She said that they wanted to tell me something. I told Mary that I didn't really want to bother them, but Mary delivered their messages anyway. The reading was utterly amazing. My father and mother's personalities were exactly as they were when they were alive - Dad was quiet, thoughtful and intelligent, and Mom was bubbly, funny and loving.

Two things stood out for me, however. One of my mother's messages to me was that she was so happy in heaven, and that it was great fun to be with her family - she said she was having a ball. She also said that she had a tiny waist and looked the way she did when she was thirty-five, with no pain. My mother had gained a lot of weight as she got older, and suffered from paralyzing sciatica.

The other message gave me goose bumps - my mother said that she wanted to thank me for naming my daughter's middle name after her - Mom's name was Marie, and my daughter's name is Lily Marie. The only catch - Mom died a year and a half before Lily Marie was born, and I had never discussed children's names with my mom when she was alive - I wasn't even sure that I was going to have children. So Mom obviously knew about my daughter and her middle name - and Mary - who knew nothing about me - was able to deliver that wonderful message.

Mary grew up in Saco, Maine in a big family, where she was one of six children. When she was little, Mary used to lie on her back on the grass and talk with the angels. "I would imagine being in the clouds with them, playing games. They always gave me good advice and have always been there for me."

Mary has known she was gifted since she was a little child, but she simply thought everyone else had the same ability to see the future the way she did. However, after being incessantly teased by her five brothers and sisters – who definitely were not psychic and made fun of Mary, saying she was "an ESP – Extra Stupid Person" – she learned to shut her ability off at an early age. But not entirely.

"Since there were so many of us in the house, there were a lot of chores," Mary remembers. "My dad used to pull the sticks off a broom and say 'The person who picks the shortest stick has to do the dishes.' Well, needless to say – I never had to wash the dishes. My siblings slowly began to take me seriously, and today they all come to me for readings. But back then, as a child growing up, I began to shut down this part of myself so I could fit in."

Mary grew up and did "normal" things – she went to college, left school and worked at a ski resort, and eventually moved out west to Utah with her boyfriend and his dog, in pursuit of adventure. "I just wanted to have fun and do something that I was passionate about, but I chose not to pursue my psychic ability at that time so that I could appear to be normal among my friends."

After Mary moved to Utah, she started a helicopter ski guide service in Park City. In addition, Mary managed a local cable TV station, *Park City TV,* where she produced a metaphysical TV show and a local morning show called *Park City Today.* "That was over thirty years ago and, believe it or not, that show is still on the air today," says Mary. "We covered local news and weather, but we also interviewed city officials, Olympic stars and famous tourists who visited the town."

Mary got married and had two daughters, and in 1990, she and her family moved back to her home state of Maine, where she opened a metaphysical bookstore called *Light of the Moon.* The name and the location of her new bookstore were given to her in a dream. "I began to embrace my psychic ability again after reading books about Edgar Cayce. There were different psychic readers in the store every day, but one day a reader didn't show up and the calendar was booked, so I had to bite the bullet, and I took over doing readings that day. I was finally 'out of the psychic closet' and I loved it!"

Eventually, Mary and her husband got divorced, and when the *Light of the Moon* bookstore closed a few years later, she started doing private and group readings for clients. In addition, Mary hosted *Spiritual Adventure Tours* to her homeland, Ireland, where she shares a dual citizenship with the U.S. Then, she decided to move back to Utah to be with her daughters, who were living there at the time. "I worked with the 2002 Olympics, which were taking place in Utah, and I met Michael, who works in the aviation industry. After the Olympics were over, Michael went to his home in Port Townsend, Washington, and several months later I moved to Port Townsend to be with him. We got married and moved to Sacramento, where I'm based today."

Mary gives readings to loyal clients across the country, and often travels to give seminars on developing intuitive ability. Mary is particularly gifted as a medium, and has an uncanny ability to pick up on people who have passed to the other side – sometimes when no one is even aware that a particular person has died.

"I remember I read this one woman, and I kept getting messages from this guy named Dave who was on the other side," Mary says. "The woman, who was in her thirties, insisted that that couldn't be true. She said that her brother was alive. He was still young and although they had been estranged for some time, she had no reason to believe that he had died. But Dave kept coming through as we sat there – he wanted to tell his sister that he was finally okay.

"After our reading, the woman called the police in Boston, which is where her brother lived, to see what they might know. It turned out that her brother had been homeless for the last years of his life, and had recently been found dead on the street. My client was shocked, but relieved to have made contact with her brother, who finally seemed to be at peace."

Mary believes that everyone has the ability to connect to their loved ones on the other side. "But given our busy lifestyles, or in the quest to be 'normal,' we've learned to value logic and reason above our intuitive knowing. Thankfully, times are changing and people are listening to their yearning for more connection, and are finally seeking out the answers."

After decades studying Shamanism and other healing methods, Mary has created her own healing sessions called *Igniting the Flame Within*. "My mission in life is crystal clear – I'm here to ignite the healing power within each of my clients, and help them connect with their divine guidance. My method ignites the healing power within the seekers, and gives them the tools for their own personal growth. My workshops, tele-seminars, and private sessions are designed to clear out old patterns and blocks, and give you the clarity to connect with your personal guides and loved ones, while at the same time creating more peace, abundance and joy in your life. As you connect with your psychic abilities, you will find the spark within and ignite the flame that empowers you to greatness."

Mary has a unique perspective of the afterlife, since she has spoken to many people who've passed on and shared their experiences with her. "Mostly, people who have passed on are really, really happy," explains Mary. "They're surrounded by love, family and friends, and look and feel as they did when they were at the best, healthiest and most attractive time in their lives."

Although our deceased loved ones are aware of what's going on in our lives, it's not their sole focus. According to Mary, "The biggest misconception is that these souls are still attached to the material world – that they actually care about all the minutiae that we, still here on Earth, are dealing with everyday. They don't – they've moved on, and they wish their living loved ones the best, but they're not up there in heaven, looking at us and passing judgment. They're having the time of their lives!"

REBECCA FEARING

Rebecca Fearing is a psychic medium and healer from Southern California who does national and international readings for people, including celebrities, entrepreneurs, business professionals and also for law enforcement agencies. She has a quick, energetic style, and she often communicates with deceased loved ones to gain insights into her client's past, present, and future direction. Rebecca wants people to know, "I never chose to be a professional psychic. Like other gifted psychics, it usually chooses you."

During my reading with Rebecca, she correctly identified several of my family members by name, including loved ones who had passed on years ago, and whom I had not heard from before. She also described complex family issues that were still unresolved, but she assured me that it is important to simply move on with my life and to leave the past in the past.

When Rebecca was three years old, she discovered something that her mother and grandmother were trying to hide from her. "My mother and grandmother bought my sister a brand new dress and they hid it under the bed because they didn't get me one as well," remembers Rebecca. "I had no way of knowing this physically, but I knew about this psychically. So I started to have a tantrum, and I stomped over to the bed where they had hidden the dress and I reached down and pulled it out from under the bed. Then they took another outfit of mine and turned it inside out so that I would think that it was new, but I wouldn't have it." This was when Rebecca realized she was intuitively gifted.

Rebecca's next psychic experience happened when she was five years old, near the time of the Kennedy assassination. "My grandmother and my mother really liked John Kennedy and they would always sit in the kitchen and talk about him. Even though I was very young, Kennedy was a familiar topic of conversation around our house, and I knew who he was. So when I heard that he was shot, I told my grandmother, 'Did he just die?' I thought that he had already died, because I had a vision of him dying months before it actually happened."

Sometimes, as a grade school student, Rebecca's strong intuition would manifest itself. "We always had to wear uniforms, so it was always a big deal when we could have a free dress day. On this particular Easter Sunday in 1965, I really wanted everybody to see me at Our Lady of Peace Catholic Church in this really pretty yellow Easter dress. However, my mother informed me that we were going to visit my great grandmother and aunt's family in Ontario, California. So I wore the dress in Ontario instead.

"The next free dress day we had at school, I decided to wear my pretty yellow Easter dress, but when I got to school everyone said they had already seen me in this dress on Easter Sunday at church, even though I had been in Ontario at the time. This was the first of two times that I believe that I bi-located myself, meaning that I appeared in two separate locations at the same time."

When she became a teenager, some of Rebecca's classmates began to notice her intuitive ability. "I just knew everything that was going on with people, and I didn't really keep it quiet," explains Rebecca. "Sometimes I would see ghosts at a slumber party, or I would give psychic predictions to my friends. This happened more and more often, and the people around me began to realize that I had these intuitive abilities."

After high school, Rebecca got a job at Universal Studios. "I was a mailroom girl at Universal, and I basically delivered the mail and also worked as a temp," Rebecca says. "And I thought that I might want to become an actress, so my mother and grandmother enrolled me in Lee Strasberg's acting school. At first, I enjoyed acting and did very well. But then, during one scene, my acting partner slapped me really hard in the face, and I didn't like that at all. I kind of went into shock, and I realized that acting wasn't for me, so I quit."

Rebecca began working at a series of odd jobs for the next few years, including working as a clerk in a liquor store, working as a nanny, and she also still worked part time at Universal. However, during this period, she had a near death experience, which made her realize she should pay more attention to her intuitive gifts.

"One night, I had a dream which was actually a premonition," recalls Rebecca. "In the dream, I saw a black crow that was wearing a big cap that said Death on it, and I knew that if I went out that night that I would die. But I went out anyway, and as I was crossing the street, I was hit by a speeding car. Somehow, I was okay, but the car that hit me was very damaged, with a cracked windshield and a twisted fender."

Rebecca continues, "It was a miracle. I guess I was protected by angels. I went to the hospital, and my leg swelled up, but all I had was a scratch on my toe. I realized that I should have paid attention to my psychic ability and not gone out that night, but I ignored the warning. That incident completely changed how I viewed my psychic ability, so I began to take it seriously after the accident. It really woke me up."

Interestingly, Rebecca began to have strangers come up to her and tell her that she was going to become a famous intuitive and healer. "This happened more than once. I would start laughing and say, 'I would never do that!' The one encounter that I remember the most was when George, this old psychic on Venice Beach, stopped me and my mother, and said, 'You know, you're going to be a well known psychic and healer, and a man in a red robe watches over you and protects you.

"George asked my mom and me if I could wait there for a moment, because he had some people that he wanted me to meet. The next thing I know, he brought a whole crowd of people over, and they surrounded me and were shaking my hand, very excited to meet me. Then George told the crowd, 'One day, this woman will become a famous psychic and healer!' I'll never forget that experience!"

In the early 1990s, one of Rebecca's friends suggested that she take a job on a new psychic hotline, which was one of the first in the country. "This hotline was one of the first reputable psychic hotlines. It was a legitimate hotline, and there were other gifted psychics working there. It was actually good for me, because I got a lot of experience doing back to back readings all day. But after a while, when the hotline started training less gifted psychics, I decided to quit."

Rebecca continued to do readings, and she eventually took a job at a magic club at Universal Studios called Wizards. "I used to wear a purple robe and hat that made me look like a wizard, and there were other psychics at the club who gave readings, but I became so popular that I finally decided to start my own psychic practice," Rebecca says. "I never advertised or solicited, but thanks to a lot of positive word of mouth, I had so many clients that I decided to open an office, and I've been doing psychic readings ever since."

After years of doing readings for clients, Rebecca has come to understand more about spirituality, the divine and the universe. "My main message to people is that heaven is real. I know that we live in a multidimensional universe just like the physicists and the scientists say," explains Rebecca. "We live in a very amazing universe, but right now, we don't understand exactly how it all works. Or maybe it's that we don't remember exactly how it all works. But I believe that we're on the cutting edge of understanding this extraordinary and magnificent universe."

Rebecca has a big picture view of humankind that she wants to share with others. "Basically, we all want the same things. No matter what religion or culture or economic status you're in, everybody wants to have a nice, happy life, to love and to be loved, and to have something that you can be proud of. I've seen people who go from ground zero to accomplishing amazing things, and I feel that nothing is impossible. It's very simple. We have divine intervention, angels are real, and there is a heaven, regardless of your religion."

However, Rebecca cautions people that they need to be responsible for their behavior in this life. "I've learned that you are accountable for your actions, once you are *conscious*. Some people are unconscious or they suffer from mental illness or other things that are out of their control. But once you become conscious and you know that your behavior is wrong, you need to be accountable. And you will be. Everything is recorded. Everything is noted. So we can redeem ourselves by being conscious and doing a better job while we're here."

SUZANNE GIESEMANN

Suzanne is a retired U.S. Navy commander who served as a commanding officer, as special assistant to the Chief of Naval Operations, and as aide to the Chairman of the Joint Chiefs of Staff. After earning a Master's Degree in National Security Affairs, she taught political science at the U.S. Naval Academy. She completed overseas assignments in Panama and Japan, and earned military decorations, including the Combat Action Ribbon and the Defense Meritorious Service Medal.

Suzanne is also a highly gifted psychic medium, who only discovered her intuitive gift in her early 40's, after she retired. After a long career in the military, where Suzanne rose to become a U.S. Navy commander, her transition to becoming a highly respected intuitive counselor was a surprise to her and to everyone else. The juxtaposition of these two strikingly different worlds she has experienced is amazing indeed.

Unlike many other gifted intuitives, as a child, Suzanne was completely unaware of her intuitive abilities. "My parents were almost anti-religion. I wasn't even encouraged to seek spiritual answers to anything," remembers Suzanne. "I see that now as a blessing, because I've come to my spiritual understanding through personal seeking rather than what other people told me to believe. I had no idea that there was a spirit world and no idea that there was a greater reality. And certainly no idea that if there were one, that I could communicate with those in it."

Suzanne grew up and attended Millersville State College, a small college in Pennsylvania, where she majored in Spanish, with a minor in Russian and French. Her dream was to join the navy, and being proficient in a number of languages would prove helpful to a military career.

"When I was five years old, my brother, who is quite a bit older than I am, joined the Air Force, and I thought that was just the greatest lifestyle, serving his country, traveling all around the world, and I thought that's for me, especially as a foreign language major," Suzanne says. "I knew I would get to use my languages, so that is exactly how it worked out."

Suzanne joined the U.S. Navy right after she graduated from college. She thrived in the military environment and quickly rose through the ranks.

"In the navy, you have different assignments every couple of years, every two to three years. So I had nine different tours of duty in my twenty years in the navy," Suzanne explains. "There are various ranks, and I just went through the typical ranks of ensign, lieutenant junior grade, lieutenant, lieutenant commander, commander. I had a variety of jobs because I joined the navy before most women were allowed on ships."

Eventually, Suzanne worked her way up to being named commanding officer of a shore-based unit, and she became the special assistant to the Chief of Naval Operations. "This was the head of the navy. Then, ultimately, I was asked by the Chairman of the Joint Chiefs of Staff – the head of the entire United States Military – to be his right-hand man, so to speak. His aide-de-camp."

During her military career, Suzanne flew on Air Force One with the President of the United States, President George W. Bush, on one occasion. "In addition to that one flight on Air Force One, I was in the presence of President Bush about a dozen other times as aide to the chairman. "One fateful day, she was on a military plane on September 11th, 2001 that had to be diverted.

"On 9/11, the chairman and I, and just a handful of immediate staff members, were on a plane to England because the chairman was going to be knighted by Queen Elizabeth," Suzanne recalls. "While we were out over the Atlantic, we got word of the attack on the World Trade Center, so we turned around and came back. By the time we got back into U.S. airspace, we were the last aircraft still in the air. We actually saw the World Trade Center from the air as we returned to Washington; we saw the devastation to both the World Trade Center and the Pentagon as our plane flew back and landed."

After 9/11, instead of grieving like most of the country, Suzanne had to go to work in the Pentagon, which had also been attacked by the terrorists. "It was one of those cases where they tell all non-essential personnel to stay home – but as an aide to the chairman, we were essential. People didn't realize that the Pentagon actually burned for three days, but it did. It was very sobering, because they were still searching for remains while we were working in the building. Everybody in the Pentagon was ultimately issued a gas mask."

Suzanne continues, "They put up sign boards of the people who had been killed and I would walk by them every day, with their personal stories and their smiling faces looking at you and these were just regular people. That was an eye opener for me, and that's what really started me down my spiritual path, asking why these things happen and are those people really gone. That was real hard for me, and that started me on my way to where I am today. I felt a spiritual pull, and I tried to delve into traditional religion, but it just didn't speak to my heart."

In 2003, Suzanne was eligible for retirement, and she decided to retire and enjoy her free time with her husband. "I retired, and the very next day my husband and I took off on our sailboat," Suzanne recalls. "We sold our house, we sold our cars, and we sailed across the Atlantic Ocean and around the Mediterranean for a little bit, and life seemed idyllic."

But Suzanne's perfect life would soon be interrupted by a tragedy that shook her to her core. "We were off the coast of Croatia when our family tracked us down to share the news that no parent ever wants to hear. They told us that my husband's daughter, my stepdaughter Susan, who was 27-years-old and a sergeant in the Marine Corps, had been crossing the flight line at her duty station when she was struck and killed by lightning. To make things even worse, Susan was six months pregnant with our first and only grandchild.

"I replayed that moment so many times in my life. You just want to hit the rewind button. You just can't believe this is real. How can somebody who was so vibrant suddenly be gone just like that? And all your hopes and dreams died. She was only married seven months earlier. We flew home in a state of shock.

"The moment that was a real turning point for me was the viewing the night before her funeral. I was staring down at the open coffin containing this body in a Marine dress uniform, and I just said out loud repeatedly, that's not Susan. There was such a difference between, as anybody who has seen a dead body knows, between a body filled with a spirit and a lifeless body, and I knew then and there that you couldn't have killed her vibrant spirit."

So Suzanne decided to learn what happens to our spirit after we die. "I wanted to find out if what I'd read in books about the afterlife was true. That's what led to the most wondrous, unexpected spiritual journey for me. We miss Susan every day, but what a gift she gave us – because I started to read more spiritual books and develop my own ability as a medium, and now I'm able to use my ability to help thousands of people know that our loved ones are still with us."

In fact, Suzanne's deceased stepdaughter Susan often helps her from the other side when Suzanne is doing a reading. "It's Susan who's helping me now with my readings. I hear others in my readings. I hear them like my own thoughts. But when Susan is present, I hear her voice and it is almost impossible to re-create a loved one's voice. One of the first things we forget is what they sounded like. But she talks to me in her own voice and gives me information about the person I'm reading."

In addition to doing readings, Suzanne is also an accomplished author, and has written a number of books, including her first metaphysical book, *The Priest and the Medium*. Throughout her life, including her amazing transition from being a military leader to becoming a psychic medium, Suzanne has evolved greatly, and she wants to share what she's learned with other people.

"This life is not all there is, and if we keep our focus so firmly in this physical world, we shut out the magic, the miracle, of which we are a part of in the next greater reality," Suzanne explains. "Life continues on for all of us. Not only does it give us the hope that our loved ones are still with us, and the knowledge that we will see them again, but it takes away the fear of death and shows us that it's really, really important to love each other here and now, because life is ongoing and we're here to learn how to love each other."

When asked where our spirits "go" when we die, Suzanne shared her views in an interesting analogy. "Here's a good question for you. Are the actors on your television in the TV? No. Where are they? It's a signal that's in the air. That is what your TV picks up. If your TV breaks, where does the signal go? It's still all around you. Is the real you in your body? No. The real you is a signal. You are a spirit. You are vibrations.

"But when the body dies, just like when a TV set breaks, where does the spirit go? It doesn't go anywhere. Your signal still exists eternally everywhere in this nonphysical realm. It doesn't go anywhere. So your loved ones are still very much with you. It's a state of awareness, which is what we are – pure awareness."

ROBERT HANSEN

Robert Hansen, raised in a skeptical, law enforcement family, became an amazingly gifted psychic medium who has helped thousands of people connect with their loved ones after losing them in often sudden and tragic circumstances. Robert worked as a special education teacher before becoming aware of his gift. Unlike many mediums, who have had intuitive experiences as children, Robert wasn't aware of his gift until he was much older. Robert uses a down-to-earth, no-nonsense approach that enables him to educate people about what happens to us after we die, and to connect clients with their family members and others who've passed on.

During my reading with Robert, I was astonished at just how accurate he was - particularly regarding specific details that no one could know. When my mother came through, Robert said that she regularly visits my daughter - her granddaughter who was born a year and a half after my mom's death - and that she visits my daughter at night, in the room with the "stars on the ceiling." Yes, there are glow-in-the-dark stars on the ceiling of my daughter's room. His level of detail enabled me to realize that my mom - who never met her granddaughter here on Earth - actually is watching over my daughter, and knows her very well.

For 25 years, Robert Hansen was living an ordinary life, working as a special education teacher on Long Island, raising four children with his wife, Katie, when everything changed. One day, when he was in his early forties, he began hearing messages from the dead.

"I tell people I lay down one evening and I woke up and the world that I knew had died and everything shifted," Robert says. "I grew up in a Catholic family and my upbringing was very law enforcement based, and my family was saying to me, 'You've got to be kidding, Robert – you were raised in a family of cops and now you're doing psychic stuff?' All I could say to them was, 'You know,

I didn't ask for this – I didn't just say one day, oh, this would be a cool thing to do, let's go be a psychic.' This came to me as an act of grace, or a gift, and it came to me when I was at a certain receptive, mature point in my life to really understand and appreciate it."

What event triggered Robert's intuitive gift? According to Robert, one day near Thanksgiving, he decided to help a homeless woman who asked him for money at the karate studio where he taught martial arts. Instead of just giving her money, he told the woman that he would give her twenty dollars if she would do a small task in return – such as taking out the garbage or sweeping the floor. She returned day after day, doing some *work* in return for her *pay*. Soon, over the course of a few weeks, her dignity began to return.

"And after I gave her the money, I got in my car, and I heard this voice that said 'Thank you for helping one of my children,'" Robert recalls. "And it scared the pants off of me. But after that, I began receiving messages from spirit all the time. And I started helping children who had crossed over connect with their parents here on Earth."

Today, after doing thousands of readings, being studied by noted paranormal researcher Dr. Gary Schwartz, and being featured in the *New York Times*, Robert still jokes about his late start as a psychic medium.

"Most other mediums come into it after a near death experience or after a childhood accident," Robert notes. "I was just a regular guy from a cop family. In fact, I was the guy who said, 'I want you to prove it to me,' before I'd believe anything – a real skeptic. So it probably didn't happen until I was in my forties because I was too much of a banana head prior to that, an immature jerk, and the souls probably said, 'This guy's gonna blow everything, we can't go to him – he's an idiot. So we'll wait until he grows up a little bit, and then he can talk on our behalf.' That's probably what they said."

Robert's gift as a teacher translated well to his work as a medium. Every year, he gives hundreds of workshops and seminars both at his studio in Merrick, New York and at restaurants, fundraisers and other events. The seminars are usually attended by people who've lost loved ones they want to reach, or those who would like to know more about psychic development.

"I always tell people that there are three types of people who attend a session," Robert says. "The psychic nut jobs who would buy into anything a psychic says, the cynics who roll their eyes and won't believe anything you say, and the third type of guest – which is the best – intelligent skeptics. I always tell my guests to be intelligent skeptics – that's a term I learned from Dr. Gary Schwartz, the prominent paranormal researcher, and I think that it's very well stated."

During his sessions, Robert commonly gets many questions about death and the afterlife. "A lot of people say that their loved one is 'on the other side' – they use the term so loosely. But when I ask them where the other side is, they don't know. Because there is no 'other side' – the souls are here with us."

Robert also counsels grieving parents, many of whom have lost a child and are worried about what's happened to the child after he or she died. "I've worked with many parents who've lost a three-year-old, a four-year-old, or a seven-year-old, and they're paralyzed by fear that their little girl, who died of leukemia, is only two years old and is wandering around on this dark other side, alone. And they really think that. So I try to bring an energy of other souls that they know, and the family will say, 'Oh my God, that's my brother-in-law, that's my father – and I tell them 'They have this child.' So they feel much, much better."

Interestingly, Robert has a very specific view about what becomes of married couples in the afterlife – a view that differs from the norm and often upsets his clients. "People often say to me, 'My dad passed away ten years ago and my mother just died – are they together?' And they want to hear that they are because it has a romantic – what I call a Hallmark Card feeling to it.

"Actually, it is very rare for a couple to be together after they die, very rare. Because their consciousness as a unique human being evolves differently. It's not what it was like here, and that carries over to there – it doesn't work like that. But people get upset, so

I simply say 'They're around each other, their presence is nearby,' and that's true."

However, Robert does believe that our loved ones help us make the transition from life to the afterlife when we die. "When you die, or what I call 'get ready to go home,' there is this window – we call it a portal – in which a soul or souls that you know will come across to guide you to your new evolution. There is a moment of connection, and people are comforted when they hear that."

Overwhelmingly, people ask Robert where we go when we die. According to Robert, our soul's consciousness chooses one of two doorways: one, the soul stays in the unmanifested, meaning without structure or form; or two, the soul seeks a new life process in which to continue evolving in the human form – which is the idea behind reincarnation.

"A lot of people believe that you wind up in a place when you die – like purgatory or limbo or heaven or hell, which is really not true," Robert believes. "But they don't 'go' anywhere – they're a consciousness evolving – they don't go to a location, like heaven. Heaven is not a location – it's a state of consciousness. And very, very few people reach that 'heaven' state of consciousness – you have to be one-hundred percent fully illuminated – or spiritually conscious – in this incarnation, like Buddha or the Christ figure, and very few people reach that level of consciousness during their life."

Although human beings are flawed and are certainly not perfect, it is Robert's hope that more people will strive to reach a higher level of consciousness during their incarnation on the Earth plane. "If people take the time to just listen, and to pay attention to their inner voice, their inner guidance, they'll take a giant step to becoming the best person they can be. And by elevating their consciousness as a human, they'll also be elevating their soul on the spiritual plane as well."

KIRA KAY

Kira Kay is a gifted intuitive who was born in Australia and now resides in Berlin, Germany. She first experienced her precognitive abilities as a teenager, but kept her gift to herself and went to college, graduating with a degree in business law. Finally, in her mid-twenties, Kira decided to explore her spiritual path, to find her true purpose in life. She quit her job in the hospitality industry, and began studying with a series of mentors to get a handle on her immense intuitive gifts. Today, after embracing her strong intuitive gift, Kira helps clients from around the world - including celebrities, spiritual leaders and ordinary people - discover the true purpose of their lives and their soul's journey.

I learned about Kira from Dean Radin, the highly-respected scientist who is studying 'psi' when I interviewed him for this book. According to Dean, Kira is "a psychic's psychic. She has an excellent intuitive ability." I found this to be true during my reading with Kira. She sees the beauty in every being, and helps her clients awaken to their own inner beauty, and to their soul's purpose as well.

Kira Kay grew up in Australia as a happy child, going to school and playing with her friends. And because her parents chose to live in very distant, secluded areas of Australia, Kira had a sense of freedom and a profound connection to nature that most children don't experience. "I'm grateful that my parents chose to live in very far away areas – you could agree that the southern middle of Australia in the desert is remote!" Kira laughs.

"My parents chose to live remotely to give their children a lot of freedom for our self-discovery and to explore nature and the life around us. I have to say that my parents were quite unusual in the amount of freedom they gave us to roam around in nature. My mother was a lover of animals, so we always had a menagerie of animals around us."

For example, Kira's mother bought Kira a wild horse, a Brumby, for her 11th birthday. "Brumbies are wild horses which have never been touched by humans," Kira explains. "Mum had been visiting a station, Fossil Downs in Western Australia, that is known for its wild Brumbies. She decided, spontaneously, to buy me a wild Brumby because I loved horses. They cut one out from the herd, put the horse on the back of a truck and drove the thousand or so kilometers to where we lived. And that was my birthday present!"

Kira believes that nature is a great teacher, and interacting with nature can help us get in touch with our own intuition. "Nature can illuminate one's path in life, as well as giving us a wider perspective on how life itself really works. I used to get up before the sun and ride out with my horse and the dogs and arrive home after sunset. My parents were never concerned, as there were very few other humans in the area, so it was essentially nature, the animals and myself. I think in my childhood, and certainly in my teens, I didn't understand the impact of what a gift I had grown up with, but today I understand the value of nature and its teachings."

But Kira's idyllic childhood would eventually be interrupted by a tragic event. When she was 15, Kira had a precognitive dream that her mother was going to die. "My mother had previously had breast cancer when I was a very young child, but she'd been in remission for years," Kira says. "I woke up from that dream very disturbed, and when my father told me later that day that my mother had been re-diagnosed with cancer – this time, it was liver and bone cancer – I was in utter shock. I thought that I had caused it to happen to her somehow. I felt responsible." Kira didn't talk to anyone about her dream, and decided to keep it to herself.

About a year later, Kira's mom died. "I had an enormous amount of guilt that it was my fault, because I had that dream and now my mom was dead. It was a very confusing time – I didn't know anything about the word 'psychic' back then. I had no clue what was going on."

A few years later, Kira had another precognitive dream – this time, it was about her father dying. "About seven days after I had that dream, my brother ran into the place where I worked at the time and said 'Dad died.' It was an incredible shock. Dad died of a heart attack under a tree, just as it had been in the dream. By this time, I'd heard about psychic ability and precognitive dreams, but I was still so confused."

Although Kira tried to keep her abilities "bottled in," she began having a series of extremely vivid precognitive dreams for about four years. "It was so intense that I couldn't watch TV or listen to the radio, because I'd get confirmation about what I was dreaming, such as tragic world events. In fact, I didn't want to dream anymore, so I basically tried not to sleep at night. I would just try and nap so that I wouldn't fall into a deep sleep and have these intense dreams."

Even though Kira was having these strong intuitive experiences, she managed to finish her degree in business law at the university. However, when she began looking for work in her field, she knew that she needed to move in a different direction. "I realized that – although I'd finished this intensive study at school – I really didn't know what was coming next, so I went to visit my brother, who lived in a different part of the country, in a forest. He lived in the outskirts of Melbourne, in Victoria, which is in the foothills of the Snowy Mountains. It was a very pristine, beautiful place."

What happened next would answer many of Kira's spiritual questions, and change her life forever. "When I was staying with my brother, I remember going for a walk, and then sitting on a rock, deep in the forest, and a voice inside of me said 'Find out who you are, find out what life is about.'" When Kira heard that message, "it was crystal clear, alive, simple and profound – a sense and feeling that I've learned to recognize over time. There was a profoundness, a certainty, an absoluteness that was simple and clear."

But Kira decided to keep this spiritual epiphany to herself for awhile. "At the time, I didn't talk to anyone about that particular profound moment. I just remember walking back down the mountain, feeling deeply connected within myself, and it was pouring with rain; that is fairly classic Melbourne weather. It was sunny where I'd been sitting up on the rock, and by the time I walked down the hill it was pouring with rain. I just felt really clear and certain that I needed to go back home to my house in Perth, and that my life was going to totally change."

After her visit with her brother, Kira, who had been working in the hospitality industry as a manager in a five-star hotel, returned to Perth, quit her job and set out on a spiritual journey. "Almost immediately, I started to meet several spiritual teachers, who helped me quite a bit. I learned how to go to a deeper place of wisdom within myself, where I could access information more easily."

Kira contacted her brother to let him know that she had made big changes in her life, and that she was now on the right path. "When I got home to Perth, I do remember that I told my brother about my choices, and I think that he was probably relieved that I was back together again, and not as depressed and lost as I was when I arrived at his home some weeks before!"

Kira decided to start doing readings for clients, and she designed a business card for herself. But she didn't put the word "psychic" on the card. "I didn't want to use the word 'psychic' on the card, because I had such a judgment about that word," Kira explains. "I wanted to call myself a 'life skills counselor,' but eventually I realized that I needed to get over my problem with calling myself a psychic, so I finally started calling myself a psychic and printed that business card! By acknowledging that I have psychic abilities, I was able to move forward and do the work that I'm supposed to do."

When Kira does a reading, she sets her own ego aside and simply brings forth the information for each client she reads for. "When I'm giving a reading, I have very little sense of myself. Of course, I know that I'm speaking, but I set my opinions and my own humanity to the side, so that I have the freedom to simply and clearly state what is coming through for the client. Sometimes I'll even say a word that I don't understand because it's in another language. But each reading is different and highly personal. It's between the universe and my client."

Today, Kira travels to Nepal twice a year to do volunteer work with earthquake victims. In addition to doing readings for clients, she gives workshops and meditation retreats so that other people can develop their intuitive abilities. "For me, this is a very deep passion that I have – from my perspective, if we all access this level of knowledge or wisdom, we could not persist with wars or with destruction. It would not be possible, because we would be awakened, and could see each other on such a different level.

"I see now that this is my path – to support others and to help them move deeper into that higher level of consciousness. I consider that being a human being is truly a gift, and I feel that if I can help others appreciate this gift that we have here right now, then I feel that I have accomplished my work."

GREG KEHN

Gregory Kehn is a big man with a gentle demeanor, and he approaches his readings with great sensitivity to the soul who's crossed over, and great caring and concern for their loved ones who are still on Earth. Greg is a fourth-generation spiritualist and medium who does readings for people from across the country. He grew up in Ohio and today splits his time between Florida and Lily Dale, New York.

When Greg delivers messages during a reading, he often gets a clear picture of the situation, and he offers pathways and solutions about how to resolve the issue at hand. He can pick up on subtle personality traits of the people his clients are asking about, which confirms that he's tuning into the right soul or spirit. After doing readings for clients for almost four decades, Greg can provide a unique perspective on communicating with the other side.

Unlike many intuitives, Greg grew up in a household that was very supportive of his gifts. Both his grandmother and mother were also gifted mediums in their own right, and they often took Greg with them to spiritualist churches and spiritualist camps. Greg witnessed his family using their abilities to help others, and they encouraged him to do the same. From the age of five, Greg was able to do readings for people, and he enjoyed being able to help them.

"I've been dedicated to this work since I was a little kid," says Greg. "When my father would ask me, 'What do you want to do when you grow up?' I said that I wanted to work in the local Healing Temple, and I want to counsel people and do readings for them. And that was when I was eight or nine years old."

Greg also had a special ability that few others had – his spirit could travel out of his body to visit and help others. "I remember getting off the school bus one day, and feeling very strongly that something was wrong with my friend, the little girl next door,"

says Greg. "I felt she was very, very sick – I felt her high temperature and sweating – so I went over to her house and her mom
said that I couldn't come in because I might catch something.
Afterwards, I went home and my mom said, 'I know you're upset
that you can't see your friend – why don't you go help her? You
know what to do.' So I went in my bedroom and I laid on the bed
and focused on sending her energy and healing so she would
become healthy."

Although Greg was in his own bedroom and his sick friend was
in her house next door, Greg felt her high temperature, and the
chills she was experiencing. "I worked on her for a little while, and
again later that evening when I went to bed. And the next day, the
girl's mother came over to tell us that her fever had broken and
that she was okay," remembers Greg. "But the mother said that her
daughter insisted that Greg had come to help her and was in her
room – that she could see me. Her mother thought her daughter
must have been delirious, but I was there in spirit, at the foot of her
bed, working on her, and her mother couldn't see me. I had many
experiences like that as a child."

Greg often used his intuitive ability to avoid being bullied at
school. Other boys picked on Greg due to the fact that he was a big
boy. "When I was twelve, I was over six feet tall and weighed 225
pounds," says Greg. "And on top of that, some of the other kids
knew I was psychic and it scared them. One guy was planning to
beat me up to impress his buddies, and I sensed it before it happened. So I told him I knew what he was going to do, and it freaked
him out so much he left me alone."

Some of Greg's teachers were also aware that he had special
intuitive gifts. "One time, I felt that my teacher was really worried
and disconnected from being in the class, so I told her, 'Don't
worry – the baby's healthy. You're going to have a beautiful little
girl.' She looked at me and said 'How did you know I was pregnant –
I just found out myself?' And I said, 'Well, I see things, and I saw
the spirit of the baby you're carrying around you, and I saw that
you lost your last baby and are worried about this baby – but don't

worry – the baby you lost prepared you to have this one. She'll be healthy.' And the baby that my teacher eventually had was just fine. She treated me with a lot of respect after that."

Greg has an "insider's" view of heaven, mostly because he regularly communicates with souls who have passed on, but also because he became ill with a serious illness and "died" when he was eleven. "I was very sick – I had some sort of an infection or virus in my chest, and my lungs were all filled up with fluid and I had a temperature of 106," says Greg.

"During that week, I went to heaven three times. I left the body and went through the tunnel of light and I was on the spirit side completely. It was beautiful, it was amazing. I mean, I've never seen sharper greens and blues in the water, and you could see everything so clearly and in such a brilliant manner – but regardless of how bright it was, you were never squinting your eyes. And the quality of your life there – the quality of the energy – was just complete openness, complete honesty. There was nothing that would be a threat, nothing that you felt you'd have to protect yourself from – it was just so peaceful."

One of the most striking things Greg noticed was that everyone in heaven was young and in their prime. "You can choose to come back as your most vibrant self, when you were strong, healthy and energetic. The way you looked when you were at your best during life. And you're with everybody that was important to you – everybody that you love. In fact, when I crossed over during my illness, I saw my grandmother and several other relatives of mine that died before I was born."

When Greg was a teenager, he studied to become a minister at the Spiritualist Church that he attended, and he became an ordained minister at the age of sixteen. After high school, Greg became certified as a master car mechanic in California, Ohio and Pennsylvania. He took a full-time job for the Ford Motor Company, where he overhauled motors. But he continued doing readings for people in the evenings and on weekends, and he also went to Lily Dale in the summer to do readings.

Eventually, Greg's work as a medium became more in demand. He would come home from his day job at Ford and his answering machine would be full of messages from people who wanted readings. So he decided to quit his job at Ford to dedicate his life to his mediumship and healing work.

"I just reached a point where I was doing so many readings for people, that my job at Ford became an obstruction for me, and I had only worked there for a couple of years, so I decided to quit," explains Greg. "The job was taking time away from my healing work and my readings, and I realized that I could make a living helping people. I just needed to trust – to allow myself to trust and just go in this new direction. And when I let go of it, everything went fine. I was busy doing readings all of the time."

Greg begins all of his readings with a prayer. "I always send a thought and prayer to God, asking him to guide me. I know He sends His angels to guide us and help us and protect us. You could call them guardian angels, or guides, they're there and they're working with us at all times."

Unlike some other intuitives, Greg doesn't interfere with the information he's given for a client. "I look at it this way – if I'm reading for you, and God hands me a package, I hand it to you. I don't open it, I don't go through it, I don't figure it out, I don't restate it, I don't pull out the information and rewrite the information my way – I get the package, I give it to you – it's that simple. You're an instrument and a channel of energy – God's energy and wisdom, which flows through you. After a reading, I usually don't even remember what I said to my clients."

Most gifted intuitives cannot accurately predict lottery numbers – and Greg is no exception. But during one reading, the correct numbers did come through. "I was reading for a woman, and her deceased husband came through," Greg recalls. "And he told his wife a lottery number to play. She was reluctant, so I said 'Go put a couple of dollars on it,' and she did, and she won. Now, she didn't win millions of dollars, but just enough to pay off all the bills. It covered every bill she had, the funeral bills, mortgage, car payments – everything. That was the only time that ever happened – it was like her dead husband knew about her financial troubles and was giving her a gift."

Greg wants people to know that there are two distinct paths that we can take – to go with the flow of spiritual energy, or to resist it. "It says in the Bible, 'Ask and you shall receive.' If we put out a prayer and ask for help, and guidance, and attunement, we're going to have a flow of energy working for us. But many times, we try to control and maneuver events to achieve the outcome we desire, and that outcome is not necessarily what's supposed to happen for us," Greg explains.

"If you listen, and go with the flow of what's supposed to happen, everything works really well, and it works quickly. But many people don't listen to spirit, and they become very forceful and aggressive and try to get the outcome they want. Many of us are busy trying to force things to happen the way they want them to happen, and it can really muck things up.

"It's like a ball floating in the middle of a swimming pool. If we swim to the ball forcefully, the waves carry it away. But if we just wade out there very gently, we can lift our hand underneath it, and the ball is in the palm of our hand. And that's what people forget. We need to change our approach when working with spiritual things. We've come to the Earth plane to learn, grow and accept. Our pathway, our outcomes and lessons have already been determined before our soul enters our body. We need to accept this and go with the flow, not try to resist our lessons in this life, or believe that we can manipulate things to get the outcome we think we want."

ELIZABETH LEE

Elizabeth Lee has loved animals since she was a child but, ironically, she hasn't been able to have pets of her own, due to the severe allergies and asthma attacks she experiences when she's around animals. A highly gifted intuitive who uses her psychic ability and telepathic skills to communicate with animals, Elizabeth enjoys using her intuitive gifts to help clients communicate with their pets, particularly when the animal is misbehaving, sick or transitioning to the other side. Elizabeth is also a Reiki Master and does intuitive healing sessions with people.

When I spoke to Elizabeth, my own dog was very ill and, although I was hoping to hear that Snowball was going to make a full recovery, Elizabeth felt otherwise. After informing me that Snowball was ready to pass on, Elizabeth sent healing energy to Snowball to make the dying process easier and more comfortable - for Snowball, myself and our family.

As a child growing up in rural Illinois, Elizabeth loved to go outside and interact with birds, squirrels and other wild creatures. "I was always drawn to animals. From the minute I was born, I wanted to be around animals all the time," says Elizabeth. "I held the baby bunnies in our yard when they were born, and I watched the chipmunks and squirrels play and run around. Unfortunately, because of my pet allergies and asthma, we couldn't have animals in the house, so my family never had dogs and cats when I was a kid."

But Elizabeth still dreamed about being with animals, and having them play an important part of her life. "So many times, when I was little, people would say to me, 'What do you want to do when you grow up?' And I would say, 'I want to work with animals.' And they would look at me and say, 'But you have asthma and pet allergies, you can't work with animals,' remembers Elizabeth. "I actually found one of my old journals, which I started writing when I was ten years old, and in one entry I wrote that I was going to work with animals one day, and that I didn't know how I would do that, but that I absolutely had to find a way to make that happen."

When Elizabeth grew up and became an adult, she decided to get some cats of her own. After she took in a stray cat, she learned that her allergic reactions had gone away. "I was finally able to have a pet without getting sick," says Elizabeth. "My nose was stuffy, but I didn't sneeze, or have rashes and bumps. It was like a miracle to me. I was in heaven!"

Elizabeth loved her cats, but began having behavioral issues with them and she hired an animal communicator to work with the family pets. Elizabeth's relationship with the animal communicator evolved into something more. "I ended up becoming friends with this animal communicator, because we both loved animals and had so much in common," says Elizabeth.

"One day, my friend asked me to help her with one of her clients, because she wasn't sure if she was getting clear information from her client's pet. So I said yes, and I listened in, and all of a sudden, I got a really clear picture of this kitty. The kitty wasn't feeling well, and her owner wanted to know her cat's prognosis. Well, I got a picture of the cat sitting on a stage as the curtain came down in front of it, and I felt strongly that the cat would be passing on in the next few days, and he did."

That was the first time Elizabeth knew that she had the gift of being an animal communicator. "After that cat died, my friend told me that she felt that I also had this intuitive ability with animals, and that I could start helping people communicate with their pets. So I started taking classes and reading and doing workshops on animal communication. And that's how I started doing this work."

Elizabeth got married to her first husband, David, but that marriage only lasted one year. Eventually, she married her second husband, Jack, and had a daughter named Serena. When Serena was a baby, Elizabeth learned that her daughter had allergy issues with the family cats, just as she had, when she was a child. "Serena became highly allergic to our cats and developed severe eczema all over her body," recalls Elizabeth. "We had to give our cats away. We had to find homes for them, and it broke my heart terribly. That was the last thing that I wanted to do. It was intense, but my daughter was pretty sick, so we had no other choice."

A few years after she found homes for her cats, Elizabeth still yearned to be around animals, so she decided to visit an animal sanctuary outside Los Angeles called the Gentle Barn. "I took Serena and a friend of hers to the Gentle Barn and we fed the horses, petted the cows, watched the goats and the chickens, and we had a really, really great day," says Elizabeth. "Unfortunately, about an hour after we arrived, I started to get very sick and had trouble breathing and began sneezing and itching, even though we were outdoors in the fresh air. It seemed as though my allergies to animals had suddenly returned with a vengeance."

Elizabeth and the girls left the animal sanctuary and drove home. When Elizabeth arrived at her house, she was at her wit's end. "I was so sick and so frustrated and so angry that I just came up in my bedroom and I yelled at the sky," remembers Elizabeth. "I said 'Why? This is so unfair. I wanted to be with animals so much, and I feel so awful right now. After I said that, I clearly heard, 'Are you willing to use your telepathic skills to help the animals?' And I said, 'Of course, yes'. And the rest is history! I felt very confused and cheated at first, but eventually I found a way to work with animals and not have an allergic reaction."

After this incident, Elizabeth decided to work with a spiritual coach who helped her formulate an animal communication business that Elizabeth could run, primarily by doing phone readings. That way, she could help animals without becoming sick from her allergies. "Thanks to my coach's help, I was able to find the courage to start my animal communication practice, and to commit to it, and put my heart into it," says Elizabeth. "That was the beginning."

Although many might wonder how Elizabeth could use her intuitive skills to help animals without seeing them in person, she has an explanation. "I don't need to be in the same room with an animal, or even in the same state, because it just doesn't matter.

It's all energetic. Time and space don't matter. I often ask clients to send me a photograph of their animal, and I just tune into the essence of the animal through their picture. I can work without a photograph, but the pictures do help me."

Elizabeth has used her intuitive abilities to heal animals from all over the country with different ailments. "I had a client who had a Bichon Frise. Her Bichon was hiding under her desk for five days. It wouldn't come out to eat and was miserable and had a terrible skin rash," "My client had taken her dog to the vet and the vet gave him steroid shots and medication, but it wasn't helping," Elizabeth recalls.

"So she called me for help, and I did some distant Reiki healing and, after just 15 minutes, I could feel the heat coming off of his little body. It was intense heat, so I worked with my guides to pull this heat out, so the dog could feel better. Later that night, my client called me to tell me that, for the first time in five days, her dog came out from under the desk, and ate, and began acting like his old self again. He didn't go back under the desk again."

In addition to calling due to physical ailments, clients often call Elizabeth to help with a pet's behavioral and emotional issues. "One client called me because whenever she left for work, her Labrador would whine and pee in the house and tear things up, and she just couldn't figure out why, and she couldn't do anything to make her dog feel better," says Elizabeth.

"So she called me, and I checked in with the dog, and the dog communicated that she felt really unsafe when she was alone at home all day. I could feel that her heart was lonely. So I asked my client if she would be willing to get another dog to keep her Lab company, and she said yes. And they adopted another dog, who became best friends with her Lab, and the whining, peeing and bad behavior never happened again."

While Elizabeth is often successful in connecting to animals, once in awhile it can take some coaxing. "Sometimes, animals aren't really interested in talking, and sometimes they don't want to show you where it hurts," Elizabeth explains. "And sometimes, they can be really angry and they turn their backs. In those cases, I just sit and talk with them, and talk to their people about them until they eventually come around and want to communicate. It's different in every case."

Elizabeth feels a special calling in connecting to animals that have passed into spirit. "I love helping people reconnect with their animal friends after they have transitioned. It's extremely healing for people to be able to feel that bond again. They can ask about how the animal's soul is doing, and they can get clarity over what happened before their animal passed and, as a result, deep grief can be healed."

Ultimately, Elizabeth believes that animals are an enormous spiritual asset to humans, and that they enrich our lives in countless ways. "I think that animals are like a gift to us, honestly. They help us. They connect us to the natural world. They have a way of getting into our hearts like nobody else can. I think that learning how to communicate with animals and honoring our relationship with them on a deeper level is very important. Because when we reciprocate that love, and reach back to our animals, it honors them."

In her sessions, Elizabeth also brings through messages from her guides, and connects with the animal's higher self. "I think that we have soul agreements with these beings. They are beings just like we are, and they're part of our soul families. Just like with humans, I believe that we live many lifetimes, as the animals do, and we can have profound relationships with these beings over and over and over again. I see animals as a gift that we should cherish and appreciate, because they make our lives so much better, and they give us the opportunity to love so deeply."

LORI LIPTEN

Lori Lipten is a shamanic medium and a professional intuitive practitioner who is dedicated to helping others "access their soul's power, purpose and potential." Gifted since she was a child, Lori tried to talk about her strong intuitive perceptions with family and friends, but quickly learned that she should keep her gift to herself because her family and others didn't "believe in such things."

When Lori was older, she was very successful in the corporate world, and she decided to pursue a master's degree in psychology. But she began to awaken and embrace her intuitive gifts, and she finally chose to follow her spiritual path. Today, as the founder of the Sacred Balance Academy and Healing Center in Bloomfield Hills, Michigan, she guides others on their spiritual journey so that they, too, can realize their soul's purpose.

When Lori was a child of about seven, she had very strong past life memories. "I remember that I used to live in an ashram, which is a Hindu temple or place of spiritual enlightenment," Lori explains. "It was very detailed, and I was kind of confused that I now had white skin and lived in a suburban home in the U.S. as a female. Not in a bad way. I was just thinking, 'Oh, this is interesting. I wonder what happened to my ashram?' I remembered that I had been Hindu, and that I had been profoundly devoted to God, and that I had spent almost my entire adult life in the service and worship of God. I remember teaching and leading others through spiritual practices, and I recall that very distinctly."

Lori tried to share stories about her past life and her ability to see angels with her family, but they weren't very receptive. "I would bring these subjects up, but was consistently met with strong looks of disapproval, so I learned to keep quiet about my intuitive experiences. It was really interesting, because I was raised in a Jewish home, but I had this affinity for angels, which was not a strong focus of the Jewish religion. My mom and dad thought that my interest in angels was strange, because they didn't know where it came from and they couldn't relate to it."

In addition to being raised Jewish, Lori's parents were both highly intellectual, and strictly rational thinkers. "My mom had a doctorate in sociology, and my father was the CEO of an engineering firm, so they were heavily science based, rational thinking intellectuals, and here I was, seeing and talking about things that they didn't really validate or didn't want me to talk about. It was like they saw me as flighty or something."

When Lori was a teenager, people started to come to her to ask her questions about their lives. "Friends and even distant acquaintances came to me for counsel," Lori recalls. "They would ask me the most bizarre questions, like, 'What do you think is going to happen to me in the fall?' And I would tell them what I saw happening. I never thought about it, until one of my friends said, 'Don't you think it's odd that everybody thinks you know the answers to everything?' And I said, 'Yeah, I do think that's kind of weird.' It was like these answers came from this natural out-flowing in my mind, but I still kept it hidden that I had any access to something other than my own information or thoughts."

Lori could always tell if a relationship was going to work out, and she angered her mother when she told her mom that one of her close friends was going to get a divorce in the near future. "My parents were playing golf with another married couple who were their dear friends. After the golf game, when we were walking away, I said to my mom, 'You know, they're going to get a divorce in the next two months.' And my mother became very angry at me and she said, 'How could you say such a terrible thing? What would make you think that?' And I told her that I didn't know – I just knew what I knew. And then two months later, they got a divorce, and I told my mother 'You know, now he's going to marry your other friend, Ruth.' And my mom just thought I was the most horrible person, and she was angry. Well, after the first couple divorced, a few months later, the man married that Ruth woman. I'll never forget that. And my mom said 'How did you know that was going to happen?' And I said, 'It's because I just know stuff.' That kind of thing happened a lot."

Lori continued to have intuitive experiences as she grew up, but when she was 17, she had her first real encounter with her guides, and it was a life changing experience, to say the least. "I went to go dancing with my friends, and we were all partying because we had just graduated from high school. I was always the designated driver, because I was a couple of months younger than everyone – they were eighteen and I was seventeen and I had a car. That day, I kept thinking that I shouldn't be driving. Something just kept telling me that. But I drove anyway. I picked up my friends and drove them to the club."

Although the drinking age was 18, the dance club let Lori and her friends in, and everybody danced, drank and had fun. "But as we were getting ready to leave, I wasn't feeling that great, so I asked someone else to drive my car," remembers Lori. "I got into my girlfriend's car instead, and sat in the middle of the front seat – it had bench seats. Everybody was chatting and saying goodbye, and the door to the car was still open. Suddenly, I heard a male voice from behind me say, 'Get out of the car,' I turned around, but I only saw my girlfriends, and I asked, 'What did you say?' and they said, 'We weren't talking to you.' So I turned back around, but I heard the male voice again, saying urgently, 'Get out of the car now!' I didn't understand what was going on, and the next thing I knew I literally got pulled up and thrown out of the car."

Lori continues, "I landed on the sidewalk, and my friends balked and said, 'What is your problem?' I just looked at them and said, 'I can't ride with you – I don't know why, but I just can't.' Then they drove off, and I turned to my friends who were going to drive my car, and I said, 'I'll go with you, but we can't drive right now – we have to wait.' And they listened to me, and we waited for about a half hour or so. Then I felt like it was okay to drive, and on the way home we saw my friends car, the one I was in earlier, and it was flipped over because they'd been in a terrible accident with one fatality. I would never have survived that accident. That was my first encounter with a spirit guide where I actually heard a voice – and the guide saved my life."

Lori told her dad about the accident the next day, and she told him that she'd heard a voice that saved her life. "I didn't know how to tell my dad, because he didn't believe in this stuff at all. But after I told him, he said, 'Listen, I don't know what that voice is, but I don't care. If you ever feel it or hear it again, listen to it.'"

Lori didn't hear the voice again with certainty until she was in her early twenties. She had been assaulted and, as a result, began to slip into a deep depression. "I began to drink too much in order to cope," Lori explains. "So I said a prayer in a state of desperation. I was alone in my apartment and I said, 'You know, God, if you're there and you can hear me, I need your help.' Suddenly, I was in a vortex of light in my apartment – golden light filled with thousands of angels – it was not like anything I had ever seen. It looked like a hologram. It was incredible. And I was filled with all this love, an unbelievable amount of love, and I heard the voice again. This time, it said, 'We love you, we hear you, and we are here to help.' Soon after, Lori joined AA, stopped drinking, and rose out of her depression.

For the next several years, Lori worked in the corporate world in PR and marketing. She got married at age 35 and had a baby girl. Lori left the corporate world to raise her daughter and earn a master's degree in clinical psychology. During this time, she had a highly spiritual experience that altered the course of her life.

"When my daughter was three years old, an angel visited me and told me about a young boy who had died and needed to speak with his mother," recalls Lori. "Although I didn't know the woman directly, the angel helped me find the grieving mother – who was the cousin of a woman in my daughter's playgroup – so that I could relay the messages from this boy, her son, who had passed on. I spoke to the mother of the boy for two hours, which helped her tremendously. After I had this life changing experience, I was guided to do psychic readings while I was attending graduate school.

"When I first started to do readings, I really didn't know what I was doing. I would have to ask my guides how to bring through clear messages at will. And they taught me. After about five or six months into doing these readings, I began to realize that almost all of the readings included some kind of contact with spirits that have crossed over. I didn't think of myself as a medium, but it became evident that I was serving that role. And I've been reading people ever since."

After Lori's father died – just two months after her daughter was born – he came through to her with some advice. "My father, who didn't believe in this intuition stuff, came to me and said, 'Hey Lori, we need to talk.' That was the best moment of my life. He said to me, 'There is a God, but this God is not at all what I thought or what a lot of people say. This God is way bigger.' And he said, 'I didn't know who you were until now, and I'm here to help you.' He talked to me for two hours. He's the one who gave me the name for my company, Sacred Balance. He said that I was here to learn how to live in the world of the divine, the world of spirit, and the world of the physical, and that I can master both, and that he was assigned to help me. My dad was one of the beings who was going to help me find my spiritual path."

Lori wants people to know that psychics and mediums are here to help others. "We need to get that message out. We are not special. I love that I have these abilities and I'm grateful for them, but there are other people with these abilities, and people need to know that. God didn't just make one of us – there are many others with these abilities, and we are here because we're needed in my opinion.

"The world is waking up. We need to wake up to who we are and how we can make this world a better place," Lori advises. "I think that's why so many more people are open to understanding the importance of intuition, and more people are embracing psychic phenomena than ever before. I believe that it's because we really do need to change what's happening in the world. We're at a pivotal time where we need to heal our world and come together – not continuing the separation that we've seen in the past. When we learn to access these abilities, and trust it and follow this divine guidance, we can fulfill our highest destiny."

LORENZO MARION

The son of a Sicilian mother and an African American father, Lorenzo Marion was fortunate to receive support from his family as he explored his intuitive gifts. Lorenzo is a psychic medium and spiritual teacher who resides in Port Charlotte, Florida, where he gives readings to clients and teaches classes and workshops about spiritual development. In addition to his work as a intuitive, Lorenzo hosts a radio show called **Spiritual Insight** *on I Heart Radio, and he is the author of two books,* **A Journey Through a Psychic's Eyes** *and* **Messages Beyond the Grave.**

When reading a client, Lorenzo quickly gets to the point and provides spiritual insights in a clear and refreshing manner. He believes that each one of us is here to learn, and that "nothing in life that happens to us is random, we are the authors of our own script." Lorenzo enjoys helping people see the big picture, and he guides them toward the right path to fulfill their soul's purpose.

Lorenzo was an ordinary kid who enjoyed playing with his friends and having fun. But when Lorenzo was six years old, he had a profound spiritual experience that made him aware of his intuitive ability. "One night, I was in my bedroom but I couldn't go to sleep, and I heard my father speaking out loud to someone, but I didn't hear anyone respond back," recalls Lorenzo.

"So, being a curious kid, I crept down the hallway and I looked into my parent's room. I saw my father talking to a woman in a rocking chair, who I realized was my grandmother, my dad's mom, who had passed on over twenty years before I was born. She turned around and looked at me, and then I went back to bed. A few days later, my dad spoke to me and confirmed that he was talking to his dead mother, and that she visits him often, and that it was okay."

Although Lorenzo was somewhat surprised by the incident, he wasn't frightened by what he saw. "My grandmother died from uterine cancer when she was just thirty-three years old. My father was only nine when she died," explains Lorenzo. "That night, I saw her clear as day sitting in the rocking chair, but there was this beautiful soft golden white light that glowed around her. She just looked at me and smiled. Children and animals are the most psychic beings on the planet, so I wasn't thinking, 'Oh my God, oh my God!' It felt natural to me because, at that age, I thought everybody could see what I saw."

When Lorenzo was eleven, he began to realize that he was different, and that other people didn't always see what he was seeing. "One night, I was watching TV with my mom, my stepdad and my siblings, and I saw a man walk into the room," Lorenzo remembers. "He was a young Caucasian man in his thirties, who was tall and slender, with dark hair and dark eyes. He just walked into the room and walked out. And I said, 'Who was that man?' I was very adamant about seeing him. But everyone in the room looked at me and said that they didn't see or hear anyone or anything. That was the very first moment that I knew I was different. After that, my psychic ability really opened up, and I began randomly seeing and hearing spirits every day."

Even though Lorenzo knew that he had a strong intuitive ability, he chose not to use his gifts to help him have an advantage in the classroom. "I didn't use my intuitive ability to give me an edge at school. It's not for us to use for ourselves, it's for us to give out to other people," says Lorenzo. "There are no free lunches. I didn't read myself. But when I turned thirteen and was in middle school, I started getting my hands on every book that I could about metaphysics, astrology, reincarnation, dream interpretation, numerology and other spiritual subjects. I knew I was different, but I didn't tell anyone that I had this gift until I got into high school."

When Lorenzo was in the ninth grade, his intuitive and clairvoyant abilities opened up more than ever before. "I'd walk through the hallways at school, and I'd feel someone's depression. I would feel that they had a sick stomach. Or I would see that someone's parents were getting divorced, or that there was a death in the family," Lorenzo says. "It was overwhelming. So I learned how to put the protection of the Holy Spirit around me, and to call on the angels that were around me."

One night, when Lorenzo was sleeping over with some other boys at a friend's house, his intuitive insights just came pouring out. "We were staying up late, and all of a sudden I looked at one of my friends, Frank, and I started talking about his dad," Lorenzo remembers. "His parents were divorced, which Frank never discussed, and I talked about his dad's new girlfriend, and that they had moved far away from Frank, and I described his dad's new girlfriend. I even talked about some health problems that his dad was having that I was concerned about. That's when my intuitive ability was 'out of the bag,' and everybody in the school knew that I was psychic."

Fortunately, instead of being bullied by his peers as other young intuitives often are, Lorenzo's abilities were embraced by his friends. "They started asking me for psychic readings, and I would do readings for my friends, and for friends of friends. Thank God I wasn't looked at as some kind of freak. It was actually the opposite. My ability was accepted. I was never bullied.

"I think it was my personality too," continues Lorenzo. "I always had a lot of friends. I was very outgoing. I was friends with everybody, not just one social group. You know how everybody has their own little clicks in school? I didn't. Everybody knew me and they just kind of embraced my psychic ability. In fact, they thought it was exciting. To be honest, I still didn't know what I was doing. I just did it."

In addition to reading his friends and classmates, Lorenzo's teachers often asked him for readings between classes, and would reward him with late passes. "I remember reading my social studies teacher. I told her that she was going to marry a fireman and have a baby," says Lorenzo. "I remember being in the classroom with her, and the bell rang and I had to get to my next class, and my teacher gave me a late pass to excuse me from being late for my next class. I found out a year and a half later that she did marry a fireman and they had a baby boy. So what I predicted came true."

After Lorenzo graduated from high school, he went to a trade school to become an audio recording engineer. He worked in audio recording for a year, but then decided to work in the education field instead, and he took a job at the Boys and Girls Club as a supervisor. Lorenzo eventually worked with autistic children and, after that job, he relocated from Long Island, New York to Florida, where he became the director of an after school program at an elementary school.

"I was doing psychic readings during the whole time I worked in education, but I didn't realize that doing readings could actually be a career for me. Finally, after seven years of working in education and doing readings on the side, I quit my job and started doing readings full time. All of my clients came to me through word of mouth. In addition to doing private readings for clients, I was invited to do readings on cruise lines, at corporate events and at dinner parties. And I've been reading full time ever since."

Recently, Lorenzo opened his own spiritual center called *The Souls Journey,* where he conducts seminars and classes on spiritual development. "I've always wanted to have one place where I could do readings and teach others how to enhance their own intuitive ability," says Lorenzo. In addition to running his spiritual center, Lorenzo hosts a radio show on I Heart Radio called *Spiritual Insight.* "We talk about spiritual topics and I do live phone readings for people who call in. It's a great way to reach people and to help them."

Although Lorenzo is now an openly gay man, when he came out at the age of twenty-one, there were some challenges. "A friend of mine always laughs because I came into this life with so many diversities," says Lorenzo. "I'm biracial, with a black father and a Caucasian mother. I'm psychic, and on top of that, I'm also a medium. And then I came out as a gay man, so I had to deal with that, which was not easy, especially in the African American community, where it's a double-edged sword to be gay. But I use all of this to help other people, because I can share my story with people who are questioning their sexuality, are mistreated because of their ethnicity, and who thought they were crazy because they had psychic abilities."

In 2014, Lorenzo created a group called *Extraordinary Kids*, which offers group sessions for children who are highly gifted in some way: psychically, musically, athletically, and academically. "I started *Extraordinary Kids* because a lot of parents of gifted kids were calling me and asking for advice on how to help their children. Often times, gifted kids feel isolated from other children and even their parents, because they don't know how to relate to their child's gift. So we offer meditations, seminars and activities that help these kids relate to other young people who are gifted, so that they finally feel that they fit in with other kids."

Lorenzo wants people to realize that life is just a temporary state, and that we're here primarily to enrich our soul. "What I've discovered from my communication with the afterlife is that our soul is only here for a very brief time, and that life is just a school for our soul to learn and to evolve, so we need to make the most of our human experience," Lorenzo says. "The afterlife is our real home. We will all be together again after we pass from the physical plane, and the important thing to remember when we're here is that we should love one another and not judge each other in this lifetime."

PETER MARKS

Peter Marks spent 25 years as a television producer. Today, he is a Connecticut-based psychic medium who is also an astrologer. He does readings for a wide variety of people, including celebrities, from all over the world, and he's a regular guest on the "Joyce Barrie and Friends" radio show on Blog Talk Radio. Peter was also a clinical mentor and an advisor for children with autism and their families. When Peter was working with an autistic teenager named Robert, who was living in a dysfunctional home, he decided to adopt Robert who, in Peter's words, he "absolutely adores."

During our reading, Peter spoke about wonderful events that were going to happen for us in the coming year, but he also correctly picked up on more mundane issues, including the fact that our basement had recently flooded and that there was a small leak in our roof that we were in the process of repairing. While Peter is primarily a psychic, he also has mediumship abilities, and a client's loved ones will occasionally come through, during a reading, to deliver an important message.

When Peter was eleven years old, his paternal grandmother died, and something unusual happened on the night of her funeral. "I was in my bed asleep, and then I woke up and saw what appeared to be a spirit at the end of my bed," says Peter. "The spirit started to converse with me, and I realized that it was my grandmother. She told me that I was going to be doing spiritual work as I started to get older, and that I was going to help people, and that she would be available for me if I needed her help in any way. So at an early age, I recognized that I was in touch with the other side."

Instead of telling his parents about this experience, Peter kept it to himself. "I was way too nervous to say anything to my family, because I was afraid of being judged or punished," recalls Peter. "So I kept my grandmother's visit to myself." But, as jarring as the experience was, Peter wasn't too frightened. "When I first saw her, I was scared. But she had this aura of light surrounding her, and it was very bright and it made me feel very loved and safe."

Peter did not feel safe in the neighborhood where he grew up, mostly because he was constantly bullied by his neighbors and class-mates. "I had a very rough childhood, because I grew up in a work-ing class neighborhood in Palisades, New York, and we were one of the only Jewish families, so I was beaten up every day," remembers Peter. "Even though both of my parents were executives and had good jobs, my father was financially very conservative, so we lived there so that he could save money and not be in debt."

Finally, when he was in high school, Peter's family moved to a safer area, a suburb of Teaneck, New Jersey, and he was able to make friends. "My father finally felt more secure with our finances, so we moved to Teaneck, and everything was much better," Peter says. "The only thing was, I was still pretty shy because of my experi-ences growing up in Palisades. But after a few weeks, I started to make friends with the other kids."

When Peter was hanging out with his new friends, he began to have intuitive experiences about his friends that he wanted to share with them. "When I was around my friends and peers, I would pick up things about them, but I wasn't quite sure how to relay the information I was getting to them. I would pick up that someone was going to be in a car accident, or become ill, or that there was going to be a death in their family. Spirits would give me infor-mation, sometimes in physical form, and sometimes in an auditory manner."

Peter decided to tell his friends about the intuitive information he was getting. "I would bring up somebody's name to a friend and he'd say, 'Oh, that was my aunt. She died years ago.' And when my friends were talking about the different colleges they were thinking of going to, I would tell them, 'I really have the intuition that you're going to be accepted to this college,' and they would come back to me later on and be laughing and say, 'Peter, I was accepted at that college. That was a good guess!'"

Peter's friends began to tell their parents about Peter's intuitive ability, and the news was met with mixed results. "My friends in Teaneck were more educated and they were open to my abilities, so some of them told their parents about me. When their parents found out that I was psychic, they became a little nervous, and they weren't too thrilled that their child was playing with me or associating with me. But when I was alone in a room with one of these parents, they would ask me questions about their lives and what the future held for them."

When Peter was seventeen, he decided to ask his parents about his intuitive gift. "I said something to my father, and my father said, 'Go ask your mother.' And I went to my mother, and she said, 'Talk to your grandmother.' My mom's mother was visiting us for the summer, so I went to my grandmother and I said, 'I have something to tell you,' and my grandmother's face lit up. And she said, 'I've been waiting for this!' I said, 'Nana, there's something strange with me because I'm picking up people who are talking to me, and I'm picking up images.' And my grandmother said to me, 'Sweetie, I have the same gift!' I was relieved that I wasn't the only one in our family who was gifted."

When Peter graduated from high school, he didn't really want to go to college, but both his parents and his guides insisted that he get a college degree. "My parents gave me two options, either to attend college or leave their house," recalls Peter. "And my guides were telling me that I had to go to college because I would be using my gift to help people in the future, and that college would enable me to relate to my future clients, who were mostly college educated."

Peter decided to go to the same college his older sister was attending. "My sister was enrolled at Ramapo College in New Jersey, which is one of the top public colleges in the eastern United States," explains Peter. "It turned out to be one of the best educational experiences of my life. I majored in sociology, psychology and business, partly because my guides told me that studying those subjects would benefit me in the future."

After he graduated from college, Peter's guides told him to turn on the radio and listen to the *John Gambling Show.* "There was a famous psychic named Yolana [Bard] on the radio show and after I listened to her interview, I called her office to book a reading. The next week, I went to New York with my sister to meet with Yolana, and I handed her pictures of my family. She correctly named everyone in the pictures, and then she said to me, 'First, I'm going to let you know that you're going to become a very well known psychic and medium. And you'll also become a TV producer.'"

It turns out Yolana was right. Shortly after Peter had his reading with Yolana, he became friends with a man named Greg, and they decided to rent television cameras and interview local merchants for a cable show they wanted to produce, called *You The Consumer.* "Back then, we were able to secure free public access on cable, so my partner Greg and I decided to interview local business and restaurant owners and, to our surprise, everybody wanted to sign on for the publicity the show generated. And I could still do readings for clients on the side."

Peter and Greg also created a show called *Medical Magazine,* and they would charge local doctors a few thousand dollars to produce an hour long show about their medical practices. "In addition to having their video segment appear on our cable TV show, the doctors could also play the video in their offices," explains Peter. "The show was very successful, and after that we attracted the attention of PBS, and we started producing national TV shows, including *America, Coast to Coast, Matters in Life and Death with Dr. Earl Grollman,* and *Dining with Bob Lape.*"

After working as a TV producer for twenty-five years, Peter decided that he needed a career change. "My guides led me into the field of autism. They wanted me to have some experience working with kids who were autistic," says Peter, who majored in psychology in college. "I started working with a psychologist at the Division of Children and Family in Connecticut, where I was living at the time. I was placed in homes with single mothers who needed assistance with parenting their autistic children."

Peter slowly began to understand why his guides had directed him to work with autistic children. "I was placed in one home with a mother and her autistic child named Robert," Peter says. "Their home environment was totally dysfunctional, because the mother would constantly go from one bad relationship to another. She was unfit to raise him. So I adopted Robert. He was fifteen at the time, and he's twenty-six today. I adore him and would do anything for him."

Amazingly, Robert told Peter that he had selected Peter to be his father even before he came into the world. "When I met Robert, he said to me, 'Dad, I chose you to be my dad when you were living in this white split level house with a big green yard.' He was describing my childhood house, where it was located, and he even knew about the kids in the neighborhood who were bullying me," says Peter. "Robert may be autistic, but he's also psychic, because there's no way he could have known what my childhood house looked like, and about the bullies. So I do believe that he chose me to be his father."

Peter believes that everyone starts their life with a beautiful, pure and pristine soul. "The wisdom I've gained is this – when we are born, we come into this world as a perfect spiritual soul. But often, we can be sidetracked from our mission here by materialism, by a desire for money, possessions, fame and fortune. The material things that the media tells us we should value and pursue. I've learned that the true gift of living, of going through life and experiencing both the good and bad, that's the way for us to grow. And as we grow, we'll be able to become the perfect spiritual being that is part of God."

Peter continues, "My advice is to listen to the messages that your soul is giving to you. If you follow the light path of the soul and you believe in God or a higher power, you'll be protected, and you'll be much more enriched in your life. If every person expresses unconditional love without judgment, it doesn't matter if you're Buddhist, Catholic, Protestant, Lutheran, or Episcopalian, or any specific religion. Love is the true culmination of everything. We're here to learn, and to love ourselves and one another. If we share our love with others, our friends and even our enemies, we'll grow, heal ourselves and enrich the world."

LOIS T. MARTIN

Lois T. Martin is a numerologist and a spirit communicator who lives in the Catskill Mountains in upstate New York. As a child, Lois wasn't aware of her gift, but as she got older, numbers began to "speak" to her. When she does a reading, Lois only needs the person's birth date, and a flood of detailed information about that individual's life comes flowing through her.

Lois has clients all over the country, and she also does speaking engagements and gives tutorials. In addition to her intuitive work, Lois hosts two radio shows on Blog Talk Radio, "I've Got Your Number" and "Spirits Speak," where she takes phone calls from listeners and interviews other psychics and mediums.

During our reading, Lois saw a number of 22s, 11s and 8s in my numerology chart, which points to highly developed spirituality, leadership qualities and success in business. Although Lois is very spiritual, she is also a funny, down-to-earth person who delivers her clients' messages with wisdom and humor in a strong, distinct Brooklyn accent, along with much laughter.

When Lois was a child growing up in Brooklyn with her mother and older sister, she wasn't aware that she had any special intuitive abilities. "I never recognized that I had any psychic gift, and I don't know of anyone in my family who said they had a gift," says Lois. In fact, the thought of becoming a numerologist was the furthest thing from her mind in those young days. "What I find ironic is that, today my whole life is about numbers but, as a child, I failed at math. I could not do conventional math, and still can't to this day."

Lois went to grade school, middle school and high school in Brooklyn, and she lived what seemed to be a normal life. "I was a total tomboy. And I loved horses. My dream was to move out West, but that wasn't happening," recalls Lois. "I used to get feelings from time to time, intuitive feelings, but it wasn't like feelings that I get today that I recognize as the third voice coming in. My psychic abilities didn't start to take form until I was in my late twenties. That's when I started to do numerology."

After graduating from high school, Lois went to school to become a court stenographer. "I went to court stenography school, Stenotype Academy in lower Manhattan because my mom wanted to make sure I made something out of my life. And I hated it. I really disliked the system and I wanted to get out. But my mom said that I had to either work or go to school. I had no choice. So I graduated from stenography school, but I never worked as a court stenographer."

The one positive event that happened at stenography school was that Lois made friends with a fellow student, a young man who was also passionate about horses. "He was my buddy. And one day, we skipped school, and he took me to Canarsie to a horse stable that he knew about," Lois remembers. "And I saw a horse in this stall, and I decided to buy it. I'd go to the stables all the time to be with my horse."

Lois did odd jobs around the horse stable in order to get a reduced rental rate so that she could keep her horse at the stable. In addition, to make money, she babysat kids in her neighborhood, and taught guitar lessons. "I didn't really have a traditional job at that time, but I didn't really need much money. I hung out at the stables. I used to exercise the race horses and clean the stables. That was fine with me."

Eventually, Lois got married, and she and her husband performed at rodeos together all along the Eastern seaboard. "I was a barrel racer and my husband was a calf roper. I also ran summer ranch programs for kids in upstate New York. I loved working with kids and horses."

Lois's interest in intuitive ability began to increase after she moved to Long Island and became friends with a neighbor, Ken, who was an astrologer. "My next door neighbor asked me if he could teach me astrology," says Lois. "At first, I loved the personality and character of the Zodiac signs, but I couldn't do the math. I wasn't really interested in the degrees, or how far one planet was from another. I was more interested in the personality of the different signs."

As Lois continued to study astrology with her neighbor, she had her first truly spiritual experience. "I was studying the Zodiac signs and other aspects of astrology, and a voice popped into my head and said, 'Everything around you is five.' I didn't know what that meant at the time, so I asked Ken. He said, 'That's called numerology.' And I said, 'Oh, well, how can I find out about numerology?' And he suggested that I read about it, so I went to a bookstore, and I bought my first book, called *Helping Yourself with Numerology*, by Helyn Hitchcock. And opening this book opened a whole new world for me, in the understanding of numbers."

Lois became fascinated with numerology. Her new numerology book by Hitchcock became her prized possession; because she didn't want the book to get soiled, she copied its contents into a notepad that she carried with her everywhere she went. "That book was like my Bible. I wanted to keep the book safe, so I copied it into a notepad. And I read that notepad over and over again, every day."

In addition to her interest in numerology, Lois also ran summer riding ranch programs for kids at sleep-away camps, up in the Catskill Mountains. "And I would do my numerology by studying during that time. I learned from asking anyone I met, 'What's your name? What's your date of birth?' And it all started to register," says Lois.

"And as I was progressing in the study of numbers, my personal friends would say to me, 'You know, you're a psychic.' And I'd say, 'No, I'm not. I'm a numerologist.' And they would say, 'No, you're a psychic.' And I did not want to accept the word. I did not want the responsibility of being a psychic."

Lois decided to take a numerology class to find out more about her intuitive gift. "There was a wonderful woman who was in Long Island at the time, named Ellin Dodge, who is a numerologist, and I went to a numerology class that she was teaching. And she said to me, 'You will be famous.' And what did that mean to me at the time? Nothing. But Ellin did get my attention. So I just studied, and studied, and studied, and really began to hone my gift."

In order to get more experience, Lois began to do readings at local psychic fairs in Long Island, along with a number of her friends, who were intuitives. "I didn't want to be called psychic, but I felt confident that I could give good readings because I had practiced on so many people already," says Lois. "And people like John Edward and James Van Praagh were there, and we would sit at these tables and do readings. More and more I started to accept the fact that this information wasn't just coming from a book or a piece of paper – I was reading it. So I finally came to the acceptance, 'Okay, I'll be a psychic.'"

After Lois identified herself as a psychic, she began to get clear messages from her guides. "I was doing a reading, and a very distinctive voice came through to me and said, 'I will be your professor. My name is Zahkeem.'" Lois recalls. "I'll never forget the voice. I turned my head around and looked behind me thinking, 'Where did that voice come from?'

"And Zahkeem told me that he had been in life form at another time in a past life with me in France. He told me that I had to take my gift seriously, and that I could not do this for the sake of just making money. He said that I was a server, serving God and helping people. And after all this time, I read my own name and date of birth, and I learned that my mission in this life is to serve mankind. I finally understood who I was and the purpose of my life."

From that point on, Lois began to teach classes and tutorials, make public speaking appearances, write for magazines, and she was featured as a guest on cable TV and radio shows. She was even honored to be one of the first Americans to be inducted into the *Association De Numerologues* in the United Kingdom. "I was evolving. I just continued to grow and grow. And today I host two radio shows, which is a very big part of my growth. The number of callers is growing steadily, and even though each show is two hours long, the time flies by."

Lois has two basic messages she wants to share with everyone. "My guides always say to me, 'Never forget KISS – keep it sweet and simple.' And I follow that advice. Because my guides say, 'All you human beings do is to complicate everything.' When something happens, you can either laugh or cry. It's your free will. I always say, 'Your attitude is your altitude.' Listen to your inner voice. When you listen, you'll listen to the entire truth. When you hear, you'll only hear half of it."

Lois's second message has to do with faith. "It's important to never lose your faith. Hold on to your faith. Because with faith comes trust, trusting in your Creator, or God, or Buddha, or whatever you call it. And once you connect to that higher power, you'll have found your perfect alignment. An alignment of mind, body, spirit and soul. We're here to follow our soul's journey, whether you understand that or not. If you're meant to understand it, you will. If you don't, you'll learn when you go home to heaven. The afterlife is there, and it's real."

JEANNE MAYELL

Jeanne Mayell lives in Boston. She has masters' degrees from the Harvard School of Public Health and the Harvard Graduate School of Education. She also has a Masters in Counseling Psychology. In addition to her impressive degrees, Jeanne is also a gifted intuitive. In her words, she brings "an academic and intellectual rigor to the world of psychic readings and intuition training."

Jeanne has trained many people how to tune into their own intuition so that they can read for themselves and make important life decisions regarding work, family and their soul's purpose. In my personal experience with Jeanne, she did not just tell me what I wanted to hear - in fact, she told me what I needed to hear, so that I could take the appropriate path for my soul's journey in this lifetime.

As a child growing up in Massachusetts, Jeanne wasn't really aware of her intuitive gift, or thought that she was different from anyone else in that way. "I just had a knowing about things and people, but I thought that was a natural ability that other people shared. I experienced a lot of synchronicity – things would just happen at the right moment. Like I remember being a high school student, and the teacher would ask the class a question, and nobody would answer. So I felt sorry for her – and I'd just open my book at random and look down, and there would be the answer – bang, right there. But I didn't think that was weird, it seemed natural that the information would jump to me."

A straight-A student, Jeanne excelled in college. "I was raised to be straight-laced and to go to college and succeed in the academic world. So I went to U. Mass and got a bachelor's degree in English literature, and later went on to get two masters' degrees from Harvard."

After she graduated, Jeanne started working in the social services area. She eventually became the director of Medicaid in

Massachusetts. Even though Jeanne wasn't doing readings for a living yet, her abilities would sometimes come through in her work.

"The first time I realized I was channeling information was during a job interview in which my prospective boss asked for my thoughts on welfare spending," Jeanne remembers. "Even though I knew very little about the subject, I found myself telling him with great conviction that health care costs were going to go through the roof over the coming decades, and if we couldn't contain them, they would outstrip the rest of the social services budget. I foresaw that in the private sector, employers would struggle to afford the costs of health insurance and people would take jobs just for the health coverage." This incident took place in the late seventies, when health costs were not as much of an issue. Impressed by Jeanne's "knowledge" and "foresight," this prospective employer hired her.

It turned out that Jeanne was right – since that time, U.S. per capita health care costs have increased twenty-fold and have become a major issue both in social services and the private sector. "I also excelled in knowing what the public was thinking. I didn't need survey data to know. I just knew, and I was usually correct. This ability, of course, was intuitive, although I didn't think of it that way."

Even though Jeanne was aware she had been very spiritual as a child, she focused on other things until the tragic death of her first husband, a young Harvard Business School professor who took his own life just as their marriage was unraveling. "When he died, even for days after that, I was reawakened spiritually and psychically," Jeanne says. "Everything started then. I remember hearing spirit guides speaking to me – telling me how to get through it, to immerse myself in nature, the rain, the trees, how the Earth would sustain me. From that point on, I connected to the other side in a very immediate way. I felt that other dimension, and could hear spirits guiding me."

Jeanne continued working in a mainstream profession for a few more years, but her heart wasn't in it. She knew she had to find out who she really was. She quit her job, followed her inner guidance every day, and became drawn to holistic health. She met her second husband, Mark, when she began writing for *EastWest Journal*, a holistic health magazine where he was the editor. "The first time I heard his voice on the phone – we had not yet met – the sound went through me like nothing I'd ever experienced. He does have a beautiful voice," she adds, "but there was an uncanny resonance."

They married and had a baby daughter, and later a son, and Jeanne began writing for other magazines, including the *Atlantic Monthly* and *American Health*. But she soon realized that journalism wasn't quite the right work for her, and that she should follow a different career path.

Right around the time she met her first husband, Jeanne picked up a deck of Tarot cards just for fun. "I felt an instant connection, like I'd been doing this all my life. Using the cards, I felt I really knew people, even complete strangers, and could see inside them, and with such love. I was transformed when giving a reading. I carried the deck everywhere, slept with it under my pillow, and offered readings to people everywhere I went."

It wasn't long before strangers started calling Jeanne and begging for readings. In 1990, Jeanne decided to give up journalism and she started reading people full time. Her career as a professional psychic took off. "I was born to do this work," she notes. "I was put on this planet to help guide people through these times." Jeanne is good at helping people with their relationships and with decisions, but her ultimate goal is to help people wake up to their true selves.

Jeanne is especially helpful when a client is at an important turning point in his or her life. "I find that I get brought in for these moments of insight that are critical to a person's whole life. And I want people to understand that having a successful reading is a collaborative process. It has to do with how open the person is – if the client is receptive, then there's a synchronicity that happens and the information that I impart is meant to come out at that time. Those are the most gratifying moments."

Regarding the future, Jeanne feels that a new order is arising in the world.

"For people to adapt and thrive in the new world, it's important for each of us to know who we truly are. For that, we must strip away who we were trained to be by an old order that sacrificed our connection to our selves. The old order has brought about the unraveling of the world's living systems. So it's essential that we get in tune with our own psychic and intuitive ability to adapt and even thrive."

Jeanne explains, "For the past 35 years, I've known that climate change was on the way, and that we needed to be more proactive if we want to survive as a species. Lately, this shift is speeding up, and there's a 'surge' coming. The surge is both in the climate and in our collective conscience. In 1985, I had a vision of young urban professionals migrating *en masse* out of New York City, people in suits and carrying backpacks, walking north. I saw them searching for refuge on higher ground."

Initially, this vision confused Jeanne. "I used to wonder if what I was seeing was a metaphor for finding a new kind of life, and now I realize it is a both a metaphor for living a more purposeful life, and this need is sparked by dramatic Earth changes. I don't see the world ending, but we are facing the greatest shift since the dawn of civilization. And now climatologists' projections are beginning to match the visions psychics have had for decades."

Jeanne wants people to know that any issue that compels them to get a reading is a worthy one. "No issue is too small, if it bothers people enough to seek intuitive guidance. Whatever a gifted intuitive can do to help you become more whole will ultimately help your soul and the entire planet."

JOANNA GARFI McNALLY

JoAnna Garfi McNally is an intuitive communicator who lives in upstate New York with her wife, Adrienne, and their four dogs. In addition to doing readings for clients throughout the U.S. and Canada, she teaches classes in meditation and psychic development, and is also a certified hypnotherapist. JoAnna comes from a long line of psychics, including her mother.

Although JoAnna has had intuitive abilities since she was a child, she learned that she had to keep her gift to herself, especially when she was around her classmates in the Catholic grade school and public high school she attended. JoAnna has a welcoming, easy to understand way of conveying information that puts people at ease and gives them a clear picture of the future.

When JoAnna was just four years old, she had her first strong intuitive experience, and the premonition she had may well have saved her younger brother from great harm. "I was lying on the bed next to my little brother, and we were watching TV," JoAnna recalls. "I saw this shadow above us, and it was coming down, so I rolled my brother over on the bed for God knows what reason, and then the ceiling came crashing down. It was like I saw the ceiling coming down before it actually happened. And my mother came in and asked what happened, and I told her that I knew that the ceiling was going to come down somehow, and I rolled my brother over to protect him. That was my first memory of my psychic ability."

JoAnna's family was supportive of her intuitive gifts, primarily because many of her family members, including her mother, her aunt and her cousin, were psychics. "My mom told me that when I was very little, around the age of two, I would sit and talk to someone every day for a whole hour, usually around three o'clock in the afternoon. She said that I was definitely having a conversation with someone, and that I would have these hour-long conversations every day for a whole year. I'm not sure who I was talking to. Today, I realize that I was communicating with my spirit guides."

When JoAnna started going to a Catholic elementary school, her intuitive abilities often caused her problems with her classmates. "I had this feeling that there was way more to everything than what I was being taught in Catholic school," says JoAnna. "I would sense things that happened in school ahead of time, and I would tell the other kids, and they'd look at me like I was crazy. But I considered myself to be a messenger. It was like all of a sudden I'd pick up on something, and my mouth went into gear. I couldn't stop it. And I would go home crying because the kids were making fun of me, and bullying me, and calling me weird, insulting names."

JoAnna also had problems with some of her teachers. "Another reason why I was having a hard time at school was because sometimes I would go off to who knows where, picking up all of this energy, and I guess the teacher would think that I was a scatterbrain, not paying attention in class. My mother would have to go to the school and talk to my teachers, but she couldn't explain it to them, or tell them, 'Well, my daughter has this psychic ability.' They wouldn't understand. So my mother would just have arguments at school with the teachers. It wasn't easy."

JoAnna struggled to fit in at the Catholic school she attended, but the experience was very difficult for her. "We had very strict nuns as our teachers, and I remember thinking, 'How long do I have to put up with this game?' They tried to teach us that God was going to punish us if we didn't behave, but I knew intuitively that God was a loving God. God was not mean. But I had to put up with what they were telling me, just to get by. Even though I acted like I was listening, I really wasn't listening. I wouldn't pay attention."

One night, JoAnna had an out of body experience where she saw Jesus and Mary, the Blessed Mother. "It was liked I popped out of my body. I knew it was a spiritual experience, because I was talking to Mary and Jesus," she says. "And I asked them, 'Why do I have to go back? Why can't I stay here with you?' I remember how peaceful and loving everything felt. And I remember them saying that

I have to go back, because there's a lot of work for me to do. The next thing I knew, I popped back into my body. I could actually feel myself popping back in. And I opened my eyes and started to cry."

JoAnna graduated from high school, and she went to school to become a dental assistant. After she got her degree, she worked for a dentist for several years, but even though she had a steady job, JoAnna's interest in the paranormal continued to grow.

"I began to read about Edgar Cayce, and I studied transcendental meditation, which really opened up my psychic abilities," says JoAnna. "Then I met a man named Russell Arnold who did Silva Mind Control, and he taught me more about Edgar Cayce, and how to scan inside a person's body to help heal them. Russell was also a hypnotist, and he used hypnosis to show me how to scan inside a person's body and see what was wrong with them physically, and to help that person heal themselves. When I'm in a hypnotic state, I can use light energy to actually repair what's wrong in their body. And the person I'm working on often tells me that they can feel an energy inside of them. They describe it as a tickling feeling."

JoAnna started to do healing work with Russell, and they were able to help some individuals who were seriously ill. "There was a fourteen-year-old boy named Michael who had been stung by a jellyfish in the ocean, and he had a severe allergic reaction that damaged his kidneys and almost killed him," remembers JoAnna. "His kidneys were so impaired that, if he survived, he would have to be on dialysis to stay alive. So Russell and I worked with Michael, and we taught him how to visualize that he could heal himself. We told him to look inside his body like Pac-Man – to visualize the good Pac-Man and the bad Pac-Man in his kidneys, and to go inside his body and attack the bad Pac-Mans by using the good Pac-Mans to heal himself."

After a month of healing sessions with Russell and JoAnna, where they continued to encourage Michael to use the Pac-Man visualizations, Michael was totally healed. "The doctors were in awe. They couldn't figure out how Michael got well," says JoAnna. "To this day, Michael's mom says that, if it wasn't for our healing techniques, she knows that her son wouldn't be with us. Michael is a grown man now. He lives in Virginia and is a holistic chiropractor. He said that he had decided to become a healer so that he could give back to humanity, and heal others as he had been healed."

JoAnna and Russell began to hold weekly meetings in JoAnna's home to discuss healing, reincarnation and other topics and, due to the growing popularity of these meetings, they decided to open their own school for healing. "We started a nonprofit metaphysical foundation called Metaphysical Concepts, and we opened an office in Fort Salonga, New York," JoAnna says, "We, along with other teachers we enlisted, taught classes about healing, past life regressions, reincarnation, astrology, numerology and meditation. Since it was a nonprofit, we didn't make a lot of money, so we did psychic readings on the side. Eventually, Russell died and our metaphysical school closed. But I'm still very busy doing readings and metaphysical work today."

JoAnna wants to let people know that they can choose their own destinies, just by believing in themselves, and letting go of emotional drama. "People don't have to suffer. They don't have to be in pain. They don't have to be angry," maintains JoAnna. "They can change all of that, if they can just open up and see the opportunities we all have, to change our lives for the better. We all need to listen to our intuition and to believe in ourselves. And one way to do this is to meditate daily, and call on your angels and spirit guides for guidance. Just ask for assistance. They're always with you."

Because she was bullied in school, JoAnna also wants to tell the parents of intuitive children that it's important to support and protect these gifted children. "Many children born today have strong intuitive abilities. And if your child has imaginary friends, or is having psychic experiences, let him or her have those experiences and your support. Let your children have their imaginary friends. Work with them. Help them. These kids are often bullied, and it's really frustrating for them. We need to nurture and support intuitive and spiritual children. With our support, we can keep their souls strong and their hearts soft, so that they can go on to do what they're meant to do on this planet – to help other people find their spiritual path."

NANCY MYER

Nancy Myer lives in Latrobe, PA, just outside of Pittsburgh, with her black lab, Herbie. She has assisted police in the investigations of almost 900 homicides... and counting. She has provided information that has helped officers solve cases, and her tips have proved to be correct about 90% of the time. Nancy has been featured on Court TV's **Psychic Detective** *and ET's* **Psychic Investigators.** *She is the author of* **Silent Witness: The True Story of a Psychic Detective.** *Her new book,* **Travels with My Father: Life, Death, and a Psychic Detective,** *was released in the fall of 2015.*

Nancy has a master's degree in writing from Seton Hall University. She has completed everything but her dissertation for her doctorate in education from the University of Phoenix, and she is currently a part-time faculty member at a community college in her area. Nancy is one of the first psychics I had a reading with, and her accuracy is astonishing and often a bit overwhelming.

When she was a child, Nancy Myer just knew when things were about to happen. She had visions, saw ghosts, and was able to predict deaths quite accurately. Although her family didn't discuss Nancy's gift, they knew they could ask a question and get the right answer.

"My grandfather's family was in horse racing and training, and he discovered that if he took me to the paddock ahead of time, I could tell him which horse was going to win the race," remembers Nancy. "My mom and dad just accepted this ability as a natural thing – they didn't make a big deal out of it, which was a good thing, because that allowed me to feel normal as a child."

Nancy's father was a specialist in the United States Foreign Service, and her family moved to a different country every two years. When she was five, Nancy's family moved to Brazil, and most Brazilians didn't speak English. "I remember trying to talk to a man at the airport in Brazil, but I didn't understand a word he was saying. Suddenly, in my frustration to understand him, I began to feel the images of what he was thinking in his mind, so I understood what he was saying. He realized that I was reading his mind, and got really spooked by it."

When Nancy and her family were living in Chile, a gypsy king who ruled over gypsies in the Chillán region of Chile, came up to her and told her she had a psychic gift. "He told me that I had all these stars around my head and that I had the gift of precognition and a healing ability. I was eight, and here he was telling me that I would work with people all over the world, helping them to solve murder cases. I was scared, but obviously he was quite accurate."

Nancy's intuitive ability was a big help to her in elementary school. "I'm severely dyslexic, so I'd use my psychic ability to get answers when I couldn't figure something out logically. And if I was stumped on a question when I was taking a test, I could look at the teacher and somehow the answer would just pop into my head. I always knew what grade I was going to get in my classes before getting a report card."

Unlike many psychics, who are often maligned by their parents and siblings because of their intuitive gifts, Nancy's parents embraced her gift and helped to nurture her abilities. "My dad worked in agriculture and animal husbandry for the U.S. Foreign Service, so he would often take me out to the farm to help him with animals that were sick," explains Nancy. "I could put my hands on an animal and feel where the pain was and what was wrong, so my dad could treat them and make them better."

One time, when Nancy was a teenager, she remembers asking her dad why she could tell when things were about to happen when other people couldn't. "He said that only a few people had that skill – he didn't use the work psychic – and that he had it, too, although my abilities were far greater than his. He also warned me not to talk about it because people often didn't react well to this ability."

Nancy graduated from high school and went on to college, where she studied English and Spanish. She married her boyfriend when she was a freshman in college and had three children – two boys and a girl. She started to work on her master's degree in Spanish, but put it on hold to take care of the children. After 15 years of marriage, she got divorced, and needed to make a living.

"I was doing readings for people for free in my house," recalls Nancy. "I finally started setting up actual appointments and charging the people I was reading, so that they wouldn't hang around all day, and I could have time for my family. That's how I got started doing readings for a living."

When Nancy does a reading, the information usually comes in through direct telepathy, or mind to mind contact. "I get information visually, through auditory sounds, smells, sensations – the whole gamut. If somebody wants information – such as finding a new location for their business – I have them give me the addresses of the properties they're looking at, and I range (see psychically) those properties to see which ones have a good energy for business, or not. People forget to consider that the Earth has its own energy, and that there are some places that – I don't care what kind of business you put in them – it will just fail, because the energy underneath that business is bad."

Nancy's gift for giving accurate psychic readings was eventually discovered by police departments and law enforcement agencies across the country, and she became a valuable resource for detectives who were trying to solve murder cases.

"Initially, they don't believe a word I say, but when I tell them intimate details about their case – details that have never been released publicly – then they come around," Nancy says. "I either scare the crap out of them or they say, 'Well, cool – this is the neatest law enforcement tool I've ever run into!' A lot of the guys are a little bit afraid of me, but they'll still use me to solve a case. Because good cops will try anything to solve a case – that's just the reality.

"You know, people are always critical of them, but I've seen detectives work around the clock trying to solve a missing child or murder case that's bothering them. And you know, just give of themselves in a way very few human beings ever would. It's impressive to me how hard these guys will work to solve one of these cases."

According to Nancy, finding a missing child is one of the most gratifying experiences of her career as a psychic detective.

"Occasionally, I've retrieved some runaways, or found a child who was missing as a result of a custody snatch. It's awesome! It's happy dance time! This child doesn't end up dead because we found them – we found them alive. Because a lot of missing children are found after they're already dead. So finding a child who's still alive is the best – it's a wonderful feeling – I love that!"

Nancy has some positive predictions for the future. "Despite all the negative talk out there, I have faith in the United States and I believe that our economy will rebound. Part of the reason that it will improve is because the 'Made in America' movement will pick up strength. This will help bring jobs back to the U.S. And the improvement in the quality of products made here will make buyers more willing to pay a little extra to get them."

Regarding recent shootings of innocent people by mentally disturbed individuals, Nancy feels that there will be legal changes that will protect all of us. "Changes will be made to laws that will allow family members to help their mentally disturbed, dangerous relatives get the mental health treatments they need in cases where they may otherwise become a threat to themselves, their families, or society in general. These changes will help save the lives of these mentally challenged adults and other people they might assault or harm."

And Nancy believes that there will be a new tax structure that will level the playing field between the rich, the middle class and the disadvantaged. "There will be something in the new process to prevent the wealthy from avoiding paying their fair share of taxes by shipping their resources overseas. This will involve some way of taxing at the source of the income, regardless of where the person who owns the business is living. So wealthy people will now have to pay their fair share."

According to Nancy, most people are intuitive, but very few people are highly gifted psychics. "I believe that psychic ability is a natural human trait that many people have a little of, and a few people have an overdose of it. Very few people have the full dose of it, and that's what can cause trouble. The true psychic with enough ability to do the work legitimately is quite rare. I truly wish this were not so, but, unfortunately, it is."

Nancy continues, "I believe that this ability is part of our survival instincts that used to be more accessible before the misuse of logic caused society to become so critical as to squash the truth out of existence. As we evolve, it seems to me that our senses give us more information, but most people discount it or think that they're crazy. In reacting this way, they ignore their psychic input and miss out on it. This ability has a place in life, and we need to learn how to use it more effectively and to use it wisely. This skill, where it actually exists, is real and useful and we need to pay attention to it."

JACK OLMEDA

Jack Olmeda is one of the most likable guys you could ever meet, and he's also a very gifted intuitive who has a special talent for reading and identifying medical issues. Jack has never advertised - all of his steady stream of loyal clients come to him through word of mouth. In addition to doing readings, Jack has often had a day job - as a banker, an accountant and more recently as a production sched-uler at a major TV network in New York City. Jack often uses Tarot cards - but his readings are based on what he sees, not the literal meaning of the cards.

Jack Olmeda discovered that he had intuitive abilities when he was about ten. "Things would just come into my mind, I would know things. My mother was very psychic. Once she went to a spiritualist who told her that I would be doing this someday, but she didn't tell me that until later in my life."

Jack began attending local spiritualist meetings with his cousin Olga, who was also very gifted, and Olga's husband at the time, a spiritualist who took Jack under his wing. "He said that I had a lot of potential, and he took me on as a student."

Jack eventually went his own way. One day, his parents were playing cards, and Jack picked up the cards and discovered that he could use them to tune into the psychic communications he was getting. "I noticed that I was able to tune in a lot faster with the cards. So I used them as a form of focus. These were regular cards. I had heard about Tarot cards. I never studied the Tarot, but I bought a deck at the age of fifteen and started using them because people really liked Tarot readings."

Throughout his teen years, Jack did readings for friends and family for free, but at the age of twenty he decided that things must change. "I was reading a lot of people that I didn't even know that well. I thought, 'I might as well charge for my readings because they take a lot of my time.' I didn't want to charge initially because I was born and raised Catholic and I felt that this was a gift from God. But the readings were taking as much time as having a regular job, so I decided to charge, even though I felt guilty for doing so in the beginning."

Although both Jack's parents had strong intuitive abilities, they didn't talk about it – especially Jack's father. "My father said he didn't believe in it, and that I shouldn't do readings because it could lead to constant headaches, and that I would be carrying around other people's problems. Meanwhile, after a couple of years, my father started asking me for readings. I think he came to accept that it was a good thing."

Even though Jack was a gifted psychic, he tried to pursue a normal life, going to college and getting a degree. "I went to Queen's College and got a degree in computers and business administration." After college, Jack married his wife, Janet, and went to work at Manufacturers Hanover Trust, where he trained to become an officer of the bank. He tried to focus on his job, but people continued to call and ask him for readings. Finally, after three years of marriage and the birth of his son, Jack decided to quit doing readings.

"I was being pulled to do psychic readings more and more, and I just didn't want to do it anymore. I was young, having fun, living my life, and being psychic was almost a hindrance in my life. And I noticed that I was picking up a lot of people's illnesses, and I would feel them – like getting a pain in my shoulder or neck – but once I told the person who had the illness about it, the pain went away from my body. So I said that I wasn't going to do this anymore."

Then one day, Jack suffered a near death experience that changed his life and brought him back to giving readings. "All of a sudden, I felt sick one night and I couldn't breathe right, but I went to work anyway the next day," Jack remembers. "But my co-workers said, 'Jack, you look like death – go to the doctor.' So I went to the hospital and my doctor took an x-ray, and I'll never forget this – I saw my doctor and his nurses running around like crazy, and I thought, 'Whoever they're running after, they must be dying or something.' And then they said, 'There you are, Mr. Olmeda,' and I realized I was the one they were looking for. I got weak in the knees and the nurses were holding me up, and my doctor said, 'One of your lungs is one-hundred per cent collapsed – we don't know how you're walking.'"

The doctor admitted Jack and inserted a tube into his chest to inflate his lung, which hurt tremendously because the patient has to be awake during the procedure. "It was very painful, and I ended up getting an infection, so they kept me in the hospital for awhile. During that time, I kept seeing this angel by my bed, and I thought 'This is it, I guess I'm going to die.' But the angel kept saying 'You need to follow the path, you need to follow the path.' So after I got better, I got more involved with medical intuitiveness and medium-ship, and did more readings."

Jack eventually got a job as a production scheduler at a major network, CBS, in New York City, and he and his wife Janet had two more children. They were now a family of five. In spite of his full schedule at work and at home, Jack continued to do readings for clients, friends and colleagues. "The people I work with are open-minded and accept me. A lot of my co-workers ask me about the three-digit lottery number. Sometimes I give it to them and they do hit, but I try not to use this ability to gamble."

Once, Jack had a dream, and his mother came to him. Jack asked his mother for a lottery number, but she didn't give him an actual number. "So I thought, well, I dreamt about my mother, so I'll play her birthday, which was March 17 – 317. I got busy and didn't play the number. So, wouldn't you know – that number came up that Saturday! And I was really upset, but I heard my mother say 'Play it again, play it again!' But I thought, there's no way the same number is going to come up two days in a row, so I didn't play it. Guess what? That same number came up again! I should have listened to my mother!"

Although Jack is highly gifted intuitive, he also has had a long career as a TV production scheduler. "It's like I have two lives, you know what I mean?" Jack says. "Because I'm able to separate; there are a lot of psychics who are not able to separate, they live that way all their life, 24/7. I don't. It's when I sit down and I know I'm going to do a reading, that's when my psychic ability really opens. I'm not on 24/7 like most psychics are. Unless I know that there's a message that I'm supposed to give that person – then it will come to me and I will tell them."

He continues, "A lot of times, I could be just talking with someone, and I would say, 'Yeah, and you should be careful about your back,' and then I'd just keep talking as if that was just part of our conversation. And I wouldn't even realize that I'd said that. And it's happened many, many other times. It just comes out of the blue."

As a medical intuitive, Jack has correctly diagnosed ovarian cancer, lung cancer and many other physical ailments. Thanks to his readings, many of Jack's clients have scheduled visits to the doctor in time to save their lives.

"I've had readings with clients who had just been to the doctor and gotten a clean bill of health. But I would see that something was wrong – say in their ovaries, for example – and send them back for another checkup. One woman I read did end up having ovarian cancer – and she had just had her annual gynecological appointment. If she had waited another year, she might not be alive today."

One of the aspects of being intuitive Jack enjoys is his ability to warn people about future events that they can control. "What I like about most of my readings is that I'm able to predict future things that can be changed. They're warnings – a lot of times, they're warnings. I will tell them, 'Be careful about such and such.' And a lot of times they'll come to me and say, 'I didn't pay attention to you, and this happened. I had a chance to change things, and I decided not to change it, and then I remember that you told me that I should go this way.' So it's more about giving warnings to people, a lot of the future stuff is warnings. But you can lead a horse to water, but you can't make him drink."

Jack likes being able to illuminate the best direction for people to take, especially young people. "I'm able to guide people, to lead them the right way. That's why I like to read young people who are starting their lives. I'll tell them, 'You need to finish school, or this and that.' I love giving that type of advice to kids, meaning people in their late teens and early twenties, so that I can help them start off on the right path. It's one of the best things I can do with this ability – to help show them the way to their best future."

LYN POPPER

Lyn Popper, who is originally from Australia, now resides in Southern California with her family. An extraordinarily gifted intuitive, she is highly accurate, and can see the future in great detail.

Lyn is one of the most amazing psychics I've had the pleasure of meeting and experiencing. She is professional, quick and absolutely certain of what she is seeing. I was truly blown away by my reading with Lyn and am glad that she's sharing her gift with others.

When Lyn was little, she had imaginary friends, just as many children do. However, Lyn felt that her friends were real. "I could tap into a place that a lot of people can't. There was this in-between world where I could talk to my friends, and there was no time, and we had long conversations."

Lyn's mother, an Australian of Irish decent, supported Lyn's intuitive abilities as she grew up, but her father was mostly disinterested. "My mother called my abilities 'fey' – which is what Irish people called having the ability to see the future, and she was very in tune and had a great sense of humor and really encouraged me. I learned at an early age to keep things quiet – especially when I went to school – especially when it was a Catholic school."

Lyn's earliest intuitive memory happened while she was sitting on the lap of her great grandmother. "She was alive and well, but I saw 'beings' calling to her," says Lyn. "They were happy beings. Then I waved goodbye to my great grandmother because I knew she was leaving. My mother heard me saying, 'Goodbye, Grandy' over and over, so she came into the room to see what was happening. I was still sitting on my great grandmother's lap, but she was dead. My mother whisked me away, but I kept telling her that my Grandy was okay."

As she was growing up, Lyn's psychic ability protected her from some difficult situations. "One day, I told my mother that I wanted to go to my friend's house for a sleepover. My mother asked me why I wanted to leave because I didn't usually go to sleepovers. I told her that I knew that I had to leave because there was going to be chaos in our house that evening."

Lyn's mother let her go, knowing that Lyn was psychic and that she probably had good reason to leave. The next day, when Lyn went back home, she found out that there had indeed been trouble at her house the night before.

"A family friend came over at eleven p.m., because her husband was being abusive to her," Lyn remembers. "Her husband followed her to our home, and my father and her husband got into a fight. My mother laughed when she told me this and said 'I wish I would have gone with you last night!'"

Later on, when Lyn was working as a TV director's assistant, her intuitive gift saved her life. "I was working on an aviation show. During a break, a colleague asked me to take a glider flight with him. Normally, I would have gone because I'm an adventurous person. But I had a very strong feeling that I shouldn't go, so I said no and urged my colleague not to go. My co-workers said, 'Don't be ridiculous,' but I still didn't get on that plane. Unfortunately, the plane crashed and my colleagues were killed."

Like her mother, Lyn's relatives thought it was wonderful that she had gifted – but they thought of ways to make it pay off. "When I was about twelve, they took me to the horse races and asked me which horse is going to win. At the time, I didn't realize that this was something that I wasn't supposed to do. But I got every horse right – yes I did! I don't do that now – I use my ability to guide and help people."

Lyn had another experience involving a game of chance when she was an adult. She and her husband were on a cruise ship on vacation, and when they happened to walk past the roulette wheel, Lyn said that the number 28 was going to come up – not once, but twice in a row. The man spun the wheel, and the number 28 came up.

"We were amazed," Lyn says. "Then I said to my husband, 'It's going to come up again,' and the dealer said, 'No way,' and we

your unconscious can guide people and help them get some clarity about whatever is going on in their lives. Understanding more about one's past lives and what one's purpose may be in this life can be a great comfort."

Lyn feels strongly that a gifted intuitive "is only a messenger. Some psychics add their own slant on what they hear or see, which I feel is dangerous. Psychics aren't here to explain the 'why' about what we see or hear; we are here only to pass on information. Also, we're not here to tell our clients what to do. It's up to the client to hear what we have to tell them, and to make their own decisions."

When Lyn does a reading, she says that the future is no different from the past. "The information that I get comes from what I call the 'no place in time' zone. Psychics can tap into this dimension and tell our clients what we see or hear. Most of my clients tell me that the information I get and pass on to them gives them comfort and hope, and much more insight into their lives."

BRETT SAN ANTONIO

Brett San Antonio had his first intuitive experiences around the age of seven or eight, but he was overwhelmed and confused about these intuitive events. Brett continued to struggle with his gift as he progressed through high school and college, where he earned a master's degree in psychology. He held a number of different jobs, including work as an elementary school teacher, a mental health counselor, and a hairstylist. Eventually, after travelling the world with his partner, he began to embrace his psychic abilities and started doing readings for clients full time.

During my reading with Brett, he picked up on loved ones who had passed, and he clarified my role in life and the mission I was embarking upon. Talking with Brett is a lovely experience, because he approaches his readings with a deep understanding of his client's spiritual direction, purpose and needs. His empathy is palpable, and it's clear that his overriding mission in life is to be of service to others.

When Brett was about seven years old, he would wake up in the night and have his first intuitive experiences, and they terrified him. "It wasn't like these angels came down into my room, or these nonphysical entities, or people that I didn't know were coming towards me," recalls Brett. "It was that I could feel the room breathing. I could hear this middle to high tone of a noise, and everything around me was just breathing. Everything would move and I would see shadows in the room and I didn't understand what it was. I was a very anxious child. I was very overwhelmed by anxiety and it was very psychologically, physically, and emotionally draining."

For the next few years, until Brett was 12, he couldn't be alone at night, and he often slept in his mother's room. "This would happen a few times a week, and I was always afraid to go to sleep. I didn't like going to sleep. I didn't like the nighttime at all," says Brett. "It wasn't like anyone was communicating with me from the other side. I didn't hear voices or see my dead grandfather. It was different. I could feel everything as if I was a part of everything, and it was all breathing around me and flowing through me and into me. I had a lot of experiences in my room with strange things around me that I didn't understand, and it made me very anxious."

In response to Brett's unusual night time experiences and resulting anxiety, his mother decided to take him to a therapist. "That's when everyone started to look at this in psychological terms," Brett remembers. "They did a lot of different psychological tests on me, and psychiatrists were checking these tests to make sure that I wasn't having some sort of psychological issue that caused my anxiety. But I always knew that this was much more than just a kid having a mental health problem."

Brett continued to go to his therapy sessions, but they weren't very helpful, partially because he stopped communicating with his counselors. "I didn't know how to articulate what was happening to me. I shut down a lot because I didn't trust any therapist. As a kid, you don't want to talk to anybody," says Brett. "And there was another thing that was going on at that time. I was bullied as a kid, mostly for being gay. Everyone used to call me a faggot. Even when I was a little kid, like third grade, I was very targeted as a child. So I didn't trust talking to people about my experiences. I just kept to myself, and went through the motions, like any kid does."

Brett's doctors diagnosed him as suffering from depression, ADHD and anxiety, and put him on medication to treat his ailments. "They put me on Ritalin, which made me very panicky. And when I was thirteen, they put me on Prozac to treat my depression. I would go into really low states. My mother used to get scared because I would isolate myself from everyone. I had panic attacks, because when I'd walk into a room I'd feel like everything was coming at me. It was like sensory overload."

After Brett started taking medication, he began to have less intuitive experiences, which was a relief to him. "During that time, I stopped having these experiences – not completely, but I just didn't have them as much anymore. They stopped happening to me so frequently, probably because they put me on medications. That was the stage of my life where I internalized what was happening to me, and I completely stopped talking about my strange experiences."

Brett went to high school and continued to be the target of bullying by his classmates. Fortunately, however, he was able to lean on his older brother and sister. "My brother was very supportive and protective of me. And both my brother and sister were very social kids. My brother was a football guy and my sister was a cheerleader. I was just kind of the odd kid out. Obviously, being bullied doesn't help. But at least I was a good student. I tried my best."

After graduating from high school, Brett attended the University of Miami, and then transferred to the University of Massachusetts to earn a degree in teaching. "I was an elementary school teacher, and I also had a BA in psychology. In college, I finally had friends. I was having fun and doing really well in school. And I had a best friend who I hung out with every single day. Her name was Lisa. It was nonstop. She was like my sister basically. She was like a part of my family."

Then, one night, Brett had a startling dream that he shared with his friend Lisa. "I told her that I had a dream that I had died, that my spirit left the physical world and that it was the most amazing experience. I had this incredible moment with her where I told her about this dream and she was really open to it," recalls Brett.

"In the dream, I was shot, and everything went black. I could hear everyone talking to me, but I couldn't interact with them. Then, all of a sudden, everything was okay. Like I knew everything, but I didn't know anything, and I was in this mist. It was almost a grey mist and I was flying through this mist, and I ended up in the ocean. I was in the water, and then I had all of these fish floating next to me, and they pulled me up to the surface, and when I got to the surface, I woke up. It was just tremendous. I can't even verbally describe the emotion I felt. It was like an all knowing state of being. It was the most intense experience I've ever had in my life. I was crying hysterically, almost like I released something profound. It was a huge relief. And I shared that story with Lisa, and she was very open to hearing about it."

The very next day, Brett got some shocking news. Lisa was going somewhere with friends, and they were traveling by motorcycle. Lisa was on the back of one of the motorcycles, and they were involved in a terrible accident, which took Lisa's life. "I remember that I had a bad cold that day, and that I was really sick at home in my apartment," says Brett. "Then I got a phone call from mutual friends of Lisa and myself. They told me that Lisa was dead, that she'd died in the motorcycle accident. I was shocked, but I didn't really grieve, for some reason. In fact, I felt a knowing that Lisa was there with me everywhere I went."

Brett continues, "After Lisa passed, I started to have this awareness around me, this knowing. I'd walk into a place, and I'd feel her consciousness coming through to me. I was laughing like her, and she'd come to me in visitations in my dreams. And I would have these synchronistic moments where I would feel her definitely connecting with me and I wasn't trying to force it or trying to understand it. I'd feel her presence around me, and I could feel her awareness of what I was seeing in front of me, her sense of perspective."

Brett graduated from college and then got a master's degree in psychology from Springfield College in Massachusetts. After receiving his master's degree, he began to work with mentally ill patients. "I was always interested in the psychology of people who were labeled schizophrenic and psychotic. I was fascinated by that," says Brett.

"I was very drawn to these mentally ill patients because there was an energetic veil around them, and I could feel it viscerally around them. And when the veil was lifted, I could see that they were being distracted by something outside of the physical environment, and it captivated me. The energy coming around them was so intense that they couldn't integrate it in a cogent way. So they were labeled as crazy. In some ways, I could empathize with them and understand them."

After working as a psychologist for awhile, Brett decided to change careers and he became an elementary school teacher at a school for disadvantaged girls. "I worked in an all girls' school for ten and eleven year old kids who had been traumatized or sexually abused. I was the science teacher, and it was a very therapeutic setting. They lived there and it was a very cohesive group of people."

Although Brett enjoyed teaching these troubled girls, he ultimately had to leave his job because what he witnessed was so upsetting to him. "I worked with these kids because life has always been about service for me. But I saw how people treated them, and how they overmedicated them and they pumped them up with so many pills and so many drugs. These were kids who were sexually abused, not just once but continually, and a lot of them were raised by drug addicted parents who were physically abusive. So it was very painful to watch these girls being provoked by the staff, and then ultimately physically restrained by staff members, all because they were very traumatized children. I had to leave the field and take some time to decide what I wanted to do next."

By this time, Brett was in his mid-twenties, and he made another complete career change. "I decided to go to cosmetology school. I was going to be a hairstylist," he recalls. "Ever since I was a little kid, I always played with hair. But I was told that you weren't supposed to do that for a living – that hair school is for people who don't make it. But I didn't care anymore. I went to cosmetology school and I started to cut hair. And that's when I met my husband and everything really started to change for me."

Brett and his husband, Micah, who is an engineer, decided to take some time off and travel to other countries after Micah's company went public. During the year that they traveled, Brett's psychic abilities began to flourish again.

"We were in San Juan, Puerto Rico, hanging out at this bar, and I went up to this woman and started talking to her," says Brett. "She didn't speak English very well, but she could understand me. So I started telling her all about her life, and I gave her all this advice, and I said 'Who is David?' And I told her about her relationship with David. It was like I knew everything about her."

Even Brett was surprised by these sudden revelations regarding this virtual stranger. "I just knew everything that was going on with her. I wasn't trying to be psychic or anything. It just came out of me. And my husband was sitting there and he said 'How the hell do you know these things about this woman?' And I told the woman that she has a picture of David in a uniform, and that he has two kids, and she just started praying to Jesus. She was clutching her necklace, and I could see that she was fearful. It was a very intense experience."

From that time on, Brett continued to have these psychic experiences with different people several times a week, and he decided to begin to explore his intuitive abilities. "I would know things about people in a way that was beyond what you'd just naturally assume about them. This was different. I was full on in the zone, and I had that knowing," explains Brett. "I didn't know what it was. I don't like to use labels like clairvoyant, and I didn't know any of those words. I was just doing it, and it was profound."

Brett's intuitive abilities continued to increase at a rapid pace. "So I bought a deck of cards and thought that maybe I was psychic or something. But the cards didn't work. I was not connected to the cards. And I heard this voice inside my head saying, 'You don't need the cards, all you need is you.' This is the first time I heard this voice. It was a voice within me, not outside of me. I'll never forget it."

During this period of spiritual awakening, Brett began to realize that he needed to develop his gift and read people on a full time basis. "At first, I said 'I don't want to be this person, this psychic person. I was very reluctant to do it, but I knew that it was a service. I did it for free when I first started. I put an ad on Craigslist, saying 'Free Readings.' Then I got all these calls from people and the whole roof just came flying open. I was talking with people and connecting them to people who've passed, and it just blew me away. I didn't understand it, and I was very humbled by it.

"At the beginning, I was still sort of reluctant to give readings. But I just felt this knowing that this was my mission, that this was what I was supposed to be doing. And I loved doing it for free, without conditions. But my husband said, 'You shouldn't go back to cutting hair, you should do this for work.' And at first I said no, this is a free service to help people. But it just exploded and a lot of people wanted readings from me. So I decided to do psychic readings full time. And I haven't stopped ever since."

Brett believes that we're all here for a purpose, and that the true path to happiness is to spend our lives doing what we're passionate about. "Everybody is divinely here, and everyone is good at something. When you understand that, and become aligned with that part of yourself, you'll find what they call heaven on Earth," Brett explains.

"It's about having faith and trust in all that you are and all that there is. If you are here now, you've been here many, many times, and we need to remember that we're all old souls. That's my mission, to remind people that they're old souls. And to tell them that everything they're doing here is of service, and that they should do what they love, and do what they're good at, because they'll help others by being on their true path. There is so much resonance waiting for us if we just surrender to our purpose and allow it to happen."

Brett continues, "I know that once we just trust and allow ourselves to be divinely guided, everything that we're doing will have a rhythm to it, like a symphony. All the notes will come together, and the beginning and the ending will all come together in a very, very harmonic way."

SALLY SILVER

Sally Silver, a proud, self-proclaimed "Maine-iac," was born in Maine, and today she still resides in a remote part of Maine. She is a down-to-earth, no nonsense person who combines a Will Rogers humor and sensibility with an astonishingly accurate intuitive ability, combined with a big-picture perspective. Sally knows that everything in the universe boils down to this truth – that we're all part of the One True Source.

She often comes up with down home phrases I call "Sally-isms" that make me laugh, but also make me think, like "There are many paths up the mountain, but there's only one mountain." Or "You do the possible, God will do the impossible." Or "Man plans, God laughs." Sally has an irrepressible wisdom and a funny, common sense view of life that is both infectious and enlightening at the same time.

When Sally was a baby, her parents brought her home to an old house that was built in the 1700s and that had been vacant for 50 years before Sally's family moved in. The house, which had previously been owned by a missionary named Dr. Mary Cushman, who made numerous missionary trips to Africa, had been used as a hospital, where Dr. Cushman could treat her patients. As a result, the house was filled with spirits, and Sally believes that this house played a large part in her early intuitive development.

"It was a gorgeous, old, three story colonial house, and when we moved in, it was filled with Dr. Cushman's belongings, including her black leather medical kit," remembers Sally. "My parents moved Dr. Cushman's things up into the attic and, as a child, I used to go up in the attic and just touch these things, and I would hear stories from them, and I'd hear African music and voices, and I'd see the places Dr. Cushman had visited when she was a missionary. These things would tell me interesting tales, and I thought it was just my imagination. I didn't realize that I was experiencing psychometry, which is sensing information from things that you touch – it was just a lot of fun to play with these things and learn from them. I could travel without leaving my attic."

But the spirits in the house also visited Sally at night, in her childhood bed. "The house was full of energy, and full of spirits. When I'd go to bed at night, and when I was in that in between state as I was falling asleep, I'd hear children laughing and people talking, and I didn't know where it was coming from. I remember going to bed, and sometimes a doorway would appear beside the bed, and it would open, and this beautiful blue lady would come through the doorway and she would sit on the end of my bed and she would talk with me. Then she would go back through the doorway, and the whole thing would just disappear. As a child, I thought this blue lady was an angel or a spirit or something from the other side. She was very benevolent."

But some of these spiritual visitations would be too overwhelming for Sally. "There were also times when the spirits would get a little bit too close to me, and that was a little unnerving," says Sally. "I was lying in bed one night, and I felt the presence of a spirit by the head of my bed, and then I felt like someone sat on the corner of the bed. My pillow was pressed down, like someone was leaning over me and, believe me, that was spooky. I was about as big as a basketball in the middle of that bed, and I yanked the covers over my head."

According to Sally, when children learn about their intuitive ability, it was usually challenging. But for Sally, when she was a young girl, it was fun. "In the preadolescent days, when your hormones are leaving you wide open and you're learning so much, this is when a budding psychic will begin to bloom and begin to internalize these things, and you think that a lot of this stuff is your own imagination, and you don't quite trust what's happening," explains Sally. "You need to have someone that you can talk to about your experiences, someone who can confirm that these experiences are real, and support you – just one person who believes in you."

Thankfully, Sally had that spiritual support from her mother. "My mom was very supportive of my intuitive ability. I would get up in the morning and Mom would always say, 'Well okay Sally, what did you dream last night? What were they about?' And I would just tell her all these things that I was dreaming. I was a teenager, and her support helped me a lot. My mom believed in me, and always did throughout my life."

Although Sally didn't share her intuitive ability with all of her classmates, she got some attention when she posed as a psychic at her eighth grade class fair. "We had a school fair where you make things and sell them, like fudge, or play games. So I volunteered to be a fortune teller. I wore a harem suit with blousy pants and I had a turban on and makeup and big hoop earrings, and the whole nine yards. They stuck me in a side room with a school desk, and I told fortunes for a dime or something like that."

Sally continues, "One of the girls freaked out because the fortune that I told her was so good that she couldn't believe it. She actually went home and got her sister so that her sister could get a reading. I was just telling stories that I could see around people, like I could see stories around objects. So, at the age of thirteen, I started to do psychic readings for people."

After Sally graduated from high school, she went to nursing school at McLean Hospital School of Nursing in Belmont, Massachusetts. That year, when she was eighteen, Sally met her husband, George, who was also attending nursing school to become a psychiatric nurse. "Before nursing school, he was in the U.S Navy as a corpsman. After nursing school, he went back into the navy as a naval officer. He was the first male nurse ever in the United States Navy. That was a big deal back then – I've actually got newspaper clippings somewhere that they wrote about him."

Sally had two sons, and was a stay at home mom for the next 11 years. "I didn't work as a nurse, and I wasn't doing any psychic stuff during those years. All of my time and energy went to my family – my husband and my boys." But Sally's world changed when her husband died suddenly, two weeks before Sally's 30th birthday.

"After George died, I came back to Farmington, Maine, bought a house, and went on Social Security so I could raise my boys. I had a widow's pension," Sally explains. "That very first year after I moved back to Farmington, a friend, who knew that I had psychic ability, came running into my house to tell me that there was a new psychic awareness class at the University of Maine in Farmington. So I audited that class. It was taught by a woman by the name of Kay Mora. After taking her class, I went right into her apprenticeship program, and Kay got me started teaching psychic development classes."

Prior to taking classes in psychic development, Sally didn't have a clear understanding of her intuitive gifts. "I was what they called a wild talent. I had all of these psychic abilities, but I had no control over them," says Sally. "The psychic development classes I took with Kay allowed me to gain control over my visionary states, over some of my dream states, over astral travels, and over the healing aspect of psychic ability. We did the whole nine yards, so I was finally able to understand and hone my abilities."

Around this time, Sally met the man who would become her second husband. "I got tangled up with this big, tall, handsome Frenchman named John," Sally laughs. "John was a wild man. He was the oldest of six brothers in a family of twelve. He was a contractor, and he was also naturally psychic and an excellent healer. We lived in a log cabin in northern Maine, about twelve miles from the Canadian border."

Sally began to get very involved with her intuitive and spiritual work. "I opened a crystal business called Crystal Mania, and started working with crystal healing. I traveled around the area and did healing circles everywhere. A healing circle is when you get a group of people together and you work with the healing energy. There's usually a leader that leads the energy. And, typically, we put someone in the center of the circle, and do the laying on of hands to heal that person."

Although things were going well for Sally, after nine years of marriage, she and her husband decided to get a divorce, and Sally moved to Pine Island, Florida to live with her mother, who had become very ill. "The day after I arrived in Florida, I went to a healing center in Cape Coral called the Center of Eternal Light and began to study under a master teacher named Reverend Richard Smith. And I continued to learn about healing, channeling, astrology, *feng shui*, and other spiritual disciplines, which helped me to grow.

"I thought that I already knew it all, but when I became involved with the psychic community in Florida, I realized how inexperienced I was. I met many wonderful, gifted people, but I also met some pretenders and charlatans, and I quickly learned how to see the difference between truly gifted people and the wannabees."

Sally took a job at the Center of Eternal Light, and taught psychic development and healing at the Center for seven years. After that, she took a job at a New Age bookstore called Planet Earth Book Center, which provided her with many opportunities to expand on her intuitive abilities. "I worked there five days a week, eight hours a day, doing readings for thousands of people," recalls Sally.

"It gave me the opportunity to really polish my psychic ability, and to hone my gift. At the time I went to work there, Planet Earth had been around for over twenty-five years. It was the oldest New Age book store in the state of Florida. And a lot of gifted people congregated at that bookstore. From a psychic perspective, that was probably the most intense growth period I had ever experienced. I was so happy and fortunate to work with some very gifted, highly enlightened people who taught me a lot about spirituality and how to best use my psychic abilities."

Sally continued to do readings, teach classes and participate in a psychic healing circle for the twelve years she lived in Florida. "After a few years, my mom passed away, and I returned to Maine to be near my family and eight grandchildren, which continue to be a source of joy for me," says Sally. "I thought I would retire and live a simple life, but spirit had other ideas. Today, I have a weekly psychic development class, teach astrology, do phone readings, travel around the state doing lectures and classes, and I mentor several different developing healers and mediums so that they can improve on their gifts."

Now that Sally has been doing readings for more than four decades, she believes that she understands the messages she's supposed to impart to other people. "I've learned that God is love. There is no meanness in this love. There is no hatred. There is no anger. There is no doubt."

Sally often uses stories to teach others, and she shared the following story, which conveys an important message about life, spirituality and the choices we make. Sally tells the story:

"An old Indian grandfather took his young grandson down to the river to teach him how to fish. And they were sitting there, fishing, watching the river go by, and they were talking about all the things that happen in the world and how people are, and the things that they do, and the difference between right and wrong. And the young boy looks up at his grandfather. 'Grandfather,' he said, 'sometimes I feel like I have two wolves warring inside of me, and one of them makes me do bad things, and the other one wants me to be good.'

"And the grandfather looks down at him, and he said, 'You know, that's true, son. There are two wolves that are warring in each one of us. One of the wolves is hatred and anger and greed and pride. And the other wolf is goodness and love and mercy and peace and joy.' And the little boy looked up at his grandfather with his big brown eyes and he said, 'But grandfather, which one will win?' And the grandfather says, 'The one that you feed son. The one that you feed.'"

LORRAINE SMITH

Lorraine Smith had a career in marketing and she also worked as a corporate meeting planner. After her mother died and appeared to Lorraine from the other side, Lorraine chose to embrace her intuitive gifts and follow a new career path. She received a degree in mediumship from Delphi University, and became an ordained spiritual minister at the Universal Life Church. Born in Massachusetts, Lorraine relocated to Florida and now resides in Harrison, Tennessee, where she works as a psychic full time.

While Lorraine answers specific questions during a reading, she often takes a big picture approach when reading a client, and provides her client with the insight, clarity and spiritual tools to help the client follow the path that he or she was meant to follow. She believes that we all have a direct connection to our higher self, and that by exploring that connection, we can change our lives for the better.

Lorraine Smith grew up in Randolph, Massachusetts, where she shared a two-bedroom house with her three brothers, her sister and her mother. "We were very poor. My father left when I was eight years old. We didn't even own a car. I always knew that I was intuitive, but I didn't have visions or anything. I just knew things, and sometimes I would hear voices. But we were raised Catholic, so you had to be quiet about such things."

When she was twelve, Lorraine and her brother almost drowned, but the voice she heard saved both of their lives. "My brother and I were in this pond on a cow farm, and we were floating on an inner tube," Lorraine recalls. "We never learned how to swim because we didn't live near a lake or have a pool. So my brother, who was five years younger than me, fell through the middle of the inner tube, and I slipped through the middle, too. There I was, on the bottom of the water, and my brother was there next to me. We would have died, but I heard a voice telling me to pick up my brother and lift him as high as I could, and to walk out to the edge of the pond, which I did. That voice saved our lives."

Lorraine went to grade school and high school, and after she graduated, she got a job as a secretary. "When I got out of high school, I worked at the John Hancock Life Insurance Company in Boston. I was an administrative assistant, and I did mostly secretarial work."

When she was in high school, Lorraine was dating her boyfriend, Jim, and when she was nineteen, they got married. "I met him when I was a senior in high school, and a couple of years later, even though we were pretty young, we decided to get married. Jim worked at a local gas station, and then he went to plumbing school and eventually became a master plumber."

Lorraine attended college while working in the sales and marketing department of a jewelry manufacturer. "I worked for the marketing director, worked with our advertising agency and I was also a corporate meeting planner," Lorraine says. "During those years, Jim and I became parents, first having our son Jimmy and then our daughters, Patti and Lorene. We were living a pretty normal life."

When Lorraine was forty-one, she and her husband decided to move to Cape Coral, Florida. "My husband was starting to get arthritis in his hands and his knees, and he couldn't work as a plumber during the winter months," explains Lorraine. "So we decided to move to Florida and start a family plumbing business so he could make a living."

After moving to Florida, Lorraine started to connect more deeply with her intuitive abilities, which she hadn't focused on while she raised her family. She took several psychic development classes and metaphysical workshops, and learned how to channel and to receive messages for other people. "I had a teacher, an older woman, who would put the students in a circle and encourage us to give each other psychic mini messages as we went from person to person," recalls Lorraine. "I was surprised, because all of these words of wisdom would come pouring out, and I remember thinking, 'Where did that come from?' I was just naïve. I had no idea that what I was actually doing was channeling for these people."

For a time, Lorraine attempted to do readings for others by using Tarot cards, but she soon learned that the cards didn't enhance her intuitive gifts in any way. "I took three different classes with the Tarot cards, and I would play with the deck and try to memorize the meanings of each card, but I found out that no matter how many classes I took, there seemed to be a problem with using the cards, because they actually distracted me from the reading. The cards were too physical for me to work with. As I laid them down on the table and tried to read them, my psychic ability closed off. But if I put the cards away and just let go, spirit would speak through me."

In 1998, Lorraine's mother passed away after a long illness. "A few years later, I saw her in a vision, surrounded by golden-white light, walking towards me and presenting me with a huge bouquet of white flowers, handing me 'the gift of Spirit.' It was a mystical experience unlike anything I have ever experienced before, and it changed my life forever! It was this vision and visitation from my mother that ultimately opened me to my channeling abilities and provided access to the Divine, cosmic information and energies of the universe."

Lorraine continued to develop her intuitive ability, and she decided to enroll at Delphi University in north Georgia to study mediumship. "Delphi University is a metaphysical university. The people who were enrolled in the program were already gifted, like me, but the teachers helped us learn how to develop our gifts in the most sacred way," says Lorraine. "It was in that program that I found out how to pray and call in the energies and how to open up even more. I do my best work when I come to it in a sacred way, working through God, the Holy Spirit and the angels. The information comes in so much stronger and feels more accurate."

After receiving her certification in mediumship from Delphi University, Lorraine began doing professional readings for clients, as well as doing readings at psychic fairs, home parties and other events. "Thanks to positive word of mouth, I became so busy that I was able to start working out of my house. I've never had to advertise. People just find me. It's the weirdest thing. And they're calling me from all over the country and the world. I get calls from Canada, Brazil, England and Ireland and many other countries. The other day, a woman from Scotland called me, because she'd heard about me from a friend in Florida. That's how my clients find me."

Lorraine would like people to know that she proudly represents the "late bloomers" in the development of intuitive gifts, and that her story will hopefully encourage people to not give up on their potential, no matter how old they are.

She feels that we all will benefit if we learn to tap into the purest energy from our Higher Self. "The most important thing I've learned is to honor what I call The Mighty 'I AM' Presence, the Spark of God within us. The name of God is 'I AM.' So when I'm doing a reading session, I've learned to call in the 'I AM' Presence, the Higher Self of the client and my own Higher Self, to give messages that are only for the highest good of the client. By doing that, it keeps us at the purest form of energy. The more we honor that Spark of Creation, the Mighty 'I AM' Presence, the more it changes our lives. The more we stay in our power, the more we stay in our truth, which is 'I AM – meaning you are – the Spark of God.'"

Lorraine advises, "The more we honor the 'I AM' Presence within us, the more our vibration rises and the heaviness of the world leaves us. It just changes your world. We need to become grateful, more aware of nature, and more aware of the love in other people and the love in ourselves. By honoring the Spark of God within us, we can change the world."

KELLE SUTLIFF

Kelle Sutliff is a bubbly and effervescent mom of three who lives in Boston with her husband, her teenagers and two Pembroke Welsh Corgis. Kelle is a highly gifted psychic medium. She gives consistently accurate psychic readings, and has clients all over the U.S. and the world.

In addition to her work as a psychic medium, Kelle, a former radio show host, is a psychic investigator and the author of **Listen Up! The Other Side Is Talking.** *She is renowned for her predictions, including her predictions about important world events. She was the number one psychic listed on Google on New Year's Day when searchers typed in "Psychic Predictions for 2016." A former PR person and real estate sales rep, Kelle tells it like it is, and she gets right to the point when doing a reading.*

Kelle's earliest memory of being in contact with spirits from the other side happened when she was nine years old. "I remember waking up one morning and saying to my mom that Grandma Sloan was in my room last night, talking with me about different things. And I told my mom that Grandma Sloan had this specific dress on, and I told her some of the things that Grandma said to me. And my mom said, 'Oh really, that's great Kelle, put your uniform on and get ready for school.'"

Kelle continues, "In my life, growing up, there were a lot of 'oh reallys' about stories like that that I would share with my mom and my family. It's like they saw that I had an intuitive gift, but it was always kind of 'Hush, hush, don't tell anybody about it.' So I learned that you should keep quiet about these things."

When asked what her grandmother said to her, Kelle explained, "She would talk about her passing, how she died of cancer, and she wanted to let my mother, her daughter, know that she was okay. She also wanted to tell me that she loved me. I was Grandma Sloan's youngest granddaughter, and I'm the only one in the family that practices as a psychic medium. Grandma Sloan was also very intuitive, so I think that she came to me when I was a child to validate that I also had the gift, and to comfort me."

Kelle was the youngest of four children, and she has an older brother and two older sisters. As she was growing up, Kelle often had dreams at night where she would be talking to people.

"As a child, I always remember dreaming of people I didn't know, and these people would be in my dreams and I would be talking with them at night. I didn't know anything else – I thought that's what everybody did when they slept. I would have these experiences where people would come in and they would just talk to me and then they would leave. I thought that was normal."

Kelle was raised Catholic and went to 12 years of Catholic grade school, middle school and high school. During this time, she kept her intuitive experiences to herself. "You never really talked about this other side of things," Kelle says. "Then, when I was in my early twenties, I met a family friend of ours who was a priest. His name was Father Wally and he actually co-officiated my wedding, when I got married in my late 20s."

Kelle explains, "Father Wally, believe it or not, was a very spiritual man, but he was also a very intuitive man. He would actually talk about his psychic experiences as a priest, and he was into this kind of alternative world and crystals and all kinds of spiritual, intuitive information. So to me, as a child, and growing up Catholic and growing up with my religious faith, I was like 'Holy moly, a priest is actually talking about this psychic stuff.' I didn't believe it. So I was able to talk to him, and thanks to his guidance, I finally had some comfort and support about who I was and about my psychic experiences."

Thanks to Father Wally, Kelle was able to open up more to her intuitive abilities throughout her twenties. But as she reached her late twenties and early thirties, Kelle began to shut down and move away from being psychic.

"At that time, to be honest, I kind of shut my psychic ability off, because I still didn't want people to know that I was gifted," Kelle says. "When you're a psychic medium, you know that no one grows up and says, 'Hey, I want to be a psychic medium!' It evolves. You pick it obviously for your soul path, but it just really kind of evolves over your lifetime. There were times that this ability tried to come forward in my life in many, many ways, but I would shut it off. And you do have control as a person to say, 'Okay, I am ready for this,' or, 'I'm not ready for this.' You really have to accept your job with this work – in my opinion – because then you will learn how to do it the right way."

Kelle decided to embrace her gifts as a psychic and as a medium shortly after having her three children. "I had three kids in three years, and one day I was making formula in my kitchen, and I said, 'You know what? I am ready to do the psychic thing again," explains Kelle. "And as soon as I said that, a spirit opened up the veil to me while I was feeding my babies. I started to have those experiences where people were coming to me in my dreams. I was crossing people over to the other side, guiding them into the light. I was literally a conduit for the other side. So I said, 'Okay, I've got to figure out what I'm doing with this gift.'"

Kelle started studying with others to learn more about how to use her abilities so that she could better direct her gift and help others. She signed up to take classes at a local bookstore called *Open Doors,* where she could learn about different aspects of intuitive ability. "I did a year of intense study, learning all about being a medium and being a psychic. And I did all of this being the mom of a three-year old, a thirteen-month old, a two-month old, and a husband who traveled two weeks out of the month. And my immediate family all lived out of state. So, of course, I was always hiring babysitters to come and watch the kids. Today, I look back and think, 'How in the world did I do all of that?' But I trusted that God had a plan for me, and I got that part of my life in order. It took a lot of work and dedication."

Kelle was able to study with teachers from England, Ireland and Scotland through her course work, and she really began to understand who she was and why she'd had this intuitive ability even as a child. "I realized that I'd been a medium my whole life, even when I was a little girl, because I had an energy or light that could help people cross over to the other side. And it was at that moment that I said okay, I don't know what this all means, but I am going to do this right and go forward with it.

"And I continued to study with famous mediums from Boston, and they helped me learn how to develop my boundaries as a psychic medium, how to connect, how to get spirits through, and how to keep grounded when reading people."

How did Kelle's husband Tom, who works in the high tech computer industry as an electrical engineer, react to learning that his wife and the mother of their three kids was a psychic medium? "At first, he said, 'Really? Can you help me with lottery numbers, please?'" laughs Kelle. "But as time went on, and I had more psychic experiences, my husband accepted my gift, and has been impressed by it ever since – especially with my accuracy in client readings, and with predictions about upcoming world affairs."

Kelle also gets tons of support from her three kids, who are aware of what she does and are very proud of her work. "My kids are my biggest cheerleaders," says Kelle. "I've taught them how important intuition is, and we even do this little thing at our house on Tuesdays that I call Psychic Tuesdays, where I practice their intuition with them because they're all very evolved. They are very intuitive kids. You need to work with your intuition and learn the right way to use it, because then you don't lose it, and you don't get intimidated by it or fearful of it."

But in a world where intuitives and mediums are often misunderstood, and even maligned by others, did Kelle's kids ever get teased or put down regarding their mother's profession? "It's really funny. My kids have never gotten any flack because of what their mother does for a living. In fact, twice this week my girls have taken my business cards to give out to their friend's mothers, and their teachers will say, 'Oh my God, what your mom does is so cool.'

"I've actually read a few of the families of my kids' friends, especially when a child has lost one of their parents. Everybody just knows that this is what Mrs. Sutliff does. And I love their friends' reaction, especially as teenagers, because they can be funny about the whole subject, but then they're also very curious about what I do and how I get my information. I have some great conversations with those kids, plus I feed them all the time. They have to listen to me if they want food!"

Kelle believes that the world is finally coming to terms with intuition and psychic ability, and that we're now ready to accept these gifts and allow people with intuitive ability – which is really all of us – to become accepted. "It's funny. I went out to dinner with my husband and some of his colleagues, and after dinner, people pulled me aside and said, 'Hey, we heard that you're psychic, is this true?' And I told them, 'Yes, I'm a psychic medium.' And they were very encouraging. I think that today it's so much easier to tell people what I do for a living and who I am, versus fifteen years ago, when if you said you were a psychic medium people would go, 'Oh, she's a whack job.' Today, people are more intrigued and curious.

"I think the veil of consciousness is so much thinner today, and that so many more people are having their own experiences with their intuitiveness. Now, when I meet people, they'll tell me a story about how they've connected with someone who's passed on, or how their intuition guided them to start a new business, or similar stories. And I think that's made it easier to do the work that I do. So – although it took years for me to finally 'come out of my psychic closet,' the world was much kinder than it would have been a long time ago. And I absolutely love what I do."

According to Kelle, it's important for people to remember that our passed loved ones want to communicate with us. "It's their job and soul purpose for them to let you know that they're okay and that *you* will be okay too," Kelle explains. "How can they not connect to you, as you are connected to them by the most powerful link of all, love. They never forget about you. And now, they have access to communicating through divine energy. It is a lot different than how you're used to communicating with your loved ones, but a bond can still be created.

"How do I communicate with them, you ask? You start to communicate by using signs and symbols with them. It's that simple because spirit is simple. They're not complicated. This is a huge communicative tool from the other side that you have access to. You can't pick up the phone and say hello anymore, but you can ask them to give you a sign. However, it's up to you to initiate this contact."

Kelle wants us to know that spirit sends us signs constantly, but we're often too busy to recognize them in our hectic lives. So she has some advice for people who want to connect with their deceased loved ones. "Ask for signs that are obscure. For example, say to your passed loved one, 'Dad, I want to know that you're okay and that you're with me. Can you show me a golf ball today?' And sometime during the day, you may hear someone talking about golf, or you'll see an actual golf ball, or a friend will phone you and ask you to 'play nine.' You'll be inundated with so many golf ball references that it almost becomes funny. And yes, spirit always shows up with humor, and not tears in their communications with us, so be ready for a good laugh!"

Most importantly, Kelle wants people who are grieving the loss of a loved one to know that they are in a happy place on the other side, and that they want you to be happy too. "Spirit does understand your grief, and some days it will be really tough for you. That's why symbolism is so important when communicating with them. Signs are their way of comforting you. Your loved ones who've passed will never put you on 'hold' when you ask for that sign, and they'll never disappoint you when they communicate back to you. Keep aware and remember that there is no 'call waiting' in heaven!"

JUDITH SWANSON

Judith Swanson, who is from the Boston area, began losing her sight at the age of 12 and was legally blind by the time she was 44. Regardless of her ability to see, or perhaps because of this, Judith has a unique ability to tune into loved ones who have crossed over to the other side and to bring great detail to her readings.

Trained as a special education teacher, Judith, who has two children of her own, loves working with children. In addition to her work as a medium and a medical intuitive, Judith is a spiritual energy healer who helps people heal by clearing their energy and releasing negativity so that they can be as healthy and happy as possible.

When Judith was six years old, she would sit and watch football games with her father every Sunday. That's when she learned that she had intuitive ability: she could often predict which team would win.

"My dad and I would watch the football games together, and he would call his bookie and bet on the game," remembers Judith. "And when you called a bookie, you had to have a code name, because it was illegal to bet. And my dad's code name was Holiday. So he would call the bookie and say, 'It's Holiday – I'm going to put Little Holiday on the phone,' and that was me. And I would get on the phone with the bookie and I would tell him who was going to win. So the bookie even began to call me to see who was going to win other types of games."

Judith's dad was Italian and he owned one of the top construction companies in New England. "He had many people working for him on a lot of different jobs. On Sunday mornings, my family would go with him to different job sites. I was about ten or eleven at the time. It was all dirt and construction, and we would walk around the job with him, and I would see someone and say, 'Dad, I don't think that person should be working for you.' He would say, 'Why?' and I would say, 'Because he's not honest, and he's not good for the company.' Little by little, my dad was asking me all kinds of things about which employees would be good to work with him – he could tell that I knew. So that's how it started."

Her father supported her gift, but Judith's mother never talked about it. "My mom never commented on it. She was always cleaning," recalls Judy. "She was a loving mother who spent her time caring for four very active children."

Judith was careful to keep her intuitive gifts a secret from the kids at school. "I would never share my intuitive ability at school. No, never. I just knew that. No one ever told me not to, but I just knew you just don't talk about these things."

Judith was raised Catholic and she went to church with her family every Sunday. "We would go to church because my mom really wanted us to go to church every Sunday. We would be kneeling down and I would be beside my dad, and the priest would be talking about 'Don't do this, don't do that' – you know, sin – but my father would say to me, 'Don't ever feel guilty – just do the best you can in life. I don't care what you do. It doesn't matter to me. I don't want A students. I want B students with common sense.' He was so wise really. That's the kind of dad that he was."

As a pre-teen, Judith would have intensely spiritual experiences with nature. "When I was young, I would play outside. I spent a lot of time outdoors as a child, and I could see an energy field, like an aura, coming off the animals, especially bunnies and birds. I remember that they would fly off and the energy would just stay around. And I could feel and see the energy of trees, because they hold much intuitive wisdom to share with us."

One day, Judith's dad brought home a book called *The Autobiography of a Yogi* for her older brother to read. After Judith saw the book in their family room and started to read it, she had an epiphany. "I could not put this book down. I started to cry at one point because I thought, 'Ahh – someone finally understands how I feel about God and nature.' Someone really gets it – how when I was with nature, I went into a rapture, because I felt so connected to the natural world, and I couldn't believe how beautiful it is."

Judith was afraid to share her heightened intuitive awareness and feelings with the kids in middle school, so she kept to herself. "I wasn't very social. I'm an extrovert now, but as a kid, I was an introvert," Judith explains. "I don't think there was any place for my gifts then. I didn't think that I could share this stuff – all of my feelings of being so connected to nature, and seeing energy, and being psychic. There was no one I could tell, except for my dad. He was wonderful. I used to tell him about this. Being psychic was such a big part of who I was, who I am, and I had no way to express it."

When she reached high school, things got better for Judith. "The first two years of high school, I was still very quiet. Then when I got to junior year, I started to get more social – I even started dating this wonderful guy. And as I got older, things improved. Now I'm very extroverted, because most of the people I surround myself with are healers who are really into the energy world – so I'm in a solid place now."

Judith went to Lesley University in Cambridge, Massachusetts. She earned a degree in special education and got her first job as soon as she graduated.

"Immediately after I graduated, I got a job in Special Ed and I loved it. I loved kids, and still do," notes Judith. "I taught them in a very different way than most people do. I found ways around the problems that they had and the principal couldn't believe how well these kids learned. I just went way out of the box to help them. And I loved them – I could see their essence. I could see beyond their ADHD and beyond things that would drive other teachers crazy."

Eventually, Judith's teaching career would come to an end due to her vision loss. "As a kid, I had night blindness – it started when I was around twelve. Before that, I used to lie outside and just look up at the stars, and one night I remember just going up into the dark spaces between the stars, and I remember merging with those dark spaces, just absolutely knowing that within that nothingness there is everything. When that experience was over, I knew that it wasn't the physical matter where everything was – it was the places in between, the nothingness. That's what I tap into when I do readings – I call it love nothingness now."

After Judith left teaching, she wanted to continue to help others with her gifts of healing and her intuitive ability. "I attended the Barbara Brennen School of Healing, which had a four year healing science program. I quickly learned that it's not healing 'techniques' that heal – it's love that is the true healer."

In Judith's second year of healing school, she became confused about her psychic ability, mediumship and healing work. So she went outside and stood under her favorite tree. "I said to God, 'Please let me know if this work is my purpose for being on Earth.' Within two weeks, the local newspaper called me to interview me about my healing work, and they ran an article about me that appeared in seventeen area newspapers. After that article, I had a full list of clients just through word of mouth. It just exploded like you wouldn't believe. People just started coming to me, and before I knew it, I was reading people full time."

Now, Judith uses her intuitive ability to help her clients grow their businesses. Although Judith enjoys reading people, she also encourages them to explore their own intuitive ability, and often teaches clients how to enhance their ability. "The most important thing is that they come and they get opened up spiritually. They learn about themselves and their own ability, and I'm happy when they learn to listen to their inner voice. By learning to live within the heart and to tap into that inner wisdom, it will be easier for us to live in this overwhelming world we're in now."

LEANNE THOMAS

Leanne Thomas channels angels from the angelic realm. She is a former elementary school teacher who has a M.A. degree in English Language Arts and Educational Leadership. Leanne, who is originally from Santa Clara, California, loved teaching children and intended to continue teaching as a career, until her intuitive abilities became very strong and too pronounced to be ignored. She hopes to open a school one day "where children can develop their psychic abilities while learning reading, writing and arithmetic." She also recently created a deck of "Angelic Oracle Cards" which enable people to receive guidance from their angels.

I was impressed by Leanne's caring demeanor and her accuracy. During my reading, my deceased sister, whom I hadn't talked to for years before her death because of a contentious legal incident, came through to apologize for her actions and for the legal harassment. It was a healing moment, and my sister, who is now on the other side, admitted that she now realizes that what she did to me was wrong. Today, thanks in part to Leanne and her insights, all is forgiven.

When Leanne Thomas was a young Catholic girl, she was raised to believe that angels, God and Jesus exist, but that we can't see them. "I remember once that I was playing in my room with my Barbie dolls, which was one of my favorite things to do. And my mom came in and asked me what I was doing, and I said I was playing with my angels and my Barbies. It just slipped out," Leanne recalls. "And mom started to talk to me about how the angels are real, God is real, Jesus is real, but that we don't get to see them. It was a typical Catholic upbringing. You were taught to believe in these heavenly beings, but you couldn't think of them in a supernatural, ghostly or spirit kind of way."

Although Leanne learned about visionaries receiving holy messages from the Virgin Mary in Medjugorje (Croatia) and other places in her catechism class, she was taught that those visions were only for holy people, not normal people like her. But when she was nine years old, she had her first vision. "My grandmother passed away one day, and that same night, a few hours later, my grandfather passed, in the middle of the night," says Leanne.

Leanne, who was in bed with her little sister, had her first vision that evening. "My grandfather came walking into my room, and I just knew he wasn't alive, he wasn't speaking to me," remembers Leanne. "And I started to do what little kids do, saying 'Please don't die grandpa. I'll be really good, I'll eat all my vegetables. I won't tell any lies.' Like how a nine year old would negotiate to get what she wants. I remember doing that while he just stood there. Then all of a sudden, I heard my mom scream, because she got a phone call and learned that my grandfather had died. That was my first experience seeing a spirit."

Leanne also had other intuitive experiences as a child, which she didn't always share with others. "I always had a knowing. I just knew things, or if something was the truth. I knew what was in all of my Christmas packages. When I was a kid, I would say 'This is a watch, or this is Cinderella.' My mom would just look at me as if I had peeked, or as if had I looked into the wrapped packages. So I also learned to not say too much, because it would cause me more trouble than it was worth to tell her how I just knew what was in the packages."

Her family didn't like to talk about psychic ability, but Leanne wasn't the only person in her family who was intuitively gifted. "My mom's sister, my Aunt Janet, is highly gifted, but she was never able to really tap into it. She had experiences, but she expressed them as weird, crazy stories, and they made her a little nuts," explains Leanne. "She's a kind, sweet person, but she's also known as crazy Aunt Janet. She was always afraid of her ability. But for me, my psychic experiences were always kind and gentle. I never felt scared. I always felt protected, like there were a lot of angels around. That was my connection. And when I look back now, I can see that my grandmother, my mom's mom, also had intuitive ability."

Angels have always played an important role in Leanne's life, and when angels appeared to Leanne as a child, she wasn't frightened. "I do remember seeing them, but I don't remember a lot. They looked like people to me, and I don't even know how I would have known that they were angels. That's the odd part. It was just part of me. It was natural for me to see the positive things, angelic things, good things, and positive outcomes."

When Leanne became a teenager, her friends started noticing that she was doing strange things, especially at sleepover camps. "When I was at dance camp or cheer camp, my friends would say that I did strange things at night. They would just call it sleep walking, but at home I would never sleep walk," says Leanne. "But my friends would tell me 'You got up in the middle of the night and started talking about something. We didn't know what you were talking about.' I remember people telling me that. But I don't have memories of it."

Looking back, Leanne believes that these sleepwalking episodes could have been related to her intuitive ability. "I really feel now that that was like a connection or a channeling or something, that because I was young and a teenager, something was trying to connect with me. I didn't feel afraid of it. I didn't feel like what happened to me was invasive or violent. I just feel like I was an open vessel."

After Leanne graduated from high school, she went to Fresno State College in California, where she was a Liberal Arts major in education. But after three years of college, she left Fresno State before completing her degree to get married and have her child, a son. Two years after getting married, she divorced her husband and went back to school. "I went back and I got my teaching credential, and then I got my first master's degree there as a reading specialist, a Master's of Arts Degree in Education, Reading, Language Arts Option."

Leanne began teaching elementary school students, and raising her young son, Tyler. One year, when she attended her 10th year high school reunion, she reconnected with a former high school friend named Troy.

"We met up at our class reunion and we became friends for about six years," says Leanne. "I was living in Fresno and he lived in the Bay Area, so it was about a three-hour drive. But we just struck up a really good friendship. It took about six years before we really started being serious about one another, but we got married and I moved to the Bay Area. I left everything. Like here I am, I'm a literacy specialist now, I'm not a classroom teacher anymore. I just made one of those decisions that I kind of make. Like I need to change my life. And it was a very positive direction for changing my life. Things were very solid."

Soon after Leanne moved to the Bay Area, she began to have a flood of intuitive experiences again. "As soon as I moved, everything amped up for me. I started to have crazy, wild experiences, and I wanted to get my hands on every kind of spiritual book I could read, but I didn't want anybody to know. So I was in the library a lot that summer. I started having synchronistic events happening around me. Anytime I went anywhere, or turned on the television, angels would be there. It would be something about angels. There would be pictures of angels, or people would be talking about them."

One day, when Leanne was conducting a teacher training class, she overheard another trainer talking about a woman who does angel readings. "She was talking about this woman who connects to angels, so I asked for the name of the woman, and I went right home and contacted her. She got back to me and we set up a time for a reading."

Leanne's meeting with the angel reader marked an important turning point in her life. "It really blew me wide open. I was crying the whole time. I could see everything that she was saying. She told me that my grandfather was going to come to me in the car on the way home from this reading and give me a song. So, after the reading, I pulled myself together and got in the car.

"As I'm driving home, the very next song that comes on the radio is *You've Got a Friend*. First, I felt my grandfather come in, like whoosh. I felt my energy rise and I felt very emotional, and then that song came on. And I knew he was sending the song to me. I don't even know how I made it home safe. I probably lost five pounds from crying. But he said that everything is going to change now. And I knew that's what he said. But at the time, I was like, 'I don't know how I know that. How do I know that he said that?' I was still questioning everything."

After Leanne had this profound spiritual experience, she decided to take a weekend workshop that included courses on how to develop psychic and mediumship abilities. But she didn't want to tell her husband. "I didn't tell him the truth. I told him that I was going to a spiritual retreat to meditate and center myself. That I needed time for myself," says Leanne. "But I knew I needed to take this course in order to find out if I'm crazy, and if I should get help, or if this psychic ability is real."

During the spiritual workshop, Leanne had a number of jarring, and often physically taxing, psychic experiences. "The course blew me wide open, and it was very physical for me," explains Leanne. "I felt that my body was being choked, thrown off a cliff, having a heart attack and a stroke. I felt how the spirit passed physically in my own body, and at one point I turned blue from being choked. Other people in the room could see it. So the teacher came right over and cleared the energy off around me."

During another exercise, a classmate would sit in a chair, and the students would share what they were feeling or sensing about the person. One time, when a female classmate sat in the chair, Leanne sensed something extraordinary, and very frightening.

"I told the teacher, 'I've got a gentleman here, and I'm falling off a cliff, and my soul leaves the body before I hit, but I hit my head first, and my head was destroyed.' And I could feel my head. It felt like my head was being bashed in, so it was excruciatingly painful, but the pain was gone in a second. As soon as I told the class and let it out, I didn't have the pain anymore. It turns out that the woman who was sitting in the chair had a friend who had fallen off a cliff. So everybody in the class was a little shocked."

After the workshop, Leanne realized that she had a true psychic gift, and that she needed to tell her husband that she was gifted.

"When I came home on Sunday morning, I told my husband. We were in bed watching the early morning news shows. I'd been worried about telling my husband about my abilities because his dad has schizophrenia and hears voices and things. So how could I tell my husband that I hear voices and things? It was traumatizing to him as a kid that his dad had that issue.

"I'd been thinking all week 'How do I say this? How do I tell him?' So I just turned to him when we were in bed that Sunday morning and said, 'I have something that I need to tell you,' and I immediately started to cry. I looked at him and I said, 'I believe that I have a gift, and I believe this is something real. I connect to people who have passed on to heaven. Dead people.' He didn't really say anything. He just looked at me. He knew I was feeling very emotional about this. So he got up, and went downstairs to get another cup of coffee. And he came back upstairs and stood in the doorway and said, 'I don't understand what's going on, or what you have, but if you say that you have this and that this is real, then it is.' That's all he said, so we just let it be for awhile."

A few weeks later, Leanne began to give readings to clients, and was invited to be a guest on Blog Talk Radio shows, where she did readings for people who called in to the show. "When I was on the radio show, the host told me that every time I was on the show, her ratings would triple," remembers Leanne. "So she invited me to be a regular guest, and I was on the show every week. That's how I really started honing in on my gifts. On the radio, you've got to get in there and go fast when doing a reading – you definitely don't want dead air. So I took to radio fairly well."

Thanks to her radio appearances, Leanne soon developed a large client base and was able to do readings full time. She calls her practice Angelic Hope, and she does Angel Readings which connect her clients to their loved ones, angels and guides. At first, her son wasn't sure about what he thought of Leanne's new profession. "He used to call it 'Woo woo,' and he would say 'Don't do your woo woo voodoo stuff on me.' He was a teenager then. He's more accepting of it now."

Leanne would like people to know that many people with intuitive gifts didn't necessarily choose to have them, and that gifted people are not charlatans and scam artists. "Initially, I didn't choose to be a psychic medium, but I do choose it now. I don't feel helpless, or like a victim in any way. I feel very honored and blessed," says Leanne. "But I didn't really know much about intuitive ability before, and when I was growing up, people always joked about psychics. It's a shame, because I would never want anybody to think that I would take advantage of them. I would never scam anyone."

In fact, Leanne loves her work because it helps so many people. "It changes people's lives," she says. "I have therapists who come to me now, because some of their clients have been to me. And they say that they can get more in an hour session with me, getting a psychic reading, than they could get from a year of therapy."

Leanne wants people to know one important principle that she's learned from her intuitive work. "People should know that psychic and intuitive ability reaches beyond our five senses. We are connecting to energy, or the soul of the spirit that moves on as energy, and it is no longer physical. So the connection is beyond the senses. And it can do tremendous good for us, if we choose to listen to the guidance we're given."

CINDY WENGER

Cindy Wenger uses her gift to give voice to a very special group who have their own language that many of us can't hear - animals. She is an empathic intuitive from Hershey, Pennsylvania who uses her ability as an animal communicator to help clients and their pets speak to each other - often shedding light on a variety of topics - including health issues, behavioral problems, changes in personality and pets who have passed on. Cindy has studied various healing and energy modalities, has obtained a certification diploma in Animal Psychology, and has a certification in the Science and Art of Herbalism.

When I first spoke to Cindy, I was very concerned about my own dog, a Bichon Frise named Snowball, who had suddenly fallen gravely ill. But as she tuned in, Cindy said, "Another dog is coming in first, a dog who passed on over ten years ago. Did you take care of a dog after your mother died, a little brown and cream colored dog?" To my surprise, I realized that Cindy was talking about Sarah, my mom's 11 year old Shih Tzu. I had taken her in after mom died, more than a decade earlier. Even though Sarah was pretty old and grumpy, I gave her plenty of love and attention until she passed, about a year later, while I was holding her in my arms.

"Yes, that was Sarah, my mom's dog," I told Cindy. "Well," Cindy said, "she wanted to thank you for taking such good care of her and for giving her so much love, even though she didn't feel well during the last year of her life. She can't thank you enough." And I realized that - even though I had pressing questions about Snowball's condition - Sarah desperately wanted to come through from the other side to thank me.

When Cindy was a young girl, she always loved animals and gravitated towards them – although she could not have any pets as a child because her mother was severely allergic to animals. But she found ways to be around animals in others ways.

"I had friends who had pets, and we used to go to the zoo, and different parks and places to feed the ducks and watch squirrels and other animals play," says Cindy. "As a young child, I just had a knowingness about animals – I just knew what they were feeling. At that time, my ability was more of a feeling thing, rather than getting actual words."

When Cindy was seven, she had her first experience where she actually heard words from the animal. It was with a neighbor's collie. "As a child matures, understanding and language become more sophisticated, so in addition to the knowingness, I also started to receive images, impressions and words. I don't remember exactly what the collie said to me back then, but I knew that they were actual words."

As Cindy got older and became a teenager, her mother finally got a black poodle named Pepe, because poodles are hypoaller-genic and don't shed. "It was really nice to finally have a pet," says Cindy. "I took Pepe everywhere with me. We had a very close bond, but I was more into being a teenager and hanging out with my friends than I was into developing my ability as an animal intuitive, so I wasn't really focused on it for awhile."

Cindy's interest in animal communication grew stronger when she was in her mid-twenties. She was married by this time, and she and her husband owned three dogs – two Keeshonds, Hagar & Heather, and a Sheltie named Hobbes. Unfortunately, the two Keeshond dogs died within five weeks of each other, at the ages of 7 and 10 – one from cancer and the second from a heart attack.

"After my dogs passed, I just felt that I had to get back into com-munication with animals. I had been concentrating on my work as a paralegal, and I had stepped away from honing my ability to talk to animals – I think the wires got a little rusty for me. But I realized that it was time to connect again."

Cindy signed up for a course on animal communication that was taking place in New York State. Gradually, her innate abilities grew, and she was back to being able to communicate with animals. "After I took the course in New York, I came back home and I was really charged – I was really excited. And I remember that I went out in our backyard and sat on the steps of our deck, hoping to talk to some of the animals that were usually in our backyard – such as squirrels and birds and rabbits."

But, for some reason, there were no animals in the yard. Cindy started to send out the mental message: "Who wants to talk to me?" so that some animal would appear and respond to her. But – despite her desire to talk to some cute, fuzzy little animal – no creatures appeared. Cindy sent out the thought again – "Who wants to talk to me?" And she finally heard a small voice saying, "I'll talk to you."

"After I heard that voice, I opened my eyes and looked around, expecting to see some cute wild animal," says Cindy. "But all I saw was a female praying mantis on the railing of our deck. And I turned around and I looked at her again, and I said, 'Okay, is that you?' And I heard, 'Yes.' So this praying mantis began to give me some insight on communicating with animals, and how yelling in my head was not a really good idea if I wanted to talk to animals – that it was better to "speak" quietly (telepathically), and to quiet my mind if I wanted to hear what the animals were saying."

Cindy and the praying mantis continued their discussion for awhile, and at the end, Cindy stuck her finger out, saying, "I'd really like to shake your hand and thank you for connecting and sharing your wisdom with me." And – to Cindy's disbelief – the praying mantis stuck out her digit and touched her front leg to Cindy's finger. Cindy, of course, was floored!

Cindy continued to practice and hone her telepathic communication skills. Eventually, she became an animal communication consultant and, as a result, has a clientele base from all around the globe. She has been featured in books, magazines, on radio, television, and various other media outlets. As Cindy says, "I've found this line of work fulfilling on many levels. Each session brings with it unexpected surprises. There's no room for boredom!"

Cindy offers individual sessions and also teaches workshops on animal communication. She has also taught animal communication skills to animal rescue organizations and their employees who work with abandoned and abused cats and dogs.

"By my working with rescue groups and teaching them how to talk to the animals they're placing in homes, they've found that they get less returns from people who adopt the animals because they know what the animal wants – so they're matching them up with the right type of home environment," Cindy explains.

"They know that – okay, this cat or dog doesn't like kids, or – okay, this pet would prefer living with an older female, or – this dog really likes a 'guy's guy' – he wants to hang with the guys and do sporty things. So the rescue groups are matching dogs and cats up with the right people – and they're having less animal returns."

Although pet owners often genuinely love their pets, Cindy finds that some clients have a difficult time grasping the fact that animals can communicate their thoughts and feelings to us. "People can believe that they're talking to their dead aunt," says Cindy, "but the fact that an animal can think, and process and have emotions – and actually talk back, like they do with me – it's really hard for people to understand and believe. It's just foreign to them."

After twenty years of communicating with animals, both living and in spirit, Cindy has found that connecting to the animal's true essence – their soul, heart, and mind – has been a healing, learning and enriching process for her and for her clients. "During sessions, I've seen that animals, as well as their humans, were relieved of stress and the emotional issues that had been plaguing them, sometimes for years," says Cindy. "By having this emotional release, there's a return to overall wellbeing and wholeness.

"The information that we get during a consultation has also been helpful in improving my clients' relationships with their animals. I believe that everyone has the ability to connect with their animal companions telepathically, even though it's something that many people don't believe that they can do."

Cindy believes that animal owners can communicate with their own pets if they follow some basic advice. "Your attitude is a key factor in creating an open dialogue between you and your pet. If you approach animals with respect, love and humility, and acknowledge that they're intelligent beings with thoughts and emotions, they'll be able to express themselves more freely, and that will deepen and enhance the bond that you have with them."

But, according to Cindy, pet owners need to learn to listen to their pets. "Believe and trust in yourself and your abilities! Don't invalidate the messages that you're getting from your pet, no matter what form they come to you in, such as impressions, feelings, or pictures," Cindy says. "Thank your animal companion for communicating with you. You'll find that it will become easier and easier to communicate with them with practice."

Cindy has some powerful, but practical, tips for pet owners. "Visualize the positive behavior you want from your pet. Picture sending is a very powerful tool," she explains. "A common challenge my clients who have dogs have is the 'recall' or come command. With picture sending, it's important to keep your picture and what you're saying the same. When we want a dog to come to us, many times we're thinking in our minds, 'Gee, I hope they don't run away.' So you're saying 'come,' but thinking 'run away.' Guess which is more powerful? You've got it – the picture you're sending to them!"

Cindy continues, "Try this. Take a moment, close your eyes and picture in your mind your dog coming to you when you say the word, 'come.' When you have the picture firmly in your mind, open your eyes and ask your dog to come. I did this with a client during a phone session and she was amazed at how easy it was, and that she had the outcome she wanted! From then on, she made sure that what she was saying and the picture she was sending were one and the same."

Finally, Cindy has these words of wisdom for pet owners. "Always remember that animals know our truth, whether it's what we're saying, feeling, or how we touch them. For instance, pet owners struggle with the tough choice of whether or not to euthanize their pet. Our pets understand this difficult emotional decision and understand that our intention is coming from a loving, humane space – to relieve them of any pain, or lack of quality of life. There's no judgment from them when we assist them with this process. They know us sometimes better than we know ourselves!"

KELLEE WHITE

Kellee White is a licensed psychotherapist in Beverly Hills, California. After years of working as a corporate executive in the food industry, Kellee sustained a serious head injury that led to bleeding in the brain and almost ended her life. As a result of the injury, Kellee began to see "dead people" all the time, and she was apprehensive, confused and often frightened by these constant apparitions. Fortunately, Kellee's family took care of her during this difficult time, and eventually she learned how to harness the spiritual energy that she was receiving and to use her new found gift as a medium to help others who've lost loved ones. Today, she is a gifted spiritual medium.

Kellee's accuracy and compassion came through during the reading she gave me. She picked up some sensitive and specific details about a painful family issue when my deceased mother came through in the reading and clarified these issues for me. She also validated that my parents deeply valued my contributions to our family when they were in the process of passing.

When Kellee White was a child, growing up in southern California, her family didn't discuss religion. Her father, a well-known jazz musician, was Jewish, and her mother, a prominent psychologist, was raised as a Southern Baptist. Religion wasn't a big part of her family's life. "Although my mother described me as a normal child, it was well known in the family that if Kellee said, 'Don't get on the airplane,' they would not get on the plane. So the family must have seen something about me that was unusual," Kellee recalls.

"I remember that I had a huge fear of death when I was a young teenager, and my mother got me some books on the subject that really helped me. But before my grandmother died, I'd ask her, 'What happens when you die?' because I had this kind of panic about it. And my grandmother told me that you die and that's it. But later on, I found out something much different."

When Kellee was about twenty years old, her grandmother became ill and died. And Kellee was shocked at what happened next. "After she died, my grandmother immediately started coming to me at night, and she would come so frequently that I couldn't sleep anymore," says Kellee. "She was constantly there, in my bedroom, telling me to take care of my grandfather. And so I told my mother about this, and I said, 'What am I going to do? What's happening here?' My mother told me, 'Well, just tell your grandmother to go away.' It was actually quite logical, so I did what she said, and my grandmother did finally go away."

After Kellee's grandmother stopped appearing to her, Kellee went on to finish college, graduating from California State University at Northridge with a bachelor's degree in child development. "Initially, I had intended to be a teacher, but after I graduated, I decided to go to culinary school in France, so I enrolled at *LaVarenne* in Paris. I wanted to be a chef, but, in those days there really weren't many female chefs, so I went to culinary school, graduated and came back to the United States. I was one of the first female chefs around at that time."

Kellee met her first husband, got married and had a baby, a daughter she named Holiday. "After I had the baby, I was a stay-at-home mom for awhile, but then my husband and I divorced, and I decided to get a job," Kellee says. "First, I went to work for Japan Airlines as their director of purchasing. And after that, I went to work for Anheuser-Busch in St. Louis as a corporate executive chef. A few years later, Anheuser-Busch closed their food division, so I went to work for Con Agra as an executive in national and international sales in their Los Angeles office. So I moved back to LA."

Kellee eventually remarried, but that second marriage ended after ten years, when her daughter was a teenager. "I was a single mother again, and I was really busy with my career, flying all over the world. I had just come back from Hong Kong and Europe, and I'd been gone for five weeks. So I promised my daughter that when

I returned from my trip, I'd take her to see Sting in concert at the Greek Theater in Los Angeles. But when I returned to the States, I didn't even know what time it was because of the change in time zones. I was really confused."

As Kellee was getting into her car to take her daughter to the concert, something life changing happened. "We lived at the beach and our car was in an underground parking garage. As I was getting into the car, my phone rang. And as I answered my phone, I smashed my head on the side of my car, slamming my frontal lobe really hard on the car as I was getting in. I didn't duck my head to get in the car like you're supposed to, and I hit my head on the car with the full force of my body."

Somehow, despite her injury, Kellee was able to drive her daughter to the concert. "After I smashed my head on the car, I blacked out for a second, and then I felt a rush of blood come straight into my head, like an explosion in my brain. But the blood didn't come out of my head, I didn't see blood," explains Kellee. "And my daughter was saying, 'Mom, Mom, come on, we have to go. What's going on?' I asked her if I was bleeding, and she said no. So I told myself, I don't know what's happened here, but, no matter what, I'm still going to this concert."

Kellee made it through the Sting concert, but she was still confused and in pain, so she had her daughter drive the car home. "Holiday was only fifteen and just had her learner's permit, but I insisted that she drive us home, even though she had to drive from Hollywood to Long Beach on the Los Angeles freeways, which she'd never done before," Kellee recalls. "It was pretty radical and, I'm sure, traumatic for Holiday, but somehow we got home in one piece."

Although Kellee knew she had injured herself, she had no idea how serious and life threatening her injury was. "I didn't go to the hospital. I was in denial because I was a single mother and, in my mind, I'd just hit my head. I didn't know the significance of a head injury, so I didn't follow up on it. And for a year and a half after I hit my head, my behavior became more and more erratic and combative."

After the head injury, Kellee's intuitive abilities came back in strong and frightening ways. While she was vacationing in Tahiti with her boyfriend, she got up in the middle of the night to use the bathroom, and she had a startling vision. "I looked up, and standing in front of me, three feet above me, was an Indian man from India wearing a turban. It was as clear as clear could be. And I started to scream at the top of my lungs because it was so frightening. I kept opening and closing my eyes, but he was still there."

Kellee fainted, and when she regained consciousness, she saw another spiritual being. "When I came to, there was this beautiful Jamaican woman wearing flowing gorgeous robes, and she was radiating such love. I had never felt such love," Kellee remembers. "And she was there for about a minute, and then I fainted again, and when I awoke, she and the Indian man disappeared out of the blue."

Kellee's boyfriend heard her screaming and came to help her. "He comforted me, and then he said something that he would never say. He said 'Those were your spirit guides, darling.' He wouldn't know how to say that or what those words meant. He was a food industry executive. They must have put those words in his head."

When they returned from Tahiti, Kellee was so sick she couldn't get out of bed, and she stopped working at her food industry job. "I was bleeding to death and didn't know it," says Kellee. "And while I was lying in bed, I heard a voice that said to me, 'Get out of bed and call Dr. Emory.' Dr. Emory is a neuropsychiatrist I had seen a few years before, for my ADHD. And I said to the voice, 'I'll call him, but I'll never get an appointment today.' And believe it or not, they got me in to see him that day. And he diagnosed me with severe brain trauma, traumatic brain injury."

Kellee's physician told her that she had a subdural hematoma, and that she had been slowly bleeding to death since she had hit her head a year and a half earlier. "Apparently, I had a five millimeter hole in my head, and it was a slow leaker. I learned later that this was the kind of injury that only three percent of the population survives."

Dr. Emory sent Kellee to the UCLA Medical Center to get further testing for her brain injury. "I went to UCLA, and they did every single medical test that they could do. It turned out that I was very ill and that I could have either surgery or medication, and we decided to go with medication. So I was medicated for a period of time to control the bleeding, and to control my erratic, angry outbursts, because I was angry all the time."

The medicine helped Kellee, but her psychic abilities returned with a vengeance. "Everywhere I went, I would see dead people. I'd walk in a room and I'd see your dad, your mom, your spirit guides, your angels, your dogs, whatever it was. I would see them all. Everybody. There was no veil," explains Kellee. "And because there was no veil, I thought that everybody wanted to see this and to hear about it. I thought everybody would want to know about their dead relatives, but it turned out that they didn't and people were scared. It was also a scary time for me, because I had to learn how to control these visions."

Kellee's intuitive gifts also began to manifest in other ways – in ways that could prove dangerous to the people around her. "Things around me started moving, and I couldn't control it. If I was upset, a fire would start right above me or right above the person I was upset with. Or glasses would just shatter when I'd walk into a room. Or televisions would become unplugged, and tables would lift and move. And this happened for about two years. I had to move out of my mother's house and go live with my brother because I felt so bad about breaking my mother's things."

Kellee moved in with her brother, a movie director who lives in the Hollywood Hills. "I lived with my brother and his wife for about a year and a half, and they took really good care of me. While I lived with them, I was able to develop my gift and to get control of my psychic energy. It took years and years to learn how to handle and focus the energy, but it finally came together. And now I'm able to help people with my gift," says Kellee.

"I loved the life I had before I hit my head, and I would always pray, 'Please let me have my old life back.' But that was never going to happen. That door ceased to exist, and I went through a lot when I became psychic. But my new life is incredible. It just took me years of pain, and prayers, and crying to get where I am today. Now I can handle the energy that I receive from the other side."

As she was doing readings, Kellee realized through her practice that people going through loss and trauma may require therapy, so she went to graduate school to become a licensed psychotherapist. In addition, Kellee and Dr. Shirley Impellizzeri host a weekly radio show, called *Both Sides Now,* which explores the psychological and the spiritual sides of life issues.

Today, Kellee lives with her boyfriend Don, "the love of my life," and does readings and works as a psychotherapist for a variety of clients, including celebrities, corporate executives, politicians and people from all walks of life. She does general readings, but she also specializes in grief counseling, trauma, loss, transitions, and she often is consulted by individuals who've lost a loved one through suicide.

"Perhaps it's because I'm also a psychotherapist, but I tend to specialize in mental illness on the other side. If there is a mental illness or suicide, the other side sends them to me. This is probably because I have compassion for those individuals, and I also have a deep understanding of the psychology behind it. An interesting component from the other side is that they give me the diagnosis, whether it's a major depression or Asperger's. So those are the ones that tend to get sent to me from the other side. I end up with a lot of suicides. And I tell the surviving families that, many times, the soul of their loved one had taken on too much in this life, and wanted to return to the other side to heal and to grow."

Kellee feels that it's important for people to have compassion for others, but also for themselves as well. "The greatest thing I can say is that you need to have compassion for your soul, and for what you've gone through," explains Kellee. "Anybody who has incarnated in the world at this time is a brave soul, a brave warrior, and having compassion for yourself is everything. Whether you were sexually abused, physically abused, emotionally abused or had physical ailments or whatever, just have a lot of compassion for what you went through. And there will be a lot of sobbing, a lot of crying, and then you can move through it and move on.

"There is no such thing as death. This life is temporary. Before we're born, we put a plan in place, and we live this life so that our souls can learn. This is why we come here. We come here for the growth of our soul. And as hard as it is to live on this planet, in this dimension, our soul grows the fastest here."

SARAH WINSLOW

Sarah Winslow lives in Maine with her family, and she does read-ings for clients all across the globe who are looking for spiritual guidance and who want to get in touch with their higher self. I was referred to Sarah by Sally Silver, who said that Sarah was gifted - and Sally was right! Sarah is a very accurate psychic medium and spiritual counselor who originally studied fine art. Sarah is com-mitted to helping people realize there is a "higher element" that we need to listen to, and that this higher source wants us to succeed and to find our path.

When Sarah gave me a reading, she touched on some sensitive issues involving one of my family members, and she validated that my negative experience with this person actually allowed me to grow and become liberated in this lifetime. She delivers her impres-sions with a gentle demeanor and a grace that is truly helpful and healing.

As a child, Sarah was very sensitive and intuitive, and she thought that everyone around her was the same way. When she was just five years old, she had an experience involving a conversation with the stars that became one of the most profound experiences of her childhood.

"I was in my room with my sister. I was asleep and I just kind of woke up," recalls Sarah. "It was a starry night and in my head I heard a voice say, 'Go to the window.' So I went to my window, and the voice said, 'Look at the stars' and I looked at the stars and the stars kind of told me things. They said that I was going to help people. They said that my life was going to be interesting, and that I would have children, and they told me that I would be okay, and to not be afraid of them. They told me to remember this con-versation, and that the stars were 'Home, everybody's Home.' And I felt really good about it, and they told me to go back to sleep, and I did. That was my strongest psychic or spiritual memory as a young child."

As she got a bit older, Sarah was aware that she was highly sensitive, and that things would affect her deeply, more deeply than most other people. "I felt the weight of the world on my shoulders. Everything made me feel overwhelmed and sad. I cried when I saw dead animals on the side of the road, and my mother had to deal with me crying in the car for what seemed like forty minutes every time I saw a dead animal that had been hit by a car. I was just really sensitive and emotional. I felt pain and beauty all the time very deeply."

Sarah did see spirits from the other side, but she tried hard to ignore these visions and visitations when they occurred. "Yes, I saw people who had passed and energy and things, but I usually tried to turn it off because it freaked me out as a kid. My parents used to take us on picnics in cemeteries because my dad was an actor and a theater buff and he would go to the graves of major writers. And I remember seeing spirits, but I just didn't say anything. I just kept quiet, because I was quite shy. I didn't like talking about these things at all – I kept trying to inwardly figure out what it all was."

Sarah continues, "It's so overwhelming to see these things as a child. But I did see things like elementals, and I liked seeing them – like elves and fairies and things of that nature. I would allow that because it made me feel good to see them."

When Sarah got older, she decided to go to art school. During that time, she began to have a lot of prophetic, mystical dreams which would foretell various events that were about to happen in her life. She also became very good at translating signs and symbols that her spirit guides were giving her that helped her understand much higher spiritual concepts. "It was becoming less about seeing visions, and more about solid information coming in. It was about truth and vision all at the same time," Sarah says.

"When I was in art school, I was dating a man who was highly troubled and very unkind to me. I would come home from school, and a voice would tell me to go look in the trash, so I would," recounts Sarah. "I would find cigarettes with lipstick on them, and I found out that my boyfriend had been having a relationship with someone else. And I would get a vision of the person, like this person has blue eyes and dark hair, and I would question him about it and he would deny it – but of course I was right. So that happened a lot. That was a bad relationship, but it let me see how intuitive I was, and I had this really amazing spiritual awakening which changed the way I viewed this ability."

Sarah eventually met a man that would become her husband and the father of her two children, but she knew right from the beginning that the relationship wouldn't last. "I knew that I was going to marry this man and have babies with him – but I knew that I wasn't going to stay with him." After Sarah and her husband split up, she began to design spiritual art cards, which she took to some local stores to sell.

"I had two babies to feed, so I meditated and was told to take my art cards to three stores, and that I would find my career and make the money I need – I was told that I would find my life there," Sarah recalls. "Two of the stores also had people who did psychic readings, so I talked to one store owner about psychic ability. She said, 'Okay, read me right now.' I said, 'Gosh, I don't know,' and then I did a reading for her. After the reading, she became quiet and got the manager and said, 'Can you read her' and I said, 'Okay,' and I read the manager. The owner bought my art cards, but she also asked me if I could start doing readings at the store on Monday, and I said yes. That's how I started doing psychic readings."

Soon, Sarah stopped making the art cards because she was very busy doing readings – first at the local store, and then at her home, in her home office, where she was able to take care of her children. Since then, her clientele has grown substantially, and she now does readings on a global basis. In addition, Sarah conducts workshops and classes about intuitive ability and mediumship across the country, and she continues to pursue one of her first loves – abstract painting.

When Sarah does a reading, she tries to inject some lightheartedness into the session with a client. "I believe a reading is supposed to be uplifting and ultimately make you laugh and smile, and make you feel good, even if your energy and heart is kind of heavy when you're getting the reading. But ultimately, I think that spiritual awakening is important, and my goal is that I try to keep my readings upbeat, creative and uplifting, even if I have powerful messages to deliver."

Sarah believes that people who are called to be intuitives are here to help the world evolve in a positive way. "I feel that the reason I had to say yes to using my psychic ability is to help people by imparting the information that they need to know, which is coming from a higher place – a place beyond our knowing and human remembrance.

"I remind people that we're here to learn, and that right now it's more important than ever to get in touch with our own inner self, and to rely on our inner guidance. I believe that people need to understand that there is a higher element coming in to help us. It doesn't have to be labeled. It's just love, really, and understanding. And good healers and psychics are here to help people crack the code, and to help them tune into their inner map to find their direction and true purpose in life."

According to Sarah, it's important for human beings to "unlearn" some of the negative things we've been told, especially that we have no inner power or "oneness" in our connection to others. "I know that we're in a time that looks strange and frightening, but I believe that we're being guided to go within ourselves to understand what's working or not working in our lives. Happiness only comes by our connections to each other and to Spirit. When we hurt the Earth, and hurt each other, we fail. But when we unite together, we thrive. And many psychics and healers are here as guides to help people become more enlightened, and to show them the way to happiness."

"Everyone who wills can hear the inner voice. It is within everyone."

Mahatma Gandhi

EIGHT

MY MEMORY OF HEAVEN
Before I Was Born

Perhaps one of the reasons I want to raise positive awareness about intuition and the importance of listening to our own inner voice is due, in part, to an experience I had many years ago.

When I was very young, I had a distinct "memory" of being in heaven before I was born. The memory was brief but vivid and, even though I've tried to write it off as just a dream that I had as a kid, I believe that it was an actual memory, not a dream. And it was so beautiful that I want to share it with you now.

Here's what I remember. I'm holding the hand of an impossibly tall being who's dressed in a white robe with a rope belt. The being, or what I now believe was an angel, was walking next to me as we entered this enormous structure which resembled an airplane hangar. It had a huge open door, like a giant garage door. This amazingly beautiful light was shining on the outside of this structure, and I knew that the light was heaven, and that all of my loved ones were in that brilliant light, and that I was temporarily leaving them behind as I pursued the adventure that I was about to experience.

Inside the giant airplane hangar, the light was dimmer, as if you entered a big garage on a beautiful summer day and noticed the juxtaposition of the light outside and the more subdued light inside. My guide, or angel, was still holding my hand as we filed into a line of other tiny souls who were holding the hands of their impossibly tall beings. There was a mist, which resembled clouds, on the surface we were walking on, and the line of beings and child souls ahead of us was long. I felt excited and nervous all at the same time, like a little child on the first day of school. I was anxious, but thrilled at the thought of what lay ahead for me, what I would learn and accomplish in the new place I was going to live.

Somehow, I knew that heaven was really "home," and that coming to Earth as a human was really "school." I was here, as we all are, to experience good things as well as challenges, so that our souls can grow and stretch. Just like that child who's attending her first day of school, I was full of positive anticipation, as well as some trepidation, but I knew that life was unfolding before me, and that it was up to me to make the most of my relatively short time on Earth, before I would return home to heaven once again.

My angel guide held my hand and emanated love, although the being was silent and didn't verbally speak to me. Each little soul in the line ahead of me was about the size of a toddler who could walk but was new to the task. As we approached the head of the line, I saw the angel beings pick up their young soul babies and put them, one at a time, on an unimaginably long, translucent slide, and the baby soul being slid down the slide, off into the distance. Then it was my turn, and my angel guide picked me up and gently placed me on the slide, and I began my long descent, excited but somehow ready for what was yet to come.

Then I was born. I don't have an actual memory of being born, but I do have distinct memories of being in a stroller as a newborn baby, looking up at the beautiful face of my mother, who was smiling and pushing the stroller down the street on a warm summer day, with a brilliant blue sky dotted with clouds visible above her head. I felt a deep sense of contentment and peace, snuggled deep in my stroller with the blankets around me and the warm sun on my cheeks. I was born in early June, so I'm not sure how old I was at the time, but that loving memory is very distinct.

When I was four or five, I loved to lie in the fragrant grass next to our house during the summer, looking up at the sky and the clouds. I felt joyful and blessed, and I'd raise my arms straight up to the sky as if to give God, my angels, and my loved ones in heaven a big hug and a kiss.

That's my memory of heaven before I was born. I know that I was there, and it gives me a deep sense of peace, and an optimistic view about what's to come.

NINE

"DRAFTED"
My First Divinely Guided PR Campaign

In 1990, I was a senior account supervisor at Hill & Knowlton in New York City. I was in charge of promoting large global food accounts, including Pepsico Foods International, the Chilean Wine Industry and Frito Lay. Although this might sound exciting, I was feeling empty and unchallenged; introducing the new "light" (lower calorie) line of Doritos, Cheetos and Lays potato chips didn't feed my soul.

I yearned to do something that mattered. I decided to use my skills to promote a cause of some kind and give back to the world. Pro bono work was allowed at Hill & Knowlton, as long as it didn't interfere with paid account work. I wanted to choose a cause that needed assistance and visibility.

One day, I was reading a story about domestic violence and they quoted a woman named Hedy Nuriel, who was the head of a national toll-free domestic violence hotline – the only national toll-free hotline in the country. Domestic violence and its affect on the children in these abusive homes was an ugly topic that, unfortunately, did not receive a lot of press in the early '90s. I cared about this issue, and worried about the children in these households, so I felt inspired, or "drafted," to raise awareness about domestic violence. It started with a few pro bono hours a week, but eventually brought me to a meeting at the White House, generated a cover story in *Time* magazine, and introduced legislation which changed the way battered woman could seek help in this country.

After I read the article, I called Hedy Nuriel and asked her if I could do some pro bono PR for her and the toll-free domestic violence hotline, which was based in Michigan. Hedy was surprised by my call, but she was delighted to hear that I wanted to do PR for the hotline for free. I began to book Hedy on some of the national morning TV shows and arranged a number of other media appearances.

This went on for about two months, and one day – out of the blue – I got a call from a man named Larry Lux. He told me that he was a marketing director at Johnson & Johnson, and that Hedy had given him my phone number. I had no idea why a marketing guy from J&J would be calling me – the hotline was a non-profit organization which is run out of Michigan. What was the connection?

Larry explained to me that Johnson & Johnson completely funded the hotline – that it was part of a cause-related marketing campaign called Shelter Aid, which had been created to promote J&J's line of feminine protection products. If you purchased Stayfree napkins or OB tampons, a portion of the proceeds went to fund Shelter Aid and the national toll-free hotline. The spokesperson for the Shelter Aid Campaign was Lindsay Wagner – the popular actress who had played Jaime Sommers in *The Bionic Woman*, a TV show that was aired in the late 1970s.

The biggest surprise was that Larry had been paying another large PR firm a substantial amount of money to promote the national hotline in the media. He said that I had placed more stories about the hotline in two months than his expensive PR account team had done in the past two years.

Larry said that he wanted to meet with me the following week, and I said that I couldn't, because I was flying to Dallas and then on to Plano to meet with Frito Lay. Incredibly, Larry told me that he was also flying to Dallas for business, and we discovered that we were both flying on the same day and on the same plane! We made arrangements to sit together, and on the 2½ hour flight to

Texas, Larry and I talked about the hotline, and he suggested that I write a formal PR proposal for the Shelter Aid account, and that he would fire his PR firm and hire me to do PR for the hotline as a consultant. I left H&K and started to promote the hotline full-time, and unbelievably, my income quadrupled!

During the next two years, I was able to generate a lot of press about the hotline and the issue of domestic violence. Even though this was a tough topic, it was like every door magically opened for me. Virtually every major women's magazine ran stories about domestic violence. *Bride's Magazine* ran a story called "What to Watch Out For Before the Wedding Bells." I thought it was a brave move for a publication that sells ads for wedding gowns and china patterns to actually encourage women to cancel their weddings if they had been battered by their fiancés. Anna Quindlen, a journalist for the *New York Times,* flew out to the hotline headquarters in Michigan with me to do a story – and she credited Johnson & Johnson with funding the hotline, even though it was her policy not to plug any companies or products. *Time* magazine ran a cover story about domestic violence after six women journalists from *Time* took me to lunch to talk about domestic violence and what needed to be done about the issue. It took three years, but the story, entitled "'Til Death Do Us Part," appeared on the cover of *Time.*

All was going well until one day when Larry called to tell me that he was leaving J & J and moving to Indianapolis because his wife had been diagnosed with multiple sclerosis and she wanted to be close to her family in the Midwest. I was sad to see him go. But what happened next made me very upset. Larry was replaced by a female marketing manager who told me that she was pulling the plug on the Shelter Aid program, and that J & J would not be funding the hotline anymore. She felt that the topic of domestic violence was not suitable for her company to promote. I was floored – where would all of these battered women go for help now?

The next week, I got a call from *Family Circle* magazine. They were running a story about domestic violence that I had placed, and their fact checker had learned that the hotline didn't exist anymore. "Can we use your office phone number as the number that battered women can call?" they asked. Wow, I thought, how could I do that? The hotline was getting more than 10,000 calls per month, up from an average of 2,000 calls when I took over. I couldn't field 10,000 calls from my office phone! I told *Family Circle* that we would have to find another option.

After we hung up, I clearly heard the words, "Call the White House, call the White House," as though a radio had been turned up very loud. Where was this coming from? I turned around to see if someone was standing there, talking to me. But no one was there. I was alone in the room. I thought maybe I was going crazy. This was the first time I had ever had an experience like this – my first strong, intuitive "inspiration," and I will never forget hearing that voice.

Certainly, calling the White House was a wild thought, and not something that I'd ever thought before. But this thought persisted – I felt compelled to do it – so I finally contacted the White House, even though I knew that the likelihood of actually scheduling a meeting with anyone there was remote, to say the least.

To my surprise, after a few initial calls, I eventually spoke with Julie Cook, Mrs. Bush's director of programs, and I was actually able to schedule a meeting with Barbara Bush's office. Because I was flying to Washington, D.C. on my own dime (that's how motivated I felt to do this), I decided to make full use of the trip, and I also scheduled meetings with Congresswoman Connie Morella's office, Senator Joe Biden's office, and the office of Senator Dan Coats. The meetings were about the need to create a federally-funded toll-free domestic violence hotline so that battered woman would have a safe place to call without their husbands finding out they were seeking help by checking their phone bills.

It was surreal, entering the White House for a meeting. They put me through two separate security stations before I could go in. They frisked me, checked my purse and briefcase and had me walk through metal detectors. This happened a decade before 9/11, so I wasn't used to all of that security, although I knew it was certainly necessary to protect the president. I call this entire episode "Mary

Ann Goes to Washington." I'm not a political person, but I was definitely on a mission to raise awareness about the need for a toll-free domestic violence hotline among key lawmakers and politicians.

And the meetings seemed to have a positive effect. Everyone I met with thanked me for bringing this issue to their attention, and Congresswomen Connie Morella told me that she was going to introduce what was called a "concurrent resolution" which would get the ball rolling to create a federally funded toll-free domestic violence hotline. I didn't know how long that process would take, but I left Washington hopeful that I at least got the wheels turning and that something would happen.

Fast forward two years or so. I was at a luncheon at the Hilton Hotel in New York City to honor outstanding women. I was seated in a roomful of amazing women, at the same table as Jane Pauley, the anchorwoman from NBC's Today Show, as well as other accomplished women. Tipper Gore, the wife of Vice President Al Gore, was at the podium, bathed in light in the huge, darkened room where the luncheon was being held. Then she spoke these words: "And I'm pleased to tell you that our administration is the first administration to fund a federally funded toll-free, national domestic violence hotline to help battered women from across the country."

Sitting at my table in the darkness, in the company of all of these great and accomplished women, I got goose bumps. It was almost like I heard a gong sound. Here I was, the person who started the process to create a federally-funded toll-free domestic violence hotline, and now it was a reality. I instantly realized that I had been divinely guided to get this legislation passed. I felt a deep sense of gratification that I had been "utilized" to help make this happen. I believe that I was "drafted" to help raise awareness about domestic violence, and I was deeply grateful that there finally was a hotline, even if no one knew that I was partly responsible for making it happen.

This is one of the most gratifying things I have done in my career, because it definitely helped people and made a positive difference in their lives.

I always say that I'm the worker bee, and that God and the powers that be are the brains behind these divinely guided missions. How else would the door to the White House open so easily for me? I'm good at PR, but a *Time* cover story is not easy to get. I learned to listen to the inspirations from my inner voice, do my best, and watch the results in amazement.

This is how I feel about my mission to raise positive awareness about intuition and the power of our own inner voice. It's time to educate people about intuition, and to encourage everyone to be open to these divinely guided inspirations from above. Once we realize that we have access to this deeper, more profound form of communication and wisdom, the doors to the universe and to our own amazing purpose and possibilities will open wider than we could ever imagine.

TEN

A VALENTINE'S DAY PHONE CALL
FROM ALBERT EINSTEIN

*T**his is a story that I was hesitant to include in this book, because it's even too bizarre for me to understand or believe, but I've been encouraged to do so by many people, regardless of how crazy it sounds. So here goes.*

One cold, Saturday afternoon, Feb. 13, 2016, I was in my home office, writing a chapter for this book. I heard my husband Eric calling my name, asking me to come upstairs because he had something to show me on his computer that I could use in my book. Now, my husband has always been supportive of my work, but he had not really participated in the writing of this book. So the fact that he was calling me upstairs to his office to show me something was highly unusual.

"I thought you'd be interested in these quotes," said my husband.

On his computer screen were some quotes about intuition and psychic ability that were attributed to Albert Einstein, who apparently became interested in these topics late in his career. I genuinely had no clue that Einstein was into the subject of intuition – no clue at all.

I asked Eric why he was showing me these quotes – which I did think would be great for this book – when he hadn't really been involved or shown much of an active interest in helping me with this book in the past. "I don't know – I just suddenly remembered that Albert Einstein had been quoted about intuition in the past, and I know that you're interviewing scientists for the book, so I looked these quotes up."

I was really grateful for my husband's input – although, again, it was a bit strange to me because he hadn't volunteered material for my book before. I went back downstairs to my own office and began to research Albert Einstein and his interest in intuition, so that I could add his story to the chapter I was writing.

When I did a Google search "Albert Einstein" and "psychic ability," an article entitled, "Why, Dr. Einstein!" popped up; it had appeared in *The New Republic* on March 9, 1932. In the article, the author, C. Hartley Grattan, ridiculed Einstein for some remarks Einstein had made about a chance encounter he had had with a young female psychic named Gene Dennis. Apparently, Einstein was on vacation in Palm Springs, and he met Dennis when they had to share a limousine to some event. During the ride, Gene Dennis gave Einstein a brief reading, which was so accurate that it amazed Einstein.

Einstein must have shared his enthusiasm with the media, because Grattan quoted Einstein as saying, *"She told me things no one possibly could know, things on which I have been working, and she demonstrated to me that she has a power to do things I cannot at this time explain. Now, I must tell some of my associates about this. It was miraculous indeed."* Grattan also quoted Gene Dennis in the story as saying, *"Dr. Einstein is indeed the most remarkable personality I have ever contacted. [Sic.] And his aura is just sublime - pure blue electric sparks, instead of color. It was just like talking to God."*

Grattan called Einstein's meeting with Gene Dennis into question, writing: *"Wonderful! Wonderful! And so the scientific method goes crashing to the ground and the world's greatest relativist becomes an endorser of a 'psychic' vaudeville act."*

Even the brilliant physicist who discovered the groundbreaking mass-energy equivalence formula, $E=mc^2$, can be subject to ridicule because he is exploring the subject of intuition.

As I continued to do my research, I found that the prominent American author, Upton Sinclair, came to the defense of Einstein in a letter to the editor which appeared in *The New Republic* Apr. 27, 1932:

> *"Sir: I have never met the young lady who gave a demonstration to Einstein, but I know that Einstein's own statement, quoted by Mr. Grattan in* The New Republic *of March 9, is strictly scientific. Einstein says that she told him things which she could not possibly have known normally. Einstein is the only person who could have passed that judgment, and it seems to me that a man of his standing has a right to expect us to assume that he did not make the statement lightly or unthinkingly. If it was so, he knew it was so; then he had to choose between doing his duty as a scientist, or shrinking from the ridicule of those who are content to judge without investigating and who proceed upon the assumption that we know all there is to know about this universe, and that certain happenings are impossible because they are new and not understood."*

I wrote for some time and continued to research my section about Einstein. We went out to dinner that night to our favorite little restaurant with our teenage daughter, then dropped her off at a sleepover, and came home and went to bed. The next morning, I woke up at 4:30 a.m., which was unusual for me, but I had been waking up earlier than normal on some days because I had ideas for the book – or rather, inspirations – which I felt compelled to get down on paper.

After doing some research about Upton Sinclair and other potential notables to include in the Great Minds chapter, I decided to go back to bed at around 7:45 a.m., and I fell asleep for about 30 minutes. I woke up at 8:15 and went into my office to check my email and continue my research. That's when this story gets downright weird.

The phone rang at 8:20 and I immediately answered it, partly because I didn't want the ringing phone to wake up my husband, and partly because I wondered if it was my daughter, calling from her sleepover. But the woman on the phone was someone I'd never spoken to before, and I wondered who could be calling us so early on a Sunday morning – especially on Valentine's Day. She said, "Good morning, I'm calling to let you know that I was meditating and saying my morning prayers, and I was directed to call you and wish you a happy Valentine's Day – **by Albert Einstein."**

I nearly lost it – but I listened.

"He wants to let you know that you're on the right path with this project, and that you're a vessel of truth, and that you're being directed to the right people to include in this project, and you're using your innate gut level feelings to verify that truth. And you recently parted ways with someone who would not be good for this project. And you have a Native American guide who's helping you."

I was completely confused. Who *was* this? Was this one of the intuitives I was supposed to interview for my book? If so, why would she be calling me so early? On a Sunday? And on Valentine's Day? So I asked her, "Excuse me, but who are you?" She replied, "I'm Edna." Okay, so this still wasn't ringing a bell, but I remembered that Kelle, a psychic in Boston, had recommended three intuitives whom I should interview for my book, and that one had an "E" name. So I quickly found the email from Kelle, but her friend's name wasn't Edna, it was Erin.

So I asked the caller, "What is your last name?" And she said "Randall."

I immediately Googled "Edna Randall," and a story in *The New York Times* from 2003 came up. It was about psychic mediums. The reporter quoted Edna Randall, John Edward and other mediums in the story. So Edna was a legitimate medium. I asked Edna, "Do you even know my name?"

She said, "No, but I know that one of your names is like my mother's name, Ann."

"Do you even know what I'm working on?"

And she said, "No, I'm sorry, I don't."

My phone number is unlisted, and the phone bill isn't even in my name, Bohrer – it's in my husband's name, which is different from mine, so I asked her, "How did you get my phone number?"

Edna replied, "Well, he gave me your phone number when he was dictating his message for you. I get numbers in sequences, so I got 878, 787 – and I said, 'That's interesting, 878, 787,' and then he gave me the last four digits of your number – 7203."

I knew that my last four digits were actually 7283, but before I could correct Edna, she said, "But he told me to take out the 0 between the 2 and the 3, and replace it with an infinity symbol." Which, of course, was the number 8, which is my correct phone number.

At this point, Edna said, "Let me read what I was given to give to you. What he's saying to me is this: *'Madam, I am still focused on the agenda of bringing humankind to the highest best good. It is about not destruction but elevation of the illumination of consciousness. In the conscious, the unconscious and the subconscious - there are five bones in the skeletal system. In Chinese, they call it the Crystal Palaces. In biological, it is the fobal, the cerebrum, the cerebellum, and the medulla. All of that is connected to a synapse electronic connectiveness, that allows the electronic charges to go into the brain to create an idea, and go down the nervous system of the spinal column, and use our bodies as the instruments that do the work that we are supposed to do here - for God, not for man - for God.'"* Edna continued, *"'Prayer makes things happen in our lives. God's assertive entitles us to be total, whole and fulfilled. Being a higher, better self, allows the law, the natural law, and the true sense of one's earnestness, reflecting God's light, to flow and to grow.'"* That was what I was dictated to give to you this morning."

I was shaking. When Edna was delivering Einstein's message, her voice lowered, and when she spoke of God, her voice became very loud, as if to emphasize that particular point.

I had started taking notes at the beginning of Edna's call, but during the call, I grabbed my tape recorder and started to record what she was saying before she began to deliver Einstein's message. Two of the words on the tape were difficult to understand – the word "fobal" in the first paragraph, and the word "assertive" in the second paragraph. But I'm glad that I had the presence of mind to tape some of our conversation, because the entire event was unbelievable and quite unnerving.

I asked Edna if I could have her phone number and call her the next day, on Monday, because I was so overwhelmed at that moment, and she said yes and gave me her phone number. Apparently, she used to be a medium, but now, she explained, she was a "servant of God," and works in a soup kitchen three days a week, helps disadvantaged children on other days, and that she channels three beings, Einstein, Nikola Tesla and Alva Vanderbilt, a socialite who was also an activist in the women's suffragette movement.

I took Edna's phone number, told her I would call her the next day, and, still shaking, went to take a shower. I looked up at the ceiling, and told the powers that be, "Can you please tone it down a little bit? This is more than I can handle!" I took my shower, and told my husband about Edna's call.

At first, trying to make sense of the phone call, he suggested, "Maybe she wants to be part of your book."

But I told him that she didn't know anything about the book, and she didn't get my name from anyone I knew.

Then he said, "Well, Einstein contacted me first – he planted those quotes about intuition in my mind the night before!" And we laughed, because it was true – it's as if Einstein prompted my husband to call me upstairs and to show me those quotes, so that I could include him in my Great Minds chapter, and then he called me the next day to confirm that I was on the right path with my book project.

This is what happened. I'm not asking anyone to believe that Albert Einstein called me through Edna on the morning of Valentine's Day. I'm just stating the facts about what happened that day. Truthfully, I was confused by this event, because it was so incredible, and seemed impossible. I was so shaken up that I had to spend the rest of that Valentine's Day, that Sunday, doing mundane things like doing laundry and making beef stew, just to feel grounded.

When I shared this story with Dean Radin and other scientists, they agreed that it was truly evidential, and that this wasn't just some strange, random event. And Dean even said that I was probably contacted by Albert Einstein, or some collection of Einstein and other brilliant energies. But the part that he thought was truly rare was the numbers. Dean said that he's only seen one other remote viewer correctly identify a code that was locked in a safe. And the fact that Edna, a nice lady who was a former medium who lived on Long Island, could pull my unlisted phone number out of the air was highly unlikely.

Still, I feel duty bound to share this story, and you can draw your own conclusions. But at least now I've told this story which, I believe, needs to be told.

AFTERWORD

I feel grateful that I've been divinely inspired to write this book, and I hope that I've produced something that will help each one of us access our own divine guidance and wisdom simply by listening to our own inner voice.

I had two major goals that I wanted to achieve while writing this book. First, my wish is that, after reading the stories of these thirty-three highly gifted intuitives, you understand that they are just regular people – like you and me – who happen to have a very special gift. The majority of these people didn't ask to be gifted, they just are; many struggled to understand their intuitive abilities as children, or as adults, depending on when their gift became apparent to them.

Often, it was difficult for these gifted individuals to make sense of their strong intuitive ability. If they told others about their gift, they were often bullied, or shunned by those around them. Many worked hard to develop their own positive relationship with their inner voice, and to harness and maximize their intuitive talent so that they could help others, and encourage them to do the same.

The second goal that I had was to share this message: that listening to our inner voice and accessing this wealth of divine guidance is much, much easier than we think. As I researched books about intuition and spirituality, I found that there are a large number of books which promise to help us "develop our psychic ability, just by following these easy steps." While many of these books do have value, a number of them make the process of developing our intuitive ability way too complicated.

If I had to go into deep trance meditation, hold certain crystals in my hands, practice sending telepathic messages to others, learn out-of-body travel, or use techniques to open my third eye or crown chakra, I would never have been able to write this book. Instead of undergoing arduous "training" to hear inspirations from my inner voice, I simply learned to take my ego down a few pegs, be humble and listen. And trust in what I'm hearing and feeling. It's as simple as that.

Do you remember this scene at the end of The Wizard of Oz? Glinda, standing in her shimmering dress, tells Dorothy, "You don't need to be helped any longer. You've always had the power to go back to Kansas." Well, like that childhood classic, we have the answers at our fingertips, just by accessing our inner voice. It's just a matter of being open to this idea, and believing in it.

I hope that everyone who reads this book benefits from embracing this simple message. That we are loved and cherished by these divine beings and that, by listening to their guidance and wisdom, we can greatly improve our own lives and the lives of others and, as a result, affect positive change that will improve the world in which we live.

GLOSSARY

Angel Guide - An angel who is serving as a guide to a psychic or medium who is giving a client a reading. An angel who is personally guiding an individual.

Angelic Realm - The special place in the universe where angels and angelic beings dwell.

Astrology - An ancient practice of utilizing the planets, stars and related transits to gain further insight into a person, relationship or situation.

Aura - An energy field, or light field, that is around an individual which can be perceived by gifted psychics and mediums. Aura's vary from person to person, and are often perceived as different colors of light.

Channeling - The ability to receive information from a higher source, including divine guidance, angels or guide, or a loved one who's passed on.

Clairaudience - The ability to receive psychic and intuitive messages by "hearing" them.

Clairsentience - The ability to receive psychic and intuitive messages by "feeling or sensing" them.

Clairvoyance - The ability to receive psychic and intuitive messages by "seeing" them.

Crossing Over - When someone passes on or transitions from this world to the next plane of existence, often from a physical body to a nonphysical form.

Divine Guidance - Receiving guidance from a wise, loving source that is helping us follow our true spiritual path. That source has been known as God, the universe, our guides or angels, and our higher self.

Gifted - Being born with a heightened sense of "knowing" that allows one to perceive information from a higher source or a loved one who's passed on.

Ghost Hunter - A psychic medium who is helping a soul transition from the physical world into the non physical realm.

Guide - A soul or being that resides on the non physical plane who assists and guides individuals on the physical plane.

Healing School - An educational entity that teaches individuals how to harness and maximize their healing abilities.

Healing Circle - A supportive group of healers who join together to use their healing abilities to help individuals and larger groups become well.

Inner Voice - An inner "knowing" which comes from a higher source which is available to everyone.

Inner Wisdom - An inner "knowing" which comes from a higher source and which transcends our human understanding, often for the better.

Intuitive - Individuals who are in tune with their "inner voice," and who have strong, distinct feelings about people, places and upcoming situations.

Intuition - A gift of "inner knowing" that everyone is born with and which enables an individual to tap into that guidance to move beyond average right-brain thinking, perception and ideas.

Medical Intuitive - A psychic or intuitive who has a particular ability to identify issues of a medical nature.

Medium - An individual who is utilized as a conduit by souls or spirits who have passed on, often to contact loved ones and others on the Earth plane to impart messages.

Metaphysical - A way of viewing things that is "beyond" the "physical," or are outside of the normal physical or material way of looking at phenomena. A common synonym for metaphysical is supernatural.

Numerologist - A psychic who utilizes the ancient practice of numerology to advise clients in a reading.

Paranormal - Beyond the scope of normal explanation or understanding.

Past Life Regression - The act of returning to a past lifetime existence through the use of meditation, channeling or psychic phenomena.

Precognition - The ability to see an event before it happens, either through a dream, a vision, or by just a "knowing" feeling.

Psychic - An individual who can tap into their guides or higher self to receive information about past, current and future issues for other people.

Psychic Communication - Using one's psychic or intuitive ability to communicate with others, either on the Earth plane or in the universal realm.

Psychic Fair - A gathering of psychics and mediums in one setting where they give readings to clients.

Psychic Medium - An individual who has both psychic ability and the ability to communicate with souls or spirits who've crossed over to the nonphysical plane.

Psychometry - The practice of divining information by holding or touching an object, such as a stone, a piece of jewelry or an article of clothing.

Reading - A meeting or session with a psychic, medium or psychic medium which often provides clarity about a given situation or a relationship.

Reincarnation - The belief that, after someone dies, their soul can return to live life again in another physical form or body.

Seer - A wise individual who has intuitive abilities that allows them to have spiritual insights and see future events.

Soul Intuitive - A psychic or medium who receives their information directly from their soul or from the soul of the individual that they're reading.

Spirit - A supernatural or paranormal being who resides in the nonphysical plane.

Spirit Guide - A spiritual entity who serves as a guide and protector of a human being throughout its life.

Spiritualist Church - A place of worship for people who follow Spiritualism, which is the belief that the world and the universe is comprised of both human, physical beings, and spiritual, nonphysical beings.

Spiritual Energy Healer - An intuitive who uses positive energy from their higher self, spirit guides and the universe to heal an individual, both physically and emotionally.

Spiritual Medium - A medium who taps into the soul of an individual's deceased loved ones to receive messages and impart important information.

Synchronistic Events - A series of similar events or experiences that first appear to be unrelated, but later are often considered to be more than meaningful coincidences.

Tarot - An ancient method of utilizing special "tarot" cards as a tool to gain additional insight about a person, a relationship or a given situation.

Tarot Cards - A special deck of cards used in Tarot readings that typically consist of 78 cards: 22 Major Arcana cards, and four groups of Minor Arcana cards consisting of 14 cards each, including The Rods, The Swords, The Cups and The Pentacles.

Contact Information for the Intuitives in this Book:

Paul Adzic

Website	paulpsychicmedium.com

Prajna Avalon

Website	PrajnaAvalon.com
Email	prajna@prajnaavalon.com

Norman Blanchard

Email	norman@normanblanchard.de

Charley Castex

Phone	(828) 251-5043
Website	charleycastex.com
Email	charley@charleycastex.com

Virginia Centrillo

Website	theppa.net (go to the members tab to find Virginia)
Email	Virginia@theppa.net

Libby Clark

Phone	+44 (0) 1623 51 5899
Email	libbyaclark@aol.com
Website	www.libbyclark.com

Eddie Conner

Email	EddieAppointments@gmail.com
Website	EddieConner.com

Gabbie Deeds

Phone	(479) 208-7240
Website	gabbiedeeds.com
Email	info@gabbiedeeds.com

Mary Deveneau

Phone	(916) 572-5094
Website	yourspiritguide.com
Email	mary@yourspiritguide.com

Rebecca Fearing

Phone	(818) 853-1123
Website	rebeccafearing.com

Suzanne Giesemann

Website	suzannegiesemann.com
Email	info@suzannegiesemann.com

Robert Hansen

Phone	(516) 868-7778
Website	robertehansen.com
Email	modrnsage@aol.com

Kira Kay

Website	www.kirakay.com
Email	bookings@kirakay.com

Gregory Kehn

Phone	(716) 595-3529
Website	www.revgregorykehn.com
Email	gregorykehn@yahoo.com

Elizabeth Lee

Website   elizabethayerlee.com
Email   elizabeth@elizabethayerlee.com

Lori Lipten

Phone   (248) 219-5982
Website   lorilipten.com
Email   llipten@gmail.com

Lorenzo Marion

Phone   (941) 875-8224
Website   lorenzomarion.com
Email   lorenzo.thesoulsjourney@gmail.com

Peter Marks

Phone   (203) 206-9353
Email   peter_mrks@yahoo.com

Lois T. Martin

Phone   (518) 989-6349
Website   loistmartin.com
Email   numberpsychic@yahoo.com

Jeanne Mayell

Phone   (781) 820-2299
Website   jeannemayell.com.
Email   jeanne@jeannemayell.com

JoAnna Garfi McNally

Phone   (631) 836-7666
Email   jgarfimcnally@gmail.com

Nancy Myer

Phone   (724) 539-1019
Website   nancymyer-psychicdetective.com

Email   nmyerdet007@yahoo.com

Lyn Popper
Email   manon1818@hotmail.com

Jack Olmeda
Phone   (516) 647-3389

Brett San Antonio
Phone   (213) 787-7043
Website   brettsanantonio.org
Email   brett@brettsanantonio.org

Sally Silver
Phone   (207) 778-2039
Website   reverendsallysilver.com
Email   rev.sallysilver@gmail.com

Lorraine Smith
Phone   (239) 549-8724
Website   lightofthebluestar.com
Email   lorraine@lightofthebluestar.com

Kelle Sutliff
Phone   (978) 420-8213
Website   psychicmediumkelle.com
Email   psychicmedium@verizon.net

Judith Swanson
Phone   (978) 808-9095
Website   judithswanson.com
Email   judithaswanson@gmail.com

Leanne Thomas
Phone   (408) 372-7064

Website   angelichope.com
Email   leanne@angelichope.com

Cindy Wenger

Phone   (717) 566-0922
Website   cindywenger.com
Email   info@peaceablekingdomac.com

Kellee White

Phone   (562) 221-8328
Website   kelleewhite.com
Email   kellee@kelleewhite.com

Sarah Winslow

Website   sarah-winslow.com
Email   sarah@sarah-winslow.com

FURTHER READING

Conner, Eddie, *Kicking the Big But Syndrome: Put Your Big But Behind You and Improve Your Love, Money and Career* iUniverse, Inc., 2004

Einstein, Albert, *The World as I See It* New York, Philosophical Library, 1949

Giesemann, Suzanne, *Messages of Hope: The Metaphysical Memoir of a Most Unexpected Medium* One Mind Books, 2011

Kripal, Jeffrey J. *Authors of the Impossible: The Paranormal and the Sacred* University of Chicago Press, 2011

Marion, Lorenzo, *A Journey Through a Psychic's Eyes* America Star Books, 2010

Marion, Lorenzo, *Messages Beyond the Grave* America Star Books, 2015

Myer, Nancy, and Steve Czetli, *Silent Witness: The True Story of a Psychic Detective* St. Martins Mass Press, 1995

Myer, Nancy, *Travels with My Father: Life, Death and a Psychic Detective* Paladin Communications, 2013

Radin, Dean, *The Conscious Universe: The Scientific Truth of Psychic Phenomena* HarperOne, 2009

Radin, Dean, *Entangled Minds: Extrasensory Experiences in a Quantum Reality* Paraview Pocket Books, 2006

Radin, Dean, *Supernormal: Science, Yoga and the Evidence for Extraordinary Psychic Abilities* Deepak Chopra, 2013

Radin, Dean, *Real Magic: Ancient Wisdom, Modern Science, and a Guide to the Secret Power of the Universe,* Harmony, 2018

Schwartz, Gary E, *The Afterlife Experiments: Breakthrough Scientific Evidence of Life After Death* Atria Books, 2003

Schwartz, Gary E, *The G.O.D. Experiments: How Science is Discovering God in Everything, Including Us* Atria Books, 2007

Schwartz, Gary E, *The Sacred Promise: How Science is Discovering Spirit's Collaboration with Us in Our Daily Lives* Atria Books/Beyond Words, 2011

Schwartz, Gary E., *Super Synchronicity: Where Science and Spirit Meet,* Param Media, 2017

Strieber, Whitley, and Jeffrey J. Kripal, *The Super Natural: A New Vision of the Unexplained* TarcherPerigee, 2016

Sutliff, Kelle, *Listen Up!: The Other Side is Talking* Tri Circle Publishing, 2014

Targ, Russell, *Limitless Mind: A Guide to Remote Viewing and Transformation of Consciousness* New World Library, 2004

Targ, Russell, *The Reality of ESP: A Physicist's Proof of Psychic Abilities* Quest Books, 2012.

ACKNOWLEDGMENTS

This book is dedicated to the two miracles and major blessings in my life – my husband, Eric and my daughter, Lily.

As my family and friends know well, this book has been a labor of love for me from the very beginning. I felt inspired, actually drafted, to write it and to share what the powers that be want people to know – that we are all loved, and that each one of us has access to amazing divine guidance and divine wisdom simply by listening to our own inner voice.

I want to thank each and every gifted intuitive who shared their stories in this book. Hopefully, after reading about their lives, people will understand that many gifted individuals are born that way, and often struggle with bullying, prejudice and other issues as they grow up and learn how to use their gifts to help others. They bridge the gap between this plane and the next, and simply communicate profound, often life-changing messages from the other side. Sometimes the information comes from a deceased loved one, and other times directly from Spirit itself. Thanks to these spiritual communicators for sharing and interpreting these valuable messages with us.

I'd also like to thank the researchers, scientists and academics who are studying "psi" and who have bravely chosen to explore paranormal topics because they believe in their inherent value. Even though much of the scientific community considers these topics to be taboo, Dean Radin, PhD, Gary Schwartz, PhD, and Russell Targ, PhD, have worked tirelessly to study intuition, psychic ability and the nature of consciousness. The findings from their important research has, and will continue to, benefit us all.

In addition, I want to thank my friends and several professionals in the publishing industry for their input and support as I was writing this book. Their advice was insightful and invaluable, and I deeply appreciate their help as I researched and wrote **_The Gift Within Us._** I especially value the guidance of my literary agent, Bill Gladstone, who truly believes in my book and who was instrumental in ultimately getting my labor of love published and available to readers.

And a special thanks to Archbishop Harry J. Flynn, a dear family friend who was interviewed for this book prior to his passing in 2019. He was a brave spiritual pioneer who not only led the committee to hold clergy accountable for sexual abuse, but who also championed the value of our ability to communicate with the divine through intuition.

Finally, I must acknowledge the powers that be, my guides, angels and loved ones on the other side for inspiring me to write this book. Often, I simply wrote down the messages and pearls of wisdom they gave to me – sometimes waking in the night to record these inspirations accurately and fully. I am highly aware that this book is a true collaboration, and that I was assisted by colleagues both on this plane and on the other side. As I've always said, I am just the worker bee on this project, and I'm happy to utilize my skills to bring these divinely inspired messages to life.

NOTES AND INSPIRATIONS